BUSINESS COMPUTING

BUSINESS COMPUTING

Rajneesh Narayan

CENTRUM PRESS
NEW DELHI-110002 (INDIA)

CENTRUM PRESS
H.O.: 4360/4, Ansari Road, Daryaganj,
New Delhi-110002 (India)
Tel: 23278000, 23261597, 23255577, 23286875
B.O.: No. 1015, Ist Main Road, BSK IIIrd Stage,
IIIrd Phase, IIIrd Block, Bangalore-560085 (INDIA)
Tel: 080-41723429
Email: centrumpress@gmail.com
Visit us at: www.centrumpress.com

Business Computing

First Edition, 2010

ISBN 978-93-80540-45-0

PRINTED IN INDIA

Printed at Balaji Offset, Delhi.

Contents

Contents

Preface

Business computing has revolutionized the business environment with the computer — assistance of many time-consuming, complex tasks such as accounting, inventory control, customer databases, shipping control, and financial analysis. Today's desktop computers are versatile and relatively inexpensive. They have replaced the typewriter and, in many cases, the personal assistant for word-processing and organizational services. Networking of all the company's desktop computers allows access to and storage of the full range of company resources and information, reducing paperwork and increasing the productive flow of information.

A computer is an electronic device, which executes software programs. It consists of 2 parts-hardware and software . The computer processes input through input devices like mouse and keyboard. The computer displays output through output devices like colour monitor and printer. The size of a computer varies considerably from very small to very big. The speed of computers also has a very large range. Computers have become indispensable in today's world. Millions of people use computers all over the world. Computers have leapfrogged the human society into another league. It is used in each and every aspect of human life. They will spearhead the human quest of eradicating social problems like illiteracy and poverty. It is difficult to imagine a world bereft of computers. This revolutionary technology is indeed a boon to the human race. May computers continue to shower their blessings to us.

World is in need of several affordable innovations in the IT Sector to leverage the advantages for the benefit of the society at large. The major sectors which are witnessing a special thrust for adoption of IT are E-Governance, insurance, banks, financial institutions, energy, defence, public tax system, ports, customs, telecommunication, education, small office, home office/ individuals etc. Large sectors with slow IT penetration rate such as textile industry and healthcare are being encouraged by the government and private sector to adopt IT.

— *Rajneesh Narayan*

1

Introduction

Computers in Business and Professions-1970 to 1980

Computers had entered business, industry and trade in the 1960s, but it was at the beginning of the 1970s that this process gathered momentum. One reason for this was the great leap forward in microelectronics, which led to an enormous increase in performance coupled with far smaller, cheaper computer systems. The increase in the use of computers was accompanied by major technical, organizational and social change at the workplace, which caused existing business processes to be largely adapted to electronic data processing, resulting in rapid growth in requirements for new work qualifications in offices and in manufacturing.

Companies first began to work with computer systems at the beginning of the 1960s. These systems were installed at computer centres. The operating costs of such a computer centre were so high that the systems had to run day and night to be profitable.

It was only large companies that generated such large volumes of data. Accordingly, it was large banks and insurance companies that first set up computer centres. A small number of highly respected computer specialists worked there-programmers who wrote the software and operators who ran the systems. Data that had been recorded was processed there and returned to office staff as computer printouts.

With the development of data communications equipment, it was no longer necessary to install peripheral devices in computer centre locations. Terminals at office workers' desks made it possible to enter into a dialogue with the computer, i.e. to directly access the data. In 1965, IBM launched the System/360 mainframe on the market, and finally established itself as the world's leading computer supplier. From this point on, IBM set the standards.

With the development of data communications equipment, it was no longer necessary to install peripheral devices in computer centre locations. Terminals at office workers' desks made it possible to enter into a dialogue with the computer, i.e. to directly access the data. In 1965, IBM launched the System/360 mainframe on the market, and finally established itself as the world's leading computer supplier. From this point on, IBM set the standards.

In the mid-1960s, a special approach to data processing was introduced. It was predominant in Germany, where the whole range of office computers was referred to as Mittlere Datentechnik, in English later dubbed mid-range systems. Various companies-many of them from the office machine industry, such as Kienzle and Philips, or newcomers like Nixdorf-launched special small office computers for commercial administration, tailored to meet end users' needs.

This approach was an extraordinary success because it bundled application software and customer training with the hardware. This all-in service led to the rapid spread of office computers through small and medium-sized companies, which could not afford their own data processing department and therefore wanted complete solutions for their business organization.

At the beginning of the 1970s, numerous newly founded software houses in the USA and Europe discovered this market opening and satisfied the exploding demand for application programs by developing manufacturer-independent standard software.

Minicomputers came onto the market in the USA at about the same time as office computers in Europe. The first was Digital Equipment Corporation's pdp-8, which was launched in 1965. These systems were the answer to the main frames that had dominated the market in the USA until then, and were a great commercial success. In particular, scientists who wrote their own programs were keen on minicomputers, which made them independent of computer centres. Minicomputers and microcomputers quickly found their way from universities to the business world.

As flexible, fast process-control computers, they were used in factories from the 1970s to plan, control and automate manufacturing processes. The increase in computer-controlled manufacturing technologies was motivated by the necessity to cut costs and to ensure more efficient, flexible and cheaper production. Computer-controlled robots initially became widespread in the automotive manufacturing sector in the early 1980s. About 60% of all computers were in use there, and replaced 20 to 26% of factory workers. From there, computers penetrated the whole world of industry.

The Role of Computers in Reshaping the Work Force

Today's versatile computers have some impact on nearly every occupation and industry in the U.S. economy, unlike past technology which usually affected only specific jobs

Computers may be the most profound technology since steam power ignited the Industrial Revolution. Computer technology is altering the form, nature, and future course of the American economy, increasing the flow of products, creating entirely new products and services altering the way firms respond to demand, and launching an information highway that is leading to the globalization of product and financial markets.

In addition to affecting the methods of production among firms, computers are changing the relationship between labour and organization. The traditional pyramid-shaped organizational structure of most corporate firm is the by-product of the Industrial Revolution, which moved work from the individual or family unit to an organizational structure.

Computer technology challenges the traditional management hierarchy, moving many organizations from a pyramid-shaped structure to a flatter structure. Historically, decisions were passed from top management to the next management layer; today, computers permit companies to communicate throughout their organizations instantaneously, without regard for traditional management structures. Such wider distribution of authority in some companies has put new emphasis on enhancing labour efficiency by replacing fragmented work with integrated work tasks. This can lead to upgrading worker skills, as shifting flexibility among the production of various goods and services requires a more highly trained work force.

This issue of the Monthly Labour Review explains how computers have affected jobs in selected manufacturing and services industries and in high-tech defence industries, and discusses an emerging market made possible by computers-the home market. This article presents an overview of the six articles included in this series; it begins by summarizing some of the rapid changes that have occurred in computer technology over the years.

Rapid Computer Technology

In the last 20 years, there have been dramatic changes in computer technology. In the 1970s, computers were time-sharing mainframe and mini computer systems which allowed dumb terminals to share informations and computing services.

The 1980s saw personal computing. The microprocessor-based computer brought computing power to the individual at the office and home. The development of user-friendly software applications allowed for more uses, however, for the most part, computing was still done in isolation. The use of local-area networks in the workplace helped users communicate beyond the desktops, but only to other users within the organization.

Network computing arrived a decade later, ringing in the age of the information highway. The Internet, a confederation of interconnected networks, connects millions of computers using existing telephone lines. With the help of special software a powerful new computing platform on which to build brand new computing applications is open to all types of computers. Network computing is possible because of speed and cost of die technology. The power of the devices and networks run by microprocessors and software is increasing at a rate never seen before, roughly doubling in performance every 18 months or so. This trend has caused the unprecedented reduction in the cost of microchip-based technology, allowing computers to be used more widely and rapidly.

The decline in costs has assumed a central role in the use of computers. As the production costs of hardware and software fall in comparison to the development cost, it makes sense for firms to sell their products at a lower cost to establish a market hold.

Production Flexibility in Manufacturing

Semiconductors. Computers have reshaped manufacturing plants, allowing manufacturing firms to serve many markets and produce a wider range of goods. Computer technology helps engineers, managers, and workers schedule the flow of materials, control quality, and change production lines as the demand for products changes. It allows manufacturers to respond quickly to demand, and deliver a larger variety of products more quickly. With computers, retailers can gather and aggregate sales data electronically, convert the data into orders and transmit the information to manufacturers. Manufacturers with computer links to production systems, distributors and customer networks can respond quickly to the markets. For manufacturers, customized runs can now compete on a cost basis with production runs of standardized products with dedicated assembly runs.

All of this depends on the speed and functions of a computers which "in turn is determined by the system design and the underlying capabilities of its components." Semiconductor devices are the basic functional components of computers upon which computer performance depends. In the first article of this series, Francisco A. Moris discusses technology in semiconductor manufacturing, and examines employment and other trends in the industry, including worker productivity, offshore employment, technology diffusion, and export growth.

Computer manufacturing. Computer manufacturing is an industry in which new rules of production call for redefining the value of a product for which the cost of raw technology is rapidly declining. Jacqueline Warnke explores consumers, demand for computers, as prices for computers decline and the economy and society take advantage of this lower-priced and higher-quality resource.

Versatility in Service Industries

During the last two centuries, technological innovations in agriculture and manufacturing have increased output, improved productivity, and raised the standards of living for the industrial economies. This was mainly the case in the past, because for technological innovations to be effectively applied required an industry with a certain size and capital intensity. Typically, service industries were in a less favourable position to apply technological innovations because of the labour intensive nature of most of these establishments.

Due to its versatility and declining cost, computer technology has been applied in many unrelated service industries such as banking, power utilities, retailers, wholesalers, and health services. Computers can fill out and check mortgage-loan forms, transfer calls, and electronically gather and aggregate sales data for retail stores, to name a few uses. Investment by service producers in computer technology has steadily increased since 1975. As of 1993, the top four private sector industries ranked by the U.S. Bureau of the Census as having the greatest percentage of employees working with a computer were service-related industries.

Banking. Investment in computer-related technologies has caused employment adjustments.

In commercial banks, for example, the application of automated teller machines (ATM's) and other related technologies have lessened the need for customers to use a bank teller. Teresa Morisi examines employment changes in commercial banks and discusses how commercial banks, forced to be more competitive after deregulation in 1980, use computer technology to cut costs and offers new products and services to attract customers.

Computer services and engineering. Computer technology has created economies of scale for many services industries, but, more interestingly, has generated a secondary effect called "economies of scope." Many service producers have found that computer technology enables them to offer more services and attract a larger range of customers. (For example, commercial banks are able to offer several methods for their customers to access their accounts, such as automatic teller machines debit cards and personal computers.)

However, some service industries are totally dependent on technology, such as computer and data processing firms which owe their existence to computer technology. William Goodman examines employment trends in computer services and engineering-two service industries that design a large range of products and play important roles in creating and changing computer technology.

The Home Market

The computer has launched the information highway, creating a whole new market segment-the home market. It is now the home market that represents a new frontier for computer and software manufactures. This market is considered one of the major opportunities for business investment over the next 20 years. As a result of the decline in cost of personal computers and the increased speed with which computers run, the buyer of a computer for die home now can obtain a high-powered machine that is able to run sophisticated software programs and link to the Internet. Laura Freeman explores this new market, examining the current market trend and its impact on employment.

High-tech Defence

The modern computer originated during World War II when funds were provided to defence contractors to create military products for intelligence uses. Up to the end of the cold war, defence contractors were instrumental in the development of computer-related technologies such as those found in space vehicles and electronic guidance systems in aircraft, missiles, and rockets. Although still on the cutting edge of technology, defence contractors increasingly have fewer defence funds for development in areas such as computers and microelectronics. Ron Hetrick examines efforts to soften this impact on defence-related private sector employment in a post cold-war era economy.

IN SUM, computer technology is changing the nature and number of jobs. Its impact is extensive because die technology, network system, and software is similar across firms and industries. This is in contrast to technological innovations in the past, which often affected specific occupations and industries. Computer technology is versatile and affects many unrelated industries and almost every job category.

In some cases, computer technology displaces workers, for example, bank tellers are being replaced with ATM's. But, while the technology is eliminating jobs, it also is creating new ones. Job growth has occurred in semiconductor and computer manufacturing as well as in computer and engineering service industries. However, die rate of job growth in these industries has been decelerating as the technology continues to improve labour efficiency.

Computerization and the emerging information highway is transforming the American economy. Computers are changing the composition and distribution of labour, improving labour efficiency, and creating new markets and new forms of organizations. The series of articles that follow discusses in more detail how computer technology is affecting employment in selected industries.

Use of Computers in Business

The proliferation of the computer has given the business world a powerful tool to use in its day-to-day operations. Many tasks that were once time consuming or difficult can now easily be carried out through the use of a computer.

Record Keeping

1. The data storage capabilities of the computer have given the

business world the opportunity to easily keep track of everything that the company does. All work orders, invoices and previous work can be easily stored for later retrieval.

Communication

2. The use of email and instant massaging services allow employees to communicate easily back and forth. This increases the amount of work done and saves money, since less time and resources have to be spent transmitting messages.

Accounting

3. Computers allow a company to easily keep track of where its money is at all times. Not only can assets and equities be tracked, but income and expenditures can be tracked as well. Some companies do all customer billing with a computer.

Data Analysis

4. Many decisions in the business world are dependent on the calculation of complex statistics. What once took people a great deal of time to perform can now be done by a network of computers in a fraction of the time.

Productivity

5. Drafting letters, designing ad copy, and many other functions once took artists and office personnel a great deal of time to draft, type and fabricate for distribution. The use of computers has made this process much quicker and more streamlined.

Managing Small Businesses, One Byte At a Time

The Internet has become a complex marketplace of ideas, products, and services. If you don't know the detailed ins and outs of integral online business processes such as accounting, e-commerce, reporting, order processing, and customer support, you may want to check out Net Ledger, a powerful small business software application from Oracle, the industry leader in business database technology.

A Powerful, Popular Web-Based Solution

Many websites devoted to business management seem to be clusters of various third-party services slapped together into one package. Others are simply well disguised portals to more expensive, sometimes esoteric services. But one popular business management service used widely today was clearly built from the ground up with the primary objective of providing businesses with tools to leverage the Web for business success, and it just keeps getting better.

The Oracle Small Business Suite, powered by Net Ledger, is a Web-based application that provides multi-user capability, online collaborations, access to your accounting system from any location via the Internet, and seamless connections to employees, customers, and suppliers. Because the suite is Internet-based, it is automatically compatible with different operating systems. You don't need to pay for hardware or software, and upgrades and backups are managed for you. It integrates complete front-office and back-office application functionality, thereby allowing companies to run their entire enterprise on a single hosted service. Although it is simple to learn, it is secure, reliable, and scalable to grow as your business grows.

Net Ledger Makes Their Small Business Service Sweeter

Because of its Oracle Small Business Suite, Net Ledger reigns as the leading provider of integrated customer relationship management (CRM) application services, and now the company has boldly entered an even more impressive frontier. In September 2004, Net Ledger announced the launch of NetCRM, built on the CRM functionality found in the Oracle Small Business Suite. NetCRM is the first online CRM application that automates the entire sales process, from marketing to lead generation, to prospect management, to sales orders and support.

In addition, NetCRM adds important new features not found in any other online CRM solution. Customizable "Dashboards," unique to NetCRM, highlight key information related to the roles of individual users within an enterprise. Graphical snapshots provide sales personnel and management with performance comparisons, and saved searches highlight the latest results of marketing campaigns. Shortcuts and quick searches keep customer information readily available, and reminders within a Dashboard make it easy to keep track of problems that must be solved and tasks that must be completed.

Selling is made easier and forecasting more accurate by NetCRM's integrated lead capturing and order processing capabilities, which allow businesses to track sales as they actually occur. An online form captures each lead, sends a personalized email auto reply, and then routes the lead to the correct person for follow-up within your sales pipeline according to customizable territory assignment rules.

Sales representatives create sales quotes or orders within NetCRM by selecting from product or service catalogues, and then sales managers receive notification on their Dashboards when sales orders require approval before closing. This close monitoring of sales transactions helps provide managers and executives with a complete and accurate view of current and future forecasts.

Because NetCRM seamlessly integrates purchase history, you can create tailored campaigns to target specific customer segments of your market. End-to-end campaign management includes system-provided templates, email campaign creation and distribution, and results measurement and analysis—all in one application. With this terrific customer intelligence built in, NetCRM allows businesses to deliver the right message in marketing campaigns much more effectively, since marketing efforts are personalized with customers' names and information they have proven their interest in. After the campaign is executed, NetCRM tracks the results and provides accurate cost-of-acquisition statistics for the entire sales cycle.

NetCRM's knowledge management technology, Net Answers, can provide huge cost savings and increase service capabilities by allowing customers to search an online database for answers to their questions without calling customer support. Companies can track frequently asked questions, standard problem resolutions, and known issues, and organize information into different levels of topics and solutions based on individual experience as well as collective knowledge.

NetCRM also provides a complete compliment of task management tools, partner relationship management features, XML server-to-server integration capabilities, various configurable user security levels, complete document management functionality, and intranet content publishing capabilities. Its numerous powerful features far outperform those provided by competing CRM products.

E-Services

e-Services or "eServices" is a highly general/generic term usually referring to the provision of services via the Internet (the prefix 'e' standing for "electronic", as it does in many other uses). It is true Web jargon, meaning just about anything done online. This page, for example, is an e-Service.

It can cause confusion when used in conjunction with "Support," as who knows the difference between "eServices" and online Support.

It is often best to be avoided for this reason, especially in Website navigation.

e-Services include "e-commerce," although they may also include non-commercial services.

Non-ecommerce e-services include (at least some) "eGovernment" services.

Electronic Commerce

Electronic commerce, commonly known as (electronic marketing) e-commerce or eCommerce, consists of the buying and selling of products or services over electronic systems such as the Internet and other computer networks.

The amount of trade conducted electronically has grown extraordinarily with widespread Internet usage. The use of commerce is conducted in this way, spurring and drawing on innovations in electronic funds transfer, supply chain management, Internet marketing, online transaction processing, electronic data interchange (EDI), inventory management systems, and automated data collection systems. Modern electronic commerce typically uses the World Wide Web at least at some point in the transaction's life cycle, although it can encompass a wider range of technologies such as email as well.

A large percentage of electronic commerce is conducted entirely electronically for virtual items such as access to premium content on a website, but most electronic commerce involves the transportation of physical items in some way. Online retailers are sometimes known as e-tailers and online retail is sometimes known as e-tail. Almost all big retailers have electronic commerce presence on the World Wide Web.

Electronic commerce that is conducted between businesses is referred to as business-to-business or B2B. B2B can be open to all interested parties (e.g. commodity exchange) or limited to specific, pre-qualified participants (private electronic market). Electronic commerce that is conducted between businesses and consumers, on the other hand, is referred to as business-to-consumer or B2C. This is the type of electronic commerce conducted by companies such as Amazon.com.

Electronic commerce is generally considered to be the sales aspect of e-business. It also consists of the exchange of data to facilitate the financing and payment aspects of the business transactions.

History

Early Development

The meaning of electronic commerce has changed over the last 30 years. Originally, electronic commerce meant the facilitation of commercial transactions electronically, using technology such as Electronic Data Interchange (EDI) and Electronic Funds Transfer (EFT). These were both introduced in the late 1970s, allowing businesses to send commercial documents like purchase orders or invoices electronically. The growth and acceptance of credit cards, automated teller machines (ATM) and telephone banking in the 1980s were also forms of electronic commerce. Another form of e-commerce was the airline reservation system typified by Sabre in the USA and Travicom in the UK.

Online shopping, an important component of electronic commerce, was invented by Michael Aldrich in the UK in 1979. The world's first recorded B2B was Thomson Holidays in 1981 The first recorded B2C was Gateshead SIS/Tesco in 1984 The world's first recorded online shopper was Mrs Jane Snowball of Gateshead, England During the 1980s, online shopping was also used extensively in the UK by auto manufacturers such as Ford, Peugeot-Talbot, General Motors and Nissan. All these organizations and others used the Aldrich systems. The systems used the switched public telephone network in dial-up and leased line modes. There was no broadband capability.

From the 1990s onwards, electronic commerce would additionally include enterprise resource planning systems (ERP), data mining and data warehousing.

An early example of many-to-many electronic commerce in physical goods was the Boston Computer Exchange, a marketplace for used computers launched in 1982. An early online information marketplace, including online consulting, was the American Information Exchange, another pre Internet online system introduced in 1991.

In 1990 Tim Berners-Lee invented the World Wide Web and transformed an academic telecommunication network into a worldwide everyman everyday communication system called internet/www. Commercial enterprise on the Internet was strictly prohibited until 1991. Although the Internet became popular worldwide around 1994 when the first internet online shopping started, it took about five years to introduce security protocols and DSL allowing continual connection to the Internet. By the end of 2000, many European and American business companies offered their services through the World Wide Web. Since then people began to associate a word "ecommerce" with the ability of purchasing various goods through the Internet using secure protocols and electronic payment services.

Timeline

- 1979: Online shopping was invented in the UK by Michael Aldrich.
- 1982: Minitel was introduced nationwide in France by France Telecom and used for online ordering.
- 1987: Swreg begins to provide software and shareware authors means to sell their products online through an electronic Merchant account.
- 1990: Tim Berners-Lee writes the first web browser, WorldWideWeb, using a Next computer.
- 1992: J.H. Snider and Terra Ziporyn publish Future Shop: How New Technologies Will Change the Way We Shop and What We Buy. St. Martin's Press.
- 1994: Netscape releases the Navigator browser in October under the code name Mozilla. Pizza Hut offers pizza ordering on its Web page. The first online bank opens. Attempts to offer flower delivery and magazine subscriptions online. Adult materials also become commercially available, as do cars and bikes. Netscape 1.0 is introduced in late 1994 SSL encryption that made transactions secure.
- 1995: Jeff Bezos launches Amazon.com and the first commercial-free 24 hour, internet-only radio stations, Radio HK and NetRadio start broadcasting. Dell and Cisco begin to aggressively use Internet for commercial transactions. eBay is founded by computer programmer Pierre Omidyar as Auction Web.
- 1998: Electronic postal stamps can be purchased and downloaded for printing from the Web.
- 1999: Business.com sold for US $7.5 million to eCompanies, which was purchased in 1997 for US $149,000. The peer-to-peer file sharing software Napster launches. ATG Stores launches to sell decorative items for the home online.

- 2000: The dot-com bust.
- 2002: eBay acquires PayPal for $1.5 billion. Niche retail companies CSN Stores and NetShops are founded with the concept of selling products through several targeted domains, rather than a central portal.
- 2003: Amazon.com posts first yearly profit.
- 2007: Business.com acquired by R.H. Donnelley for $345 million.
- 2008: US eCommerce and Online Retail sales projected to reach $204 billion, an increase of 17 percent over 2007.

Business Applications

Some common applications related to electronic commerce are the following:

Email

Electronic mail, often abbreviated as email, e.mail or email, is a method of exchanging digital messages. Email systems are based on a store-and-forward model in which email computer server systems accept, forward, deliver and store messages on behalf of users, who only need to connect to the email infrastructure, typically an email server, with a network-enabled device (e.g., a personal computer) for the duration of message submission or retrieval. Originally, email was always transmitted directly from one user's device to another's; nowadays this is rarely the case.

An electronic mail message consists of two components, the message *header*, and the message *body*, which is the email's content. The message header contains control information, including, minimally, an originator's email address and one or more recipient addresses. Usually additional information is added, such as a subject header field.

Originally a text-only communications medium, email was extended to carry multimedia content attachments, which were standardized in with RFC 2045 through RFC 2049, collectively called, Multipurpose Internet Mail Extensions (MIME).

The foundation for today's global Internet email service was created in the early ARPANET and standards for encoding of messages were proposed as early as 1973 (RFC 561). An email sent in the early 1970s looked very similar to one sent on the Internet today. Conversion from the ARPANET to the Internet in the early 1980s produced the core of the current service. Network-based email was initially exchanged on the ARPANET in extensions to the File Transfer Protocol (FTP), but is today carried by the Simple Mail Transfer Protocol (SMTP), first published as Internet standard 10 (RFC 821) in 1982. In the process of transporting email messages between systems, SMTP communicates delivery parameters using a message *envelope* separately from the message (headers and body) itself.

Spelling

There are several spelling variations that are occasionally the cause of vehement disagreement.

email is the form officially required by IETF Request for Comments and working groups and is also recognized in most dictionaries.

e-mail is a form still recommended by some prominent journalistic and technical style guides.

mail was the form used in the original RFC. The service is referred to as *mail* and a single piece of electronic mail is called a *message.*

eMail, capitalizing only the letter *M*, was common among ARPANET users and early developers from Unix, CMS, AppleLink, eWorld, AOL, GEnie, and Hotmail.

EMail is a traditional form that has been used in RFCs for the "Author's Address", and is expressly required *"...for historical reasons..."*.

Origin

Electronic mail predates the inception of the Internet, and was in fact a crucial tool in creating the Internet.

MIT first demonstrated the Compatible Time-Sharing System (CTSS) in 1961. It allowed multiple users to log into the IBM 7094 from remote dial-up terminals, and to store files online on disk. This new ability encouraged users to share information in new ways. Email started in 1965 as a way for multiple users of a time-sharing mainframe computer to communicate. Although the exact history is murky, among the first systems to have such a facility were SDC's Q32 and MIT's CTSS.

Host-Based Mailsystems

The original email systems allowed communication only between users who logged into the one host or "mainframe", but this could be hundreds or thousands of users within a company or university. By

1966 (or earlier, it is possible that the SAGE system had something similar some time before), such systems allowed email between different companies as long as they ran compatible operating systems, but not to other dissimilar systems.

Examples include BITNET, IBM PROFS, Digital All-in-1 and the original Unix mail.

LAN-Based Mailsystems

From the early 1980s networked personal computers on LANs became increasingly important-and server-based systems similar to the earlier mainframe systems developed, and again initially allowed communication only between users logged into the one server, but these also could generally be linked between different companies as long as they ran the same email system and (proprietary) protocol.

Examples include cc:Mail, Word Perfect Office, Microsoft Mail, Banyan VINES and Lotus Notes-with various vendors supplying gateway software to link these incompatible systems.

Attempts at Interoperability

- Novell briefly championed the open MHS protocol
- uucp was used as an open "glue" between differing mail systems
- The Coloured Book protocols on UK academic networks until 1992
- X.400 in the early 1990s was mandated for government use under GOSIP but almost immediately abandoned by all but a few — in favour of Internet SMTP

The Rise of ARPANET-based Mail

The ARPANET computer network made a large contribution to the development of email. There is one report that indicates experimental inter-system email transfers began shortly after its creation in 1969. Ray Tomlinson is credited by some as having sent the first email, initiating the use of the "@" sign to separate the names of the user and the user's machine in 1971, when he sent a message from one Digital Equipment Corporation DEC-10 computer to another DEC-10. The two machines were placed next to each other. The ARPANET significantly increased the popularity of email, and it became the killer app of the ARPANET.

Most other networks had their own email protocols and address formats; as the influence of the ARPANET and later the Internet grew, central sites often hosted email gateways that passed mail between the Internet and these other networks. Internet email addressing is still complicated by the need to handle mail destined for these older networks. Some well-known examples of these were UUCP (mostly Unix computers), BITNET (mostly IBM and VAX main frames at universities), FidoNet (personal computers), DECNET (various networks) and CSNet a forerunner of NSFNet.

An example of an Internet email address that routed mail to a user at a UUCP host:

This was necessary because in early years UUCP computers did not maintain (or consult servers for) information about the location of all hosts they exchanged mail with, but rather only knew how to communicate with a few network neighbours; email messages (and other data such as Usenet News) were passed along in a chain among hosts who had explicitly agreed to share data with each other.

Operation Overview

The diagram to the right shows a typical sequence of events that takes place when Alice composes a message using her mail user agent (MUA). She enters the email address of her correspondent, and hits the "send" button.

1. Her MUA formats the message in email format and uses the Simple Mail Transfer Protocol (SMTP) to send the message to the local mail transfer agent (MTA), in this case smtp.a.org, run by Alice's Internet Service Provider (ISP).
2. The MTA looks at the destination address provided in the SMTP protocol (not from the message header), in this case bob@b.org. An Internet email address is a string of the form localpart@exampledomain. The part before the @ sign is the local part of the address, often the username of the recipient, and the part after the @ sign is a domain name or a fully qualified domain name. The MTA resolves a domain name to determine the fully qualified domain name of the mail exchange server in the Domain Name System.
3. The DNS server for the b.org domain, ns.b.org, responds with any MX records listing the mail exchange servers for that domain, in this case mx.b.org, a server run by Bob's ISP.

4. smtp.a.org sends the message to mx.b.org using SMTP, which delivers it to the mailbox of the user bob.
5. Bob presses the "get mail" button in his MUA, which picks up the message using the Post Office Protocol (POP3).

That sequence of events applies to the majority of email users. However, there are many alternative possibilities and complications to the email system:

- Alice or Bob may use a client connected to a corporate email system, such as IBM Lotus Notes or Microsoft Exchange. These systems often have their own internal email format and their clients typically communicate with the email server using a vendor-specific, proprietary protocol. The server sends or receives email via the Internet through the product's Internet mail gateway which also does any necessary reformatting. If Alice and Bob work for the same company, the entire transaction may happen completely within a single corporate email system.
- Alice may not have a MUA on her computer but instead may connect to a webmail service.
- Alice's computer may run its own MTA, so avoiding the transfer at step 1.
- Bob may pick up his email in many ways, for example using the Internet Message Access Protocol, by logging into mx.b.org and reading it directly, or by using a webmail service.
- Domains usually have several mail exchange servers so that they can continue to accept mail when the main mail exchange server is not available.
- Email messages are not secure if email encryption is not used correctly.

Many MTAs used to accept messages for any recipient on the Internet and do their best to deliver them. Such MTAs are called *open mail relays.* This was very important in the early days of the Internet when network connections were unreliable. If an MTA couldn't reach the destination, it could at least deliver it to a relay closer to the destination. The relay stood a better chance of delivering the message at a later time. However, this mechanism proved to be exploitable by people sending unsolicited bulk email and as a consequence very few modern MTAs are open mail relays, and many MTAs don't accept messages from open mail relays because such messages are very likely to be spam.

Message Format

The Internet email message format is defined in RFC *5322 and a series of* RFC*s,* RFC *2045 through* RFC *2049, collectively called,* Multipurpose Internet Mail Extensions, *or* MIME. *Although as of July 13, 2005,* RFC *2822 is technically a proposed* IETF *standard and the* MIME RFC*s are draft* IETF *standards, these documents are the standards for the format of Internet email. Prior to the introduction of* RFC *2822 in 2001, the format described by* RFC *822 was the standard for Internet email for nearly 20 years; it is still the official* IETF *standard. The* IETF *reserved the numbers 5321 and 5322 for the updated versions of* RFC *2821 (SMTP) and* RFC *2822, as it previously did with* RFC *821 and* RFC *822, honoring the extreme importance of these two* RFC*s.* RFC *822 was published in 1982 and based on the earlier* RFC *733.*

Internet email Messages Consist of two Major Sections

- Header — Structured into fields such as summary, sender, receiver, and other information about the email.
- Body — The message itself as unstructured text; sometimes containing a signature block at the end. This is exactly the same as the body of a regular letter.

The header is separated from the body by a blank line.

Message Header

Each message has exactly one header, which is structured into fields. Each field has a name and a value. RFC 5322 specifies the precise syntax.

Informally, each line of text in the header that begins with a printable character begins a separate field. The field name starts in the first character of the line and ends before the separator character ":". The separator is then followed by the field value (the "body" of the field). The value is continued onto subsequent lines if those lines have a space or tab as their first character. Field names and values are restricted to 7-bit ASCII characters. Non-ASCII values may be represented using MIME encoded words.

Header Fields

The message header should include at least the following fields:

- From: The email address, and optionally the name of the

author(s). In many email clients not changeable except through changing account settings.

- To: The email address(es), and optionally name(s) of the message's recipient(s). Indicates primary recipients (multiple allowed), for secondary recipients.
- Subject: A brief summary of the topic of the message.
- Date: The local time and date when the message was written. Like the *From:* field, many email clients fill this in automatically when sending. The recipient's client may then display the time in the format and time zone local to her.
- Message-ID: Also an automatically generated field; used to prevent multiple delivery and for reference in In-Reply-To.

Note that the "To:" field is not necessarily related to the addresses to which the message is delivered. The actual delivery list is supplied separately to the transport protocol, SMTP, which may or may not originally have been extracted from the header content. The "To:" field is similar to the addressing at the top of a conventional letter which is delivered according to the address on the outer envelope. Also note that the "From:" field does not have to be the real sender of the email message. One reason is that it is very easy to fake the "From:" field and let a message seem to be from any mail address. It is possible to digitally sign email, which is much harder to fake, but such signatures require extra programming and often external programs to verify. Some Internet service providers do not relay email claiming to come from a domain not hosted by them, but very few (if any) check to make sure that the person or even email address named in the "From:" field is the one associated with the connection. Some Internet service providers apply email authentication systems to email being sent through their MTA to allow other MTAs to detect forged spam that might appear to come from them.

RFC 3864 describes registration procedures for message header fields at the IANA; it provides for permanent and provisional message header field names, including also fields defined for MIME, netnews, and http, and referencing relevant RFCs. Common header fields for email include:

- *Bcc:* Blind Carbon Copy; addresses added to the SMTP delivery list but not (usually) listed in the message data, remaining invisible to other recipients.

- *Cc:* Carbon copy; Many email clients will mark email in your inbox differently depending on whether you are in the To: or Cc: list.
- *Content-Type:* Information about how the message is to be displayed, usually a MIME type.
- *In-Reply-To:* Message-ID of the message that this is a reply to. Used to link related messages together.
- *Precedence:* commonly with values "bulk", "junk", or "list"; used to indicate that automated "vacation" or "out of office" responses should not be returned for this mail, eg. to prevent vacation notices from being sent to all other subscribers of a mailinglist.
- *Received:* Tracking information generated by mail servers that have previously handled a message, in reverse order (last handler first).
- *References:* Message-ID of the message that this is a reply to, and the message-id of the message the previous was reply a reply to, etc.
- *Reply-To:* Address that should be used to reply to the message.
- *Sender:* Address of the actual sender acting on behalf of the author listed in the From: field (secretary, list manager, etc.).
- X-Face: Small icon.

Message Body

This section needs additional citations for verification. Please help improve this article by adding reliable references. Unsourced material may be challenged and removed. *(November 2007)*

Content Encoding

Email was originally designed for 7-bit ASCII. Much email software is 8-bit clean but must assume it will communicate with 8-bit servers and mail readers. The MIME standard introduced character set specifies and two content transfer encodings to enable transmission of non-ASCII data: quoted printable for mostly 7 bit content with a few characters outside that range and base for arbitrary binary data. The 8BITMIME extension was introduced to allow transmission of mail without the need for these encodings but many mail transport agents still do not support it fully. In some countries, several encoding schemes coexist; as the result, by default, the message in a non-Latin alphabet language appears in non-readable form (the only exception is coincidence, when the sender and receiver use the same encoding scheme). Therefore, for international character sets, Unicode is growing in popularity.

Plain text and HTML

Most modern graphic email clients allow the use of either plain text or HTML for the message body at the option of the user. HTML email messages often include an automatically-generated plain text copy as well, for compatibility reasons. Advantages of HTML include the ability to include inline links and images, set apart previous messages in block quotes, wrap naturally on any display, use emphasis such as underlines and italics, and change font styles. Disadvantages include the increased size of the email, privacy concerns about web bugs, abuse of HTML email as a vector for phishing attacks and the spread of malicious software.

Mailing lists commonly insist that all posts to be made in plain-text for all the above reasons, but also because they have a significant number of readers using text-based email clients such as Mutt. Some Microsoft email clients have allowed richer formatting by using RTF rather than HTML, but unless the recipient is guaranteed to have a compatible email client this should be avoided.

Servers and Client Applications

The Interface of an email Client, Thunderbird

Messages are exchanged between hosts using the Simple Mail Transfer Protocol with software programs called mail transfer agents. Users can retrieve their messages from servers using standard protocols such as POP or IMAP, or, as is more likely in a large corporate environment, with a proprietary protocol specific to Lotus Notes or Microsoft Exchange Servers. Webmail interfaces allow users to access their mail with any standard web browser, from any computer, rather than relying on an email client.

Mail can be stored on the client, on the server side, or in both places. Standard formats for mailboxes include Maildir and mbox. Several prominent email clients use their own proprietary format and require conversion software to transfer email between them. Accepting a message obliges an MTA to deliver it, and when a message cannot be delivered, that MTA must send a bounce message back to the sender, indicating the problem.

Filename Extensions

Upon reception of email messages, email client applications save message in operating system files in the file system. Some clients save individual messages as separate files, while others use various database formats, often proprietary, for collective storage. A historical standard of storage is the *mbox* format. The specific format used is often indicated by special filename extensions:

- eml : Used by many email clients including Microsoft Outlook Express, Windows Mail and Mozilla Thunderbird. The files are plain text in MIME format, containing the email header as well as the message contents and attachments in one or more of several formats.
- emlx

  Used by Apple Mail.
- msg

  Used by Microsoft Office Outlook.
- mbx : Used by Opera Mail, KMail, and Apple Mail based on the mbox format.

Some applications (like Apple Mail) also encode attachments into messages for searching while also producing a physical copy of the files on a disk. Others separate attachments from messages by depositing them into designated folders on disk.

URI Scheme Mailto

The URI scheme, as registered with the IANA, defines the mailto: scheme for SMTP email addresses. Though its use is not strictly defined, URLs of this form are intended to be used to open the new message window of the user's mail client when the URL is activated, with the address as defined by the URL in the "To:" field.

Use

This section needs additional citations for verification. Please help improve this article by adding reliable references. Unsourced material may be challenged and removed. *(November 2007)*

In Society

There are numerous ways in which people have changed the way they communicate in the last 50 years; email is certainly one of them. Traditionally, social interaction in the local community was the basis for communication – face to face. Yet, today face-to-face meetings are no longer the primary way to communicate as one can use a landline telephone, mobile phones or any number of the computer mediated communications such as email. Research has shown that people actively use email to maintain core social networks, particularly when others live at a distance. However, contradictory to previous research, the results suggest that increases in Internet usage are associated with decreases in other modes of communication, with proficiency of Internet and email use serving as a mediating factor in this relationship. With the introduction of chat messengers and video conference there are more ways to communicate.

Flaming

Flaming occurs when a person sends a message with angry or antagonistic content. Flaming is assumed to be more common today because of the ease and impersonality of email communications: confrontations in person or via telephone require direct interaction, where social norms encourage civility, whereas typing a message to another person is an indirect interaction, so civility may be forgotten. Flaming is generally looked down upon by Internet communities as it is considered rude and non-productive.

Email Bankruptcy

Also known as "email fatigue", email bankruptcy is when a user ignores a large number of email messages after falling behind in reading and answering them. The reason for falling behind is often due to information overload and a general sense there is so much information that it is not possible to read it all. As a solution, people occasionally send a boilerplate message explaining that the email inbox is being cleared out. Stanford University law professor Lawrence Lessig is credited with coining this term, but he may only have popularized it.

In Business

Email was widely accepted by the business community as the first broad electronic communication medium and was the first 'e-revolution' in business communication. Email is very simple to understand and like postal mail, email solves two basic problems of communication: logistics and synchronization. LAN based email is also an emerging form of usage for business. It not only allows the business user to download mail when *offline*, it also provides the small business user to have multiple users email ID's with just *one email connection.*

Pros

- The problem of logistics : Much of the business world relies upon communications between people who are not physically in the same building, area or even country; setting up and attending an in-person meeting, telephone call, or conference call can be inconvenient, time-consuming, and costly. Email provides a way to exchange information between two or more people with no setup costs and that is generally far less expensive than physical meetings or phone calls.
- The problem of synchronization : With real time communication by meetings or phone calls, participants have to work on the same schedule, and each participant must spend the same amount of time in the meeting or call. Email allows asynchrony: each participant may control their schedule independently.

Cons

This section may contain original research or unverified claims. Please improve the article by adding references. Most business workers today spend from one to two hours of their working day on email: reading, ordering, sorting, 're-contextualizing' fragmented information, and writing email. The use of email is increasing due to increasing levels of globalization—labour division and outsourcing amongst other things. Email can lead to some well-known problems:

- Loss of Context: which means that the context is lost forever; there is no way to get the text back.

Information in context (as in a newspaper) is much easier and faster to understand than unedited and sometimes unrelated fragments of information. Communicating in context can only be achieved when both parties have a full understanding of the context and issue in question.

- Information overload: Email is a push technology—the sender controls who receives the information. Convenient availability of mailing lists and use of "copy all" can lead to people receiving unwanted or irrelevant information of no use to them.
- Inconsistency: Email can duplicate information. This can be a problem when a large team is working on documents and information while not in constant contact with the other members of their team.

Despite these disadvantages, email has become the most widely used medium of communication within the business world.

Problems

This section needs additional citations for verification. Please help improve this article by adding reliable references. Unsourced material may be challenged and removed. *(November 2007)*

Information Overload

A December 2007 New York Times blog post described Email as "a $650 Billion Drag on the Economy", and the New York Times reported in April 2008 that "Email has become the bane of some people's professional lives" due to information overload, yet "none of the current wave of high-profile Internet start-ups focused on email really eliminates the problem of email overload because none helps us prepare replies".

Technology Investors Reflect Similar Concerns

Spamming and Computer Viruses

The usefulness of email is being threatened by four phenomena: email bombardment, spamming, phishing, and email worms.

Spamming is unsolicited commercial (or bulk) email. Because of the very low cost of sending email, spammers can send hundreds of millions of email messages each day over an inexpensive Internet connection. Hundreds of active spammers sending this volume of mail results in information overload for many computer users who receive voluminous unsolicited email each day.

Email worms use email as a way of replicating themselves into vulnerable computers. Although the first email worm affected UNIX computers, the problem is most common today on the more popular Microsoft Windows operating system. The combination of spam and worm programs results in users receiving a constant drizzle of junk email, which reduces the usefulness of email as a practical tool.

A number of anti-spam techniques mitigate the impact of spam. In the United States, U.S. Congress has also passed a law, the Can Spam Act of 2003, attempting to regulate such email. Australia also has very strict spam laws restricting the sending of spam from an Australian ISP, but its impact has been minimal since most spam comes from regimes that seem reluctant to regulate the sending of spam.

Email Spoofing

Email spoofing occurs when the header information of an email is altered to make the message appear to come from a known or trusted source. It is often used as a ruse to collect personal information.

Email Bombing

Email bombing is the intentional sending of large volumes of messages to a target address. The overloading of the target email address can render it unusable and can even cause the mail server to crash.

Privacy Concerns

Email privacy, without some security precautions, can be compromised because:

- email messages are generally not encrypted;
- email messages have to go through intermediate computers before reaching their destination, meaning it is relatively easy for others to intercept and read messages;
- many Internet Service Providers (ISP) store copies of email messages on their mail servers before they are delivered. The backups of these can remain for up to several months on their server, despite deletion from the mailbox;
- the Received: fields and other information in the email can often identify the sender, preventing anonymous communication.

There are cryptography applications that can serve as a remedy to one or more of the above. For example, Virtual Private Networks or the Tor anonymity network can be used to encrypt traffic from the user machine to a safer network while GPG, PGP, SMEmail, or S/MIME can be used for end-to-end message encryption, and SMTP STARTTLS or SMTP over Transport Layer Security/Secure Sockets Layer can be used to encrypt communications for a single mail hop between the SMTP client and the SMTP server.

Additionally, many mail user agents do not protect logins and passwords, making them easy to intercept by an attacker. Encrypted authentication schemes such as SASL prevent this.

Finally, attached files share many of the same hazards as those found in peer-to-peer file sharing. Attached files may contain trojans or viruses.

Tracking of Sent Mail

The original SMTP mail service provides limited mechanisms for tracking a transmitted message, and none for verifying that it has been delivered or read. It requires that each mail server must either deliver it onward or return a failure notice (bounce message), but both software bugs and system failures can cause messages to be lost. To remedy this, the IETF introduced Delivery Status Notifications (delivery receipts) and Message Disposition Notifications (return receipts); however, these are not universally deployed in production.

US Government Email

The US Government has been involved in email in several different ways.

Starting in 1977, the US Postal Service (USPS) recognized that electronic mail and electronic transactions posed a significant threat to First Class mail volumes and revenue. Therefore, the USPS initiated an experimental email service known as E-COM. Electronic messages were transmitted to a post office, printed out, and delivered as hard copy. To take advantage of the service, an individual had to transmit at least 200 messages. The delivery time of the messages was the same as First Class mail and cost 26 cents. Both the Postal Regulatory Commission and the Federal Communications Commission opposed E-COM. The FCC concluded that E-COM constituted common carriage under its jurisdiction and the USPS would have to file a tariff. Three years after initiating the service, USPS canceled E-COM and attempted to sell it off.

The early ARPANET dealt with multiple email clients that had various, and at times incompatible, formats. For example, in the system Multics, the "@" sign meant "kill line" and anything after the "@" sign was ignored. The Department of Defence DARPA desired to have uniformity and interoperability for email and therefore funded efforts to drive towards unified interoperable standards. This led to David Crocker, John Vittal, Kenneth Pogran, and Austin Henderson publishing RFC 733, "Standard for the Format of ARPA Network Text Message" (November 21, 1977), which was apparently not effective. In 1979, a meeting was held at BBN to resolve incompatibility issues. Jon Postel recounted the meeting in RFC 808, "Summary of Computer Mail Services Meeting Held at BBN on 10 January 1979" (March 1, 1982), which includes an appendix listing the varying email systems at the time.

This, in turn, lead to the release of David Crocker's RFC 822, "Standard for the Format of ARPA Internet Text Messages" (August 13, 1982).

The National Science Foundation took over operations of the ARPANET and Internet from the Department of Defence, and initiated NSFNet, a new backbone for the network. A part of the NSFNet AUP forbade commercial traffic. In 1988, Vint Cerf arranged for an interconnection of MCI Mail with NSFNET on an experimental basis. The following year Compuserve email interconnected with NSFNET. Within a few years the commercial traffic restriction was removed from NSFNETs AUP, and NSFNET was privatized.

In the late 1990s, the Federal Trade Commission grew concerned with fraud transpiring in email, and initiated a series of procedures on spam, fraud, and phishing. In 2004, FTC jurisdiction over spam was codified into law in the form of the CAN SPAM Act. Several other US Federal Agencies have also exercised jurisdiction including the Department of Justice and the Secret Service.

Enterprise Content Management

Enterprise content management (ECM) refers to the technologies, strategies, methods and tools used to capture, manage, store, preserve, and deliver content and documents related to an organization and its processes. ECM tools allow the management of an enterprise level organization's information.

Definition

The official definition of enterprise content management was created by Association for Information and Image Management (AIIM) International, the worldwide association for enterprise content management, in the year 2000. The abbreviation ECM has been reinterpreted and redefined many times.

In late 2005 AIIM Defined ECM as Follows:

Enterprise Content Management is the technologies used to Capture, Manage, Store, Preserve, and Deliver content and documents related to organizational processes.

In Early 2006 AIIM Added the Following Paragraph to the Definition:

ECM tools and strategies allow the management of an organization's unstructured information, wherever that information exists.

In Early 2008 AIIM Changed the Original Definition to:

Enterprise Content Management (ECM) is the strategies, methods and tools used to capture, manage, store, preserve, and deliver content and documents related to organizational processes. ECM tools and strategies allow the management of an organization's unstructured information, wherever that information exists.

This new term is intended to completely encompass the legacy problem domains that have traditionally been addressed by records management and document management. It also includes all of the additional problems involved in converting to and from digital content, to and from the traditional media of those problem domains (such as physical and computerized filing and retrieval systems, often involving paper and microforms). Finally ECM is a new problem domain in its own right, as it has employed the technologies and strategies of (digital) content management to address business process issues, such as records and auditing, knowledge sharing, personalization and standardization of content, and so on.

History

New product suites have arisen from the combination of capture, search and networking capabilities with technologies of the content management field, which have traditionally addressed digital archiving, document management and workflow. Generally speaking, this is when content management becomes enterprise content management. *The different nomenclature is intended to encompass all of the problem areas related to the use and preservation of information within an organization, in all of its forms — not just its web-oriented face to the outside world. Therefore, most solutions focus on "business to employee" (*B2E*) systems. However, as the solutions have evolved, new components to content management have arisen. For example, as unstructured content is checked in and out of an ECM system, each use can potentially enrich the content's profile, to some extent automatically, so that the system might gradually acquire or "learn" new filtering, routing and search pathways, corporate taxonomies and semantic networks, which in turn assist in making better retention-rule decisions, determining which records or documents to keep, and which to discard, and when. Such issues become all the more important, as email and instant massaging are increasingly employed in the decision-making processes in an organization.*

*Thus, the term enterprise content management refers to solutions that concentrate on providing in-house information, usually using internet technologies. The solutions tend to provide intranet services to employees (B2E), but also include enterprise portals for "business to business" (*B2B*), "business to government" (*B2G*), or* *"government to business"* (G2B)*, etc. This category includes most of the former document management groupware and workflow solutions that have not yet fully converted their architecture, but provide a web interface to their applications. Digital Asset Management (DAM) is as well a form of ECM that is concerned with content stored using digital electronic technology.*

The technology components that comprise ECM today are the descendants of the electronic document management systems (EDMS) software products that were first released in the late 1980s and early 1990s. The original EDMS products were developed as stand-alone technologies, and these products provided functionality in one of four areas: imaging , workflow, document management, or COLD/ERM.

For the software companies, it made sense to develop different products for each of these distinct EDMS functions. At that time, most organizations that were candidates for EDMS generally wanted a solution to address just one overriding business need or application. They were looking for stand-alone solutions to address narrow application needs, many of them at the departmental level – such as imaging for forms processing, workflow for insurance claims processing, document management for engineering documentation, or COLD/ERM for distributing and archiving monthly financial reports.

The typical "early adopter" of these new technologies was an organization that deployed a small-scale imaging and workflow system, possibly to just a single department, in order to improve the efficiency of a repetitive, paper-intensive business process and migrate towards the Paperless office. Even in these early years, when the market for these software products was still relatively immature, it was clear that each of the major technologies within EDMS offered tremendous value to specific organizational processes or applications, at a time when business processes were overwhelmingly paper-based. The primary benefits that the first stand-alone EDMS technologies brought to organizations revolved around saving time or improving accessibility to information. Among the specific benefits were the following:

- Reduction of paper handling and error-prone manual processes
- Reduction of paper storage
- Reduction of lost documents
- Faster access to information
- Online access to information that was formerly available only on paper, microfilm, or microfiche

- Improved control over documents and document-oriented processes
- Streamlining of time-consuming business processes
- Security over document access and modification
- Provide reliable and accurate audit trail
- Improved tracking and monitoring, with the ability to identify bottlenecks and modify the system to improve efficiency.

Through the late 1990s, the various segments of the EDMS industry continued to grow steadily, if not spectacularly. The technologies appealed to organizations with clear problems, and which needed targeted, tactical solutions to address those problems.

As time passed, and more organizations had achieved "pockets" of productivity with the use of these technologies, it became clear that the various EDMS product categories were in fact complementary for many businesses. Organizations increasingly wanted to be able to leverage the capabilities of multiple EDMS products. Consider, for example, the needs of a customer service department, where imaging, document management, and workflow functionality could be brought together to allow agents to access any information needed to resolve a customer inquiry. Likewise, an accounting department could access supplier invoices from a COLD/ERM system, purchase orders from an imaging system, and contracts from a document management system as part of an approval workflow. And as more and more organizations established an Internet presence, they wanted to present certain portions of this information via the web, which required the capabilities to manage web content. Furthermore, organizations that had installed the software in individual departments now began to envision wider benefits, if they were to deploy it across the enterprise. Consider the fact that many business documents cross multiple departments and multiple business processes. Why not improve the management of electronic documents throughout the organization, and gain the same business benefits at an enterprise level?

Both the market and the software providers began to understand the strategic potential of software products that integrated the individual EDMS technology components into a single, integrated solution, capable of addressing an organization's complete information management needs. In fact, the movement toward integrated EDMS solutions merely reflected a common trend in the history of the software industry: the obsolescence of certain types of products and the convergence of technologies, as vendors melded them into new packages.

Consider office suites, for instance. In the 1970s and early 1980s, word processing, spreadsheet, and presentation software products were standalone products. Within an organization, however, the same users were likely to need all three products. The software vendors responded, and started packaging them as integrated office suites – a strategy that also helped address consumer demand for tighter interoperability among desktop applications.

The situation was similar in the EDMS world. Just about any company that needed document management also needed imaging, workflow, web content management, and COLD/ERM. Organizations began to demand multiple EDMS services and ways to leverage them for broad-based applications. Thus, the EDMS vendors took steps to deliver on truly integrated solutions incorporating the EDMS component technologies.

The leaders tended to be those vendors that already offered multiple stand-alone EDMS technologies. For these vendors, the early steps toward consolidation were small ones. The first phase was to offer multiple systems as a single, packaged "suite." Early suites were little more than multiple products being sold together at a reduced price, and there was a perception in the market that such suites were a strategy on the part of the vendors to capture additional seats within a customer account. Not surprisingly, market acceptance was limited – at least initially.

But in the late 1990s, these software vendors began a major surge of software development and acquisition activity, adding capabilities to their software products or buying the software companies whose products offered the functional capabilities they needed. Integrating the products into a single solution has proven to be an ongoing challenge for many of these vendors. Scalability – that is, the ability of a software product to continue to function well when it is deployed on a wide scale – also presented some significant problems, as organizations demanded solutions that could be deployed not just to multiple geographic locations, but on a global scale, to tens of thousands of users.

In response to these market demands, the major software providers put considerable development effort into addressing these issues, and they continue to enhance the capabilities of their products and to expand the types of content those products can manage. Beginning in approximately 2001, the industry began to use the term "enterprise content management" to refer to those software solutions that provide the full complement of EDMS technologies, reflecting the truly "enterprise" nature of their products.

More recently, the ECM market has seen the entry of Microsoft and Oracle Corporation, two of the largest and most pervasive providers of software, at the value end of the market.

These companies have each taken steps to develop solutions for content management – Microsoft with its various offerings in the Share Point product family in recent years, and Oracle in 2006 with its Oracle Content Management product. These two software companies look to provide software solutions with the basic ECM functionality that will address the functional requirements commonly required by the majority of organizations. The result is likely to be a stratification of the current ECM market, based on the level of content services that different organizations require.

Independently of Microsoft and Oracle, open source enterprise content management systems have emerged. These include Logical DOC, WebGUI, Alfresco, Sensenet 6.0, eZ Publish, Knowledge Tree, Jumper 2.0, Nuxeo, Plone and freedom. Similarly to the operating system, application server and database markets, these entrants hope to apply the open source distribution model of freely available and downloadable software to compete against the traditional enterprise software sales model of the incumbent ECM vendors and commoditize the ECM market.

The need for scalability and scanning facilities for hundreds of millions of documents requiring Terabyte, Petabyte or Exabyte filestores that are in compliance with existing and emerging standards such as HIPAA, SAS 70, BS 7799 and ISO/IEC 27001 may make outsourcing to certified end to end service providers a viable alternative.

Characteristics

Content management has many facets including enterprise content management, Web content management (WCM), content syndication and digital or media asset management. Enterprise content management is a vision, a strategy, or even a new industry, but it is not a closed system solution or a distinct product. Therefore, along with DRT (Document Related Technologies) or DLM (Document Life cycle Management),

ECM can be considered as just one possible catch-all term for a wide range of technologies and vendors.

A comparison of the definitions of the different application fields of ECM and WCM makes it clear that the existing system category distinctions cannot last long, whether for products and technical platforms or for usage models. Solutions that are used as pure in-house solutions today will be made accessible to partners or customers tomorrow. The content and structure of today's outward-directed web portal will be the platform for tomorrow's internal information system. In his article in Computer Woche, *Ulrich Kampffmeyer concentrated the claimed benefit of an enterprise content management system to three key ideas that distinguish such solutions from Web content management:*

"Enterprise Content Management as Integrative Middleware

ECM is used to overcome the restrictions of former vertical applications and island architectures. The user is basically unaware of using an ECM solution. ECM offers the requisite infrastructure for the new world of web-based IT, which is establishing itself as a kind of third platform alongside conventional host and client/server systems. Therefore, EAI (enterprise application integration) and SOA (service-oriented architecture) will play an important role in the implementation and use of ECM.

Enterprise Content Management Components as Independent Services

ECM is used to manage information without regard to the source or the required use. The functionality is provided as a service that can be used from all kinds of applications. The advantage of a service concept is that for any given functionality only one general service is available, thus avoiding redundant, expensive and difficult to maintain parallel functions. Therefore, standards for interfaces connecting different services will play an important role in the implementation of ECM.

Enterprise Content Management as a Uniform Repository for all Types of Information

ECM is used as a content warehouse (both data warehouse and document warehouse) that combines company information in a repository with a uniform structure. Expensive redundancies and associated problems with information consistency are eliminated. All applications deliver their content to a single repository, which in turn provides needed information to all applications. Therefore, content integration and ILM (Information Life cycle Management) will play an important role in the implementation and use of ECM.

Enterprise content management is working properly when it is effectively "invisible" to users. ECM technologies are infrastructures that support specialized applications as subordinate services. ECM thus is a collection of infrastructure components that fit into a multi-layer model and include all document related technologies (DRT) for handling, delivering, and managing structured data and unstructured information jointly. As such, enterprise content management is one of the necessary basic components of the overarching e-business application area. ECM also sets out to manage all the information of a WCM and covers archiving needs as an universal repository."

Components of an Enterprise Content Management System

Enterprise content management systems combine a wide variety of technologies and components, some of which can also be used as stand-alone systems without being incorporated into an enterprise-wide system.

The five ECM components and technologies of the ECM model were first defined by AIIM as follows:

- capture
- manage
- store
- preserve
- deliver.

The model includes in the "Manage" category five traditional application areas:

- document management (DM),
- collaboration (or collaborative software, groupware),
- web content management (WCM) (including web portals),
- records management (RM) (archive and filing management systems on long-term storage media), and
- workflow/business process management (BPM).

These "Manage" components connect capture, store, deliver and preserve and can be used in combination or separately. While document management, web content management, collaboration, workflow and business process management are more for the dynamic part of the life cycle of information, records management takes care of information which will no longer be changed. The utilization of the information is paramount throughout, whether through independent clients of the ECM system components, or by enabling existing applications that access the functionality of ECM services and the stored information. The integration of existing technologies makes it clear that ECM is not a new product category, but an integrative force. The individual categories and their components will be examined in the following.

Capture

The "Capture" category contains functionalities and components for generating, capturing, preparing and processing analog and electronic information. There are several levels and technologies, from simple information capture to complex information preparation using automatic classification. Capture components are often also called "Input" components.

Manually Generated and Captured Information

Manual capture can involve all forms of information, from paper documents to electronic office documents, e-mails, forms, multimedia objects, digitized speech and video, and microfilm. Automatic or semiautomatic capture can use EDI or XML documents, business and ERP applications or existing specialist application systems as sources.

Technologies for Processing Captured Information

Various recognition technologies are used to process scanned documents and digital faxes, among them:

Optical Character Recognition (OCR)

This converts image information into machine-readable characters; OCR is used for type;

Handprint Character Recognition (HCR)

This refinement of OCR converts handwriting or lettering into machine characters, but does not yet give satisfactory results for running text; however, for defined field content, it has become very reliable;

Intelligent Character Recognition (ICR)

ICR is a further development of OCR and HCR that uses comparison, logical connections, and checks against reference lists and existing master data to improve results;

Optical Mark Recognition (OMR)

OMR, as used for checkboxes for example, reads special markings in predefined fields with very high accuracy; it has proven its value in questionnaires and other forms;

Barcode

Barcodes on mailed forms allow for the automatic recognition and filing of returns.

Document Imaging

Document Imaging processing techniques are used to capture, improve the quality of and to view images. Functions and features include rotation, zooming, aligning, separation of pages, annotations, despeckling and other.

Forms Processing

In forms capture, there are two groups of technologies, although the information content and character of the documents may be identical.

Paper Forms

Forms processing means the capture of industrially or individually printed forms via scanning; recognition technologies are often used here, since well-designed forms enable largely automatic processing;

e-forms/web-forms

Automatic processing can be used to capture electronic forms as long as the layout, structure, logic and contents are known to the capture system.

Cold

COLD/ERM are technologies for the automatic processing of structured entry data. COLD stands for computer output to laser disk and is still in use although laser disks have not been on the market for years. The acronym ERM here stands for enterprise report management. For both, supplied output data is processed based on existing structure information in such a way that it can be indexed independently of the origination system, and transferred to a storage component that can be dynamic ("Store") or an archive ("Preserve").

Aggregation

Is a process of combining data entries from different creation, capture, and delivery applications. The goal is to combine and unify data from different sources, in order to pass them on to storage and processing systems with a uniform structure and format.

Components for Subject Indexing of Captured Information

Systems incorporate further components for subject indexing and getting captured digital information to the appropriate recipients. These include:

Indexing (Manual)

In English parlance, indexing refers to the manual assignment of index attributes used in the database of a "manage" component for administration and access;

Input Designs (Profiles)

Both automatic and manual attributing can be made easier and better with preset profiles; these can describe document classes that limit the number of possible index values, or automatically assign certain criteria; input designs also include entry masks and their logic in manual indexing;

Categorization (Automatic Classification or Categorizing)

Based on the information contained in electronic information objects, whether OCR-converted faxes, office files or output files, automatic classification programs can extract index, category, and transfer data autonomously; these systems can evaluate information based on predefined criteria or in a self-learning process.

The objective of all "Capture" components is the provision of information to the "Manage" components for further processing or archiving.

Manage

The "Manage" components are for the management, processing, and use of information. They incorporate:

- databases for administration and retrieval, and
- access authorization systems.

The goal of a closed ECM system is to provide these two components just once as services for all "Manage" solutions such as document management, collaboration, web content management, records management and workflow/business process management. To link the various "Manage" components, they should have standardized interfaces and secure transaction processes for inter-component communication.

Document Management

Document management (DM) in this context does not refer to the industry known in Europe as DMS, but to document management systems in the narrower "classical" sense. These systems control documents from their creation through to long-term archiving. Document management includes functions like:

- check in/check out for checking stored information for consistency;
- version management to keep track of different versions of the same information with their revisions and renditions (same information in a different format);
- search and navigation for finding information and its associated contexts, and
- visualizing for showing information in structures like virtual files, folders, and overviews.

However, the functions or document management increasingly overlap with those of the other "Manage" components, the ever-expanding functionalities of office applications like Outlook/Exchange or Notes/Domino, and the characteristics of "library services" for administering information storage.

Collaboration (Collaborative Systems, Groupware)

Collaboration simply means "working together." However, these solutions, which developed from conventional groupware, now go much further and include elements of knowledge management. Collaboration includes the following functions:

- jointly usable information databases;
- joint, simultaneous, controlled information processing;
- knowledge based on skills, resources and background data for joint information processing;
- administration components such as whiteboards for brainstorming, appointment scheduling, project management, etc.;
- communication application such as video conferencing, and
- integration of information from other applications in the context of joint information processing.

Web Content Management

Enterprise content management claims to integrate web content management (WCM). However, information presented on the Internet and Extranet or on a portal should only be data that is already present in the company, whose delivery is controlled by access authorization and storage. Web content management includes the following functions, among others:

- creation of new or editing of existing information in a controlled generation and publishing process;
- delivery and administration of information for the web presentation;
- automatic conversion for various display formats, personalized display and versions;
- secure separation of access to public and non-public information, and
- visualization for Internet presentation (browser, HTML, XML, etc.).

It is, however, worth noting that many in the industry do not consider WCM as an integral component to an ECM system. There are very few examples of successful implementations whereby a shared repository for documents (the core purpose of ECM) and web content are managed together. Indeed very different techniques and philosophies to structure and organize content are utilized for external facing web content than for internal facing document content.

Records Management (File and Archive Management)

Unlike with traditional electronic archival systems, records management (RM; electronic records management or ERM) refers to the pure administration of records, important information and data that companies are required to archive. Records management is independent of storage media, and can also manage information stored otherwise than in electronic systems. The following are only some of the functions of records management:

- visualisation of file plans and other structured indexes for the orderly storage of information;
- unambiguous indexing of information, supported by thesauri or controlled wordlists;

- management of record retention schedules and deletion schedules;
- protection of information in accordance with its characteristics, sometimes down to individual content components in documents, and
- use of international, industry-specific or at least company-wide standardized meta-data for the unambiguous identification and description of stored information.

Workflow/Business Process Management

Workflow (WF) and business process management (BPM) differ substantially.

There are Different Types of Workflow, for Example:

- production workflow uses predefined sequences to guide and control processes, and
- in ad-hoc workflow, the user determines the process sequence on the fly.

Workflow Solutions can be Implemented as:

- workflow solutions, with autonomous clients which users mostly work with, or as
- workflow engines, which act as a background service controlling the information and data flow, without requiring an own client for this.

Workflow Management Includes the Following Functions, Among Others:

- visualisation of process and organization structures;
- capture, administration, visualization, and delivery of grouped information with its associated documents or data;
- incorporation of data processing tools (such as specific applications) and documents (such as office products);
- parallel and sequential processing of procedures including simultaneous saving;
- reminders, deadlines, delegation and other administration functionalities;
- monitoring and documentation of process status, routing, and outcomes, and
- tools for designing and displaying process.

The objective is to largely automate processes by incorporating all necessary resources. Business process management (BPM) goes a step further than workflow. Although the words are often used interchangeably, BPM aims at the complete integration of all affected applications within an enterprise, with monitoring of processes and assembling of all required information. Among BPM's functions are:

- complete workflow functionality;
- process and data monitoring at the server level;
- enterprise application integration (EAI), to link different applications, and
- business intelligence (BI), with rule structures, integration of information warehouses, and utilities that assist users in their work.

Today, "manage" components are offered individually or integrated as suites. In many cases they already include the "store" components.

Store

"Store" components are used for the temporary storage of information which it is not required or desired to archive. Even if it uses media that are suitable for long-term archiving, "Store" is still separate from "Preserve."

The "Store" components listed by AIIM can be divided into three categories: "Repositories" as storage locations, "Library Services" as administration components for repositories, and storage "Technologies". These infrastructure components are sometimes held at the operating system level like the file system, and also include security technologies which will be discussed further below in the "Deliver" section. However, security technologies including access control are superordinated components of an ECM solution.

Repositories

Different kinds of ECM repositories can be used in combination. Among the possible kinds are:

File Systems

File systems are used primarily for temporary storage, as input and output caches. The goal of ECM is to reduce the data burden on the file system and make the information generally available through "manage," "store" and "preserve" technologies;

Content Management Systems

This is the actual storage and repository system for content, which can be a database or a specialized storage system;

Databases

Databases administer access information, but can also be used for the direct storage of documents, content, or media assets;

Data Warehouses

These are complex storage systems based on databases, which reference or provide information from all kinds of sources; they can also be designed with more global functions such as document or information warehouses.

Library Services

Library services have to do with libraries only in a metaphorical way. They are the administrative components close to the system that handle access to information. The library service is responsible for taking in and storing information from the "capture" and "manage" components. It also manages the storage locations in dynamic storage, the actual "store," and in the long-term "preserve" archive. The storage location is determined only by the characteristics and classification of the information. The library service works in concert with the database of the "manage" components. This serves the necessary functions of search and retrieval.

While the database does not "know" the physical location of a stored object, the library service manages:

- Online storage (direct access to data and documents);
- Nearline storage (data and documents on a medium that the drive can access, but for which robotics or something similar must first be set up), and
- offline storage (data and documents on a medium that is removed from system access).

If there is not a superordinated document management system to provide the functionality, the library service must have:

- a version management to control the status of information, and
- a check-in/check-out, for controlled information provision.

An important library service function is the generation of logs and journals on information usage and edits, called an "audit trail."

Storage Technologies

A wide variety of technologies can be used to store information, depending on the application and system environment:

Read and Write Magnetic Online Media

this includes hard drives as RAID (redundant array of independent disks) server drive subsystems, storage area networks (SANs) as storage infrastructures and network-attached storage (NAS) as directly accessible network storage areas;

Magnetic Tape

in automated storage units like "libraries" or "silos" with robotics for access, used like DAT in smaller environments for backup but not online access;

Digital Optical Media

CD (CD-R for write-once, read-only Compact Disc, CD/RW for read-and-write compact disk), digital versatile disk (DVD)), MO (magneto optical), and other formats can be used for storage and distribution, or in jukeboxes for online storage.

Cloud Computing

Storage of data on external servers off-site where they can be accessed via the internet.

Preserve

The "Preserve" components of ECM handle the long-term, safe storage and backup of static, unchanging information, as well as temporary storage of information that it is not desired or required to archive. This is sometimes called "electronic archiving," but that has substantially broader functionality than that of "Preserve." Electronic archiving systems today generally consist of a combination of administration software like records management, imaging or document management, library services (IRS — information retrieval system) and storage subsystems.

But it is not just electronic media that are suitable for long-term archiving. For purely securing information, microfilm is still viable, and is now offered in hybrid systems with electronic media and database-supported access. The decisive factor for all long-term storage systems is the timely planning and regular performance of migrations, in order to keep information available in the changing technical landscape. This ongoing process is called *continuous migration*. The "Preserve" components contain special viewers, conversion and migration tools, and long term storage media:

Long Term Storage Media

WORM Optical disc

Write Once Read Many (WORM) rotating digital optical storage media, which include the classic 5 ¼" in or 3 ½" WORM disc in protective sleeve, as well as CD-R and DVD-R. Recording methods vary for these media, which are held in jukeboxes for online and automated nearline access.

WORM Tape

Magnetic tapes with WORM characteristics are used in special drives, that can be as secure as a traditional WORM medium if used properly with specially secured tapes.

WORM Hard Disk Drive

Magnetic disk storage with special software protection against overwriting, erasure, and editing, delivers similar security like a traditional WORM medium. An example is CAS (content addressed storage).

Storage Networks

Storage networks like NAS (network-attached storage) and SAN (storage area network) can also be used if they meet the requirements of edit-proof auditing acceptability with unchangeable storage, protection against manipulation and erasure, etc.

Microfilm

Microforms like microfilm, aperture cards, jackets a.s.o. can be used to back up information that is no longer in use and does not require machine processing.

Paper

Paper still has applications as a long-term storage medium, since it does not require migration, and can be read without any technical aids. However, like microfilm it is used only to double secure originally electronic information.

Long Term Preservation Strategies

To secure the long term availability of information different strategies are used for electronic archives.

Migration

Continuous migration of applications, index data, meta data and objects from older systems to new ones generates a lot of work but secures the accessibility and usability of information, and allows during this process the deletion of information which is no longer relevant; conversion technologies are used to update the formats of the stored information;

Emulation

Emulation of older software allows us to run and access the original data and objects; as well as special viewer software which can identify the formats of the preserved objects and can display the objects in the new software environment.

Standards for interfaces, meta data, structures and object formats are important to secure the availability of information.

Deliver

The "Deliver" components of ECM are used to present information from the "Manage," "Store," and "Preserve" components. They also contain functions used to enter information in systems (such as information transfer to media or generation of formatted output files) or for readying (for example converting or compressing) information for the "Store" and "Preserve" components. Since the AIIM component model is function-based and not to be regarded as an architecture, we can assign these and other components here. The functionality in the "Deliver" category is also known as "output" and summarized under the term *output management.*

The "Deliver" components comprise three groups of functions and media: transformation technologies, security technologies, and distribution. Transformation and security as services belong at the middleware level and should be available to all ECM components equally. For output, two functions are of primary importance:

Layout/Design

Tools for laying out and formatting output, and publishing with applications for presenting information for distribution and publication.

Transformation Technologies

Transformations should always be controlled and trackable. This is done by background services which the end user generally does not see. Among the transformation technologies are:

COLD/ERM (Computer Output to Laser Disc)

As distinct from "Capture" components, it prepares output data for distribution and transfer to the archive. Typical applications are lists and formatted output, for example individualized customer letters. These technologies also include journals and logs generated by the ECM components.

Unlike most imaging media COLD records are indexed not in a database table but by absolute positions within the document itself (i.e. page 1 line 82, position 12). As a result COLD index fields are uneditable after submission unless they are converted into a standard database.

Personalization

This is no longer just a function of web-based portals, but applies to all ECM components; personalization gives the user just those functions and information that he needs;

XML (Extensible Markup Language)

A description language that allows description of interfaces, structures, metadata, and documents; XML is becoming the universal technology for describing information;

PDF (Portable Document Format)

An intelligent print and distribution format that enables the platform-independent presentation of information; unlike pure image formats like TIFFs, PDFs permit content searches, the addition of metadata, and the embedding of electronic signatures;

XPS (XML Paper Specification)

A XML specification developed by Microsoft describing the formats and rules for distributing, archiving, rendering, and processing XPS documents;

Converters and Viewers

Serve to reformat information to generate uniform formats, and also to display and output information from different formats;

Compression

Used to reduce the storage space needed for pictorial information; the ITU process (CCITT) is mainly used for b/w for TIFFs, and JPEG2000 for colour images; ZIP applications allow the compression of any kind of data for transfer; Document storage reduction discusses other techniques to reduce the amount of storage for both pictorial and non-pictorial information, and

Syndication

Used for presenting content in different formats, selections and forms in the context of content management; syndication allows the same content to be used multiple times in different forms for different purposes.

Security Technologies

Security technologies are cross-section functions that are available to all ECM components. For example, electronic signatures are used not only when documents are sent, but also in data capture via scanning, in order to document the completeness of the capture. PKI (public/ private key infrastructure) is a basic technology for electronic signatures. It manages keys and certificates, and checks the authenticity of signatures. Other electronic signatures demonstrate the identity of the sender and the integrity of the sent data, i.e., that it is complete and unchanged. In Europe there are three forms of electronic signatures, of different quality and security: simple, advanced, and qualified. In most European states the qualified electronic signature is legally admissible in legal documents and contracts. Finally, there is digital rights management and watermarking. This is used in content syndication and in MAM (media asset management) for managing and securing intellectual property rights and copyrights. It works with techniques like electronic watermarks that are integrated directly into the file, and seeks to protect usage rights and protect content that is published on the Internet.

Distribution

All of the above technologies basically serve to provide the various contents of an ECM to target users by various routes, in a controlled and user-oriented manner. These can be active components such as email, data media, memos, and passive publication on websites and portals where users can get the information themselves. Possible output and distribution media are:

- Internet, extranet and intranet;
- E-business portals;
- employee portals;
- email and fax;
- data transfer by EDI, XML or other formats;
- mobile devices like mobile phones, PDAs, and others;
- data media like CDs and DVDs;
- digital TV and other multimedia services, and
- paper.

The task of the various "Deliver" components is to provide information to users in the best way for the given application, while controlling its use as far as possible.

ECM Market Development

Prior to 2003, the ECM market was dominated by a number of medium-sized independent vendors that fell into two categories. Those who had originated as Document Management companies (Advanced Processing & Imaging, Documentum, FileNet, OpenText) and had begun adding on management of other enterprise content and those who had started as Web Content Management providers (Interwoven, Vignette, Stellent) and begun trying to branch out into managing other types of content such as business documents and rich media. Larger vendors such as IBM and Oracle also had offerings in this space and the market share remained largely fragmented.

In 2002, Documentum had added collaboration capabilities with its acquisition of eRoom while Interwoven and Vignette countered with their respective acquisitions of iManage and Intraspect. Similarly, Documentum purchased Bulldog for its Digital Asset Management (DAM) capabilities while Interwoven and OpenText countered with acquisitions of MediaBin and Artesia. OpenText also acquired European companies IXOS and Red Dot to shore up its software portfolio.

In October 2003, EMC Corporation began a period of market consolidation that continues today with a $1.5B USD acquisition of Documentum. This acquisition led to the creation of a new category, Information Life cycle Management (ILM) that looked at the management and storage of content holistically from end user to software to middleware, to database with a particular focus on IT governance and management; change control processes; requirements for system availability and recovery times; and service level agreements. Soon EMC's primarily competitors in the database space responded as IBM purchased FileNet and Oracle purchased Stellent in 2006. OpenText also purchased Hummingbird in 2006.

Today, OpenText, Interwoven, and Vignette remain the three primary independent ECM vendors with OpenText far outpacing Interwoven and Vignette in terms of revenue and customer base. Other ECM vendors include Infonic's Document Manager, Computhink's ViewWise, IBM's FileNet, EMC's Documentum, Laserfiche, Columbia Soft, Microsoft Office Share Point Server 2007, Hyland Software's OnBase, Xerox DocuShare, and Saperion. Ever-Team, SunGard EXP, WAVE Corporation, Objective Corporation, and Xythos Software have been added in the Gartner Magic Quadrant for ECM 2006.

In early 2007, independent analyst firm CMS Watch cited substantial turbulence among many ECM vendors, suggesting that even some of the biggest players in the market were undergoing significant changes. In addition 2007 has seen the emergence of Open Source options for ECM supplied by Logical DOC, Nuxeo, Knowledge Tree and Alfresco, along with S-a-a-S (Software as a Service) from Logical DOC Cloud or Spring CM. In 2008 Jumper Networks released Jumper 2.0 the first ECM driven by a collaborative bookmarking engine. And in 2008 Sense/Net released Sense/Net 6.0, the world's first enterprise grade, open source application suite for building integrated Enterprise Content Management (ECM, ECMS) and Enterprise Portal (EPS) solutions running on the.NET platform. Alan Pelz-Sharpe (2007-04-23). "Enterprise Content Management Marketplace: Opportunities and Risks". CMS Watch.

According to Gartner as of 2007, the ECM market leaders were Open Text Corporation, EMC (Documentum), IBM and Oracle Corporation.

Hewlett-Packard (HP) entered the ECM space with its acquisition of Australian company Tower Software in 2008.

There are a number of software companies that have sprung up to develop applications to complement ECM with specific functions and features. There are companies that provide third party document and image viewers such as LEAD Technologies, MS Technology and Accusoft. There are companies that provide workflows such as Office

Gemini, SpringCM, and docAssist. There are also several companies that provide plugins for ECMs. The Web 2.0 wave has brought new players to the market with strength in web-based delivery. Koral and EchoSign, both available on the Salesforce.com AppExchange platform, are representative of this trend.

On January 22, 2009, British software company Autonomy Corporation announced that it was acquiring Interwoven for $775 million. According to the official press release, "The combination of Autonomy's Meaning Based Computing technologies (IDOL) (with its ability to understand content) with Interwoven's suite of products (focussed on managing the interactions of people and content) will create a new set of technologies, updating and enhancing Interwoven's products by significantly reducing the levels of manual effort now required. These technologies are ready to address the new need for manage-in-place and extend Autonomy's reach into a new customer base. Interwoven's products know what the customer interactions are, and Autonomy's IDOL will allow them to know what they mean."

Gartner estimates that the ECM market is worth approximately $2.9 billion in 2007; this is expected to grow at a CAGR of 12.9% through 2011. After a plethora of industry consolidation, only three or four major companies are left in this space, and the industry as a whole is undergoing a significant transformation as Microsoft commoditizes content management components.

According to Gartner, by 2008 75 percent of Global 2000 companies will have a desktop-focused and a process-focused content management implementation (0.9 probability) and ECM will continue to absorb other technologies, such as digital asset management and email management. Gartner also predicted that there will be further market consolidation, acquisition and separation of vendors into platform and solution providers.

Currently, enterprise information management is gaining more interest from organizations trying to approach information management (whether structured or unstructured) from an enterprise perspective. EIM combines ECM and business intelligence.

Instant Massaging

Instant massaging (IM) is a form of real-time communication between two or more people based on typed text. The text is conveyed via devices connected over a network such as the Internet.

Overview

Instant massaging (IM) is a collection of technologies that create the possibility of real-time text-based communication between two or more participants over the internet or some form of internal network/intranet. It is important to understand that what separates chat and instant massaging from technologies such as email is the perceived synchronicity of the communication by the user-Chat happens in real-time. Some systems allow the sending of messages to people not currently logged on (offline messages)*, thus removing much of the difference between Instant Massaging and email.*

IM allows effective and efficient communication, featuring immediate receipt of acknowledgment or reply. In certain cases Instant Massaging involves additional features, which make it even more popular. For example, users can see each other by using web-cams, or talk directly for free over the Internet using a microphone and loudspeakers.

It is possible to save a conversation for later reference. Instant messages are typically logged in a local message history which closes the gap to the persistent nature of e-mails and facilitates quick exchange of information like URLs or document snippets (which can be unwieldy when communicated via telephone).

History

In early instant massaging programs each character appeared when it was typed. The UNIX "talk" command shown in this screenshot was popular in the 1980s and early 1990s.

Instant massaging predates the Internet, first appearing on multi-user operating systems like CTSS and Multics in the mid-1960s. Initially, many of these systems, such as CTSS'. SAVED, were used as notification systems for services like printing, but quickly were used to facilitate communication with other users logged in to the same machine. As networks developed, the protocols spread with the networks. Some of these used a peer-to-peer protocol (eg talk, ntalk and ytalk), while others required peers to connect to a server. During the Bulletin board system (BBS) phenomenon that peaked during the 1980s, some systems incorporated chat features which were similar to instant massaging; Freelancin' Roundtable was one prime example.

In the last half of the 1980s and into the early 1990s, the Quantum Link online service for Commodore 64 computers offered user-to-user messages between currently connected customers which they called

"On-Line Messages" (or OLM for short). Quantum Link's better-known later incarnation, America Online, offers a similar product under the name "AOL Instant Messenger" (AIM). While the Quantum Link service ran on a Commodore 64, using only the Commodore's PETSCII text-graphics, the screen was visually divided up into sections and OLMs would appear as a yellow bar saying "Message From:" and the name of the sender along with the message across the top of whatever the user was already doing, and presented a list of options for responding. As such, it could be considered a sort of GUI, albeit much more primitive than the later Unix, Windows and Macintosh based GUI IM programs. OLMs were what Q-Link called "Plus Services" meaning they charged an extra per-minute fee on top of the monthly Q-Link access costs.

Modern, Internet-wide, GUI-based massaging clients, as they are known today, began to take off in the mid 1990s with PowWow, then ICQ, followed by AOL Instant Messenger (AOL Instant Messenger, 1997). Similar functionality was offered by CU-SeeMe in 1992; though primarily an audio/video chat link, users could also type messages to each other. AOL later acquired Mirabilis, the creators of ICQ; a few years later ICQ (now owned by AOL) was awarded two patents for instant massaging by the U.S. patent office. Meanwhile, other companies developed their own applications (Excite, MSN, Ubique, and Yahoo), each with its own proprietary protocol and client; users therefore had to run multiple client applications if they wished to use more than one of these networks. In 1998 IBM released IBM Lotus Sametime, a product based on technology acquired when IBM bought Haifa-based Ubique and Lexington-based Databeam.

In 2000, an open source application and open standards-based protocol called XMPP was launched. XMPP servers could act as gateways to other IM protocols, reducing the need to run multiple clients. Multi-protocol clients can use any of the popular IM protocols by using additional local libraries for each protocol. IBM Lotus Sametime's November 2007 release added IBM Lotus Sametime Gateway support for XMPP.

Recently, many instant massaging services have begun to offer video conferencing features, Voice Over IP (VoIP) and web conferencing services. Web conferencing services integrate both video conferencing and instant massaging capabilities. Some newer instant massaging companies are offering desktop sharing, IP radio, and IPTV to the voice and video features.

The term "instant messenger" is a service mark of Time Warner and may not be used in software not affiliated with AOL in the United States. For this reason, the instant massaging client formerly known as Gaim or gaim announced in April 2007 that they would be renamed "Pidgin".

Cooperation

Pidgin's Tabbed Chat Window in Ubuntu

Standard free instant massaging applications offer functions like file transfer, contact lists, the ability to have simultaneous conversations etc. These may be all the functions that a small business needs but larger organisations will require more sophisticated applications that can work together. The solution to finding applications capable of this is to use enterprise versions of instant massaging applications. These include titles like XMPP, Lotus Sametime, Microsoft Office Communicator, etc., which are often integrated with other enterprise applications such as workflow systems. These enterprise applications, or Enterprise Application Integration (EAI), are built to certain constraints, namely storing data in a common format.

There have been several attempts to create a unified standard for instant massaging: IETF's SIP (Session Initiation Protocol) and SIMPLE (SIP for Instant Massaging and Presence Leveraging Extensions), APEX (Application Exchange), Prim (Presence and Instant Massaging Protocol), the open XML-based XMPP (Extensible Massaging and Presence Protocol), and OMA's (Open Mobile Alliance) IMPS (Instant Massaging and Presence Service) created specifically for mobile devices.

Most attempts at creating a unified standard for the major IM providers (AOL, Yahoo! and Microsoft) have failed, and each continues to use its own proprietary protocol.

However, while discussions at IETF were stalled, Reuters head of collaboration services, David Gurle (the founder of Microsoft's Real Time Communication and Collaboration business), signed the first inter-service provider connectivity agreement on September 2003. This agreement enabled AIM, ICQ and MSN Messenger users to talk with Reuters Massaging counterparts and vice-versa against an access fee. Following this, Microsoft, Yahoo! and AOL came to a deal where

Microsoft's Live Communication Server 2005 users would also have the possibility to talk to public instant massaging users.

This deal established SIP/SIMPLE as a standard for protocol interoperability and established a connectivity fee for accessing public instant massaging clouds. Separately, on October 13, 2005 Microsoft and Yahoo! announced that by (the Northern Hemisphere) summer of 2006 they would interoperate using SIP/SIMPLE which is followed on December 2005 by the AOL and Google strategic partnership deal where Google Talk users would be able to talk with AIM and ICQ users provided they have an identity at AOL.

There are two ways to combine the many disparate protocols:

1. One way is to combine the many disparate protocols inside the IM client application.
2. The other way is to combine the many disparate protocols inside the IM *server* application. This approach moves the task of communicating to the other services to the server. Clients need not know or care about other IM protocols. For example, LCS 2005 Public IM Connectivity. This approach is popular in XMPP servers however the so-called transport projects suffer the same reverse engineering difficulties as any other project involved with closed protocols or formats.

Some approaches allow organizations to create their own private instant massaging network by enabling them to limit access to the server (often with the IM network entirely behind their firewall) and administer user permissions.

Other corporate massaging systems allow registered users to also connect from outside the corporation LAN, by using a secure firewall-friendly HTTPS based protocol. Typically, a dedicated corporate IM server has several advantages such as pre-populated contact lists, integrated authentication, and better security and privacy.

Some networks have made changes to prevent them from being utilized by such multi-network IM clients. For example, Trillian had to release several revisions and patches to allow its users to access the MSN, AOL, and Yahoo! networks, after changes were made to these networks. The major IM providers typically cite the need for formal agreements as well as security concerns as reasons for making these changes.

Mobile Instant Massaging

Mobile Instant Massaging (MIM) is a presence enabled massaging service that aims to transpose the desktop massaging experience to the usage scenario of being on the move.

While several of the core ideas of the desktop experience on one hand apply to a connected mobile device, others do not: Users usually only look at their phone's screen — presence status changes might occur under different circumstances as happens at the desktop, and several functional limits exist based on the fact that the vast majority of mobile communication devices are chosen by their users to fit into the palm of their hand. Some of the form factor and mobility related differences need to be taken into account in order to create a really adequate, powerful and yet convenient mobile experience: radio bandwidth, memory size, availability of media formats, keypad based input, screen output, CPU performance and battery power are core issues that desktop device users and even nomadic users with connected network.

Friend-to-Friend Networks

Instant Massaging may be done in a Friend-to-friend network, in which each node connects to the friends on the friends list. This allows for communication with friends of friends and for the building of chatrooms for instant messages with all friends on that network.

IM Language

Users sometimes make use of internet slang or text speak to abbreviate common words or expressions in order to quicken conversations or to reduce keystrokes. The language has become universal, with well-known expressions such as 'lol' translated over to face to face language.

Emotions are often expressed in shorthand, such as the abbreviation LOL, BRB, TTYL.

Some, however, attempt to be more accurate with emotional expression over IM. Real time reactions such as (chortle) (snort) (guffaw) or (eye-roll) are becoming more popular. Also there are certain standards that are being introduced into mainstream conversations including, '#' indicates the use of sarcasm in a statement (alternatively (!) after the statement) and '*' which indicates a spelling mistake and/or grammatical error in the previous message, followed by a correction.

Business Application

Instant massaging has proven to be similar to personal computers, email, and the World Wide Web, in that its adoption for use as a business communications medium was driven primarily by individual employees using consumer software at work, rather than by formal mandate or provisioning by corporate information technology departments. Tens of millions of the consumer IM accounts in use are being used for business purposes by employees of companies and other organizations.

In response to the demand for business-grade IM and the need to ensure security and legal compliance, a new type of instant massaging, called "Enterprise Instant Massaging" ("EIM") was created when Lotus Software launched IBM Lotus Sametime in 1998. Microsoft followed suit shortly thereafter with Microsoft Exchange Instant Massaging, later created a new platform called Microsoft Office Live Communications Server, and released Office Communications Server 2007 in October 2007.

Oracle Corporation has also jumped into the market recently with its Oracle Beehive unified collaboration software. Both IBM Lotus and Microsoft have introduced federation between their EIM systems and some of the public IM networks so that employees may use a single interface to both their internal EIM system and their contacts on AOL, MSN, and Yahoo!. Current leading EIM platforms include IBM Lotus Sametime, Microsoft Office Communications Server, and Jabber XCP. In addition, industry-focused EIM platforms as Reuters Massaging and Bloomberg Massaging provide enhanced IM capabilities to financial services companies.

The adoption of IM across corporate networks outside of the control of IT organizations creates risks and liabilities for companies who do not effectively manage and support IM use. Companies implement specialized IM archiving and security products and services to mitigate these risks and provide safe, secure, productive instant massaging capabilities to their employees.

Practical Use in Enterprise

The popular embrace of IM technology for sharing information has quickly led to organizations adopting IM solutions for the perceived advantages that can be brought by it. As organizations are becoming more information based (McNurlin & Sprague, 2006, p. 499) the need for effective knowledge sharing, team working and collaborative environments amongst employees has become vital, especially within more geographically dispersed teams.

Typically, IM conversations tend to have a certain "character"; they are often short and only cover one topic. Media-switching and multitasking are common throughout, however IM might also be used between established coworkers and friends for longer, more intermittent conversation. In their report of IM use at the workplace Nardi et al. (2000) identifies the four primary functions of IM which are often cited in other reports. These primary functions are:

- Quick questions and clarifications
- Coordinating and scheduling tasks
- Coordinating impromptu social meetings
- Keeping in touch with friends and family.

IM is perhaps best suited to "Quick questions and clarifications" as this is the most often mentioned attribute in other reports. A user can "respond rapidly without the overhead of telephone or FTF interaction. For example, IDC reports, "Users see IM as a medium for quick, semi-permanent 'flashes' that beg a near-immediate response" (Isaacs et al., 2002). Nardi's second and third observations are enabled in part due to the "Presence Awareness" feature of IM clients in which the user knows who is "available". This is the most relevant for colleagues who share the same physical space as each other and even paves the way for other mediums to take up the task of communication e.g. F2F or Phone. The implication is that viable communication of any sort can in someway be encouraged through IM's "Presence Awareness" feature. (Issacs et al., 2002) supports this view, "IM in business might not be the main tool for of communication, it could just be the meeting point for another type of media e.g. conference calls.

Nardi's third and fourth observations focus on the social use of IM, which have also been widely publicized in other report. That IM is used for keeping in touch with friends and arranging social events has led some employers to believe that it is used primarily for this purpose. According to (Issacs et al., 2002) a market study found that "'Fear of losing employee productivity' was the greatest concern of businesses in regards to instant massaging".

The study by (Issacs et al., 2002) goes on to suggest this fear is unfounded as it was found that on average "only 13% of conversations contained personal topics", and "only 6.4% were exclusively personal".

A study published in 2008 in the Journal of Computer Mediated Communication by Garrett and Danziger found that workers who used instant massaging on the job reported less interruption than colleagues who did not. Research showed that instant massaging was often used as a substitute for other, more disruptive forms of communication such as the telephone, email, and face-to-face conversations. They found that the conversations were briefer between co-workers when using instant massaging than with the other forms of communications. Because of its unique setup, instant massaging allows users to control how and when they communicate with their coworkers. This technology gives people the ability to flag their availability or postpone responses to a more convenient time, according to one of the researchers. The study also notes that the ability to manage interruptions is most clear with the modality of text-based IM, and that such benefits are less likely with VOIP-or videoconference-based IM.

Review of Products

This section does not cite any references or sources. Please help improve this article by adding citations to reliable sources. Unsourced material may be challenged and removed.

IM products can typically be categorised into two types: Enterprise Instant Massaging (EIM) and Consumer Instant Massaging (CIM). Enterprise solutions use an internal IM server, however this isn't always feasible, particularly for smaller businesses with limited budgets. The second option, using a CIM provides the advantage of being inexpensive to implement and has little need for investing in new hardware or server software. For corporate use encryption and conversation archiving are usually regarded as important features due to security concerns. Sometimes the use of different operating systems in organizations calls for the use of software that supports more than one platform. For example many software companies use Windows XP in administration departments but have software developers who use Linux.

Risks and Liabilities

Although instant massaging delivers many benefits, it also carries with it certain risks and liabilities, particularly when used in workplaces. Among these risks and liabilities are:

- Security risks (e.g. IM used to infect computers with spyware, viruses, trojans, worms)
- Compliance risks
- Inappropriate use
- Intellectual property leakage

Security Risks

Crackers (malicious "hacker" or black hat hacker) have consistently used IM networks as vectors for delivering phishing attempts, "poison URLs", and virus-laden file attachments from 2004 to the present, with over 1100 discrete attacks listed by the IM Security Centre in 2004-2007. Hackers use two methods of delivering malicious code through IM: delivery of virus, trojan, or spyware within an infected file, and the use of "socially engineered" text with a web address that entices the recipient to click on a URL that connects him or her to a website that then downloads malicious code. Viruses, worms, and trojans typically propagate by sending themselves rapidly through the infected user's buddy list. An effective attack using a poison URL may reach tens of thousands of people in minutes when each person's buddy list receives messages appearing to be from a trusted friend. The recipients click on the web address, and the entire cycle starts again. Infections may range from nuisance to criminal, and are becoming more sophisticated each year.

IM connections usually take place in plain text, making them susceptible to eavesdropping. In addition, IM client software often requires the user to expose open UDP ports to the world, increasing the threat posed by potential security vulnerabilities.

Compliance Risks

In addition to the malicious code threat, the use of instant massaging at work also creates a risk of non-compliance to laws and regulations governing the use of electronic communications in businesses. In the United States alone there are over 10,000 laws and regulations related to electronic massaging and records retention. The better-known of these include the Sarbanes-Oxley Act, HIPAA, and SEC 17a-3. Clarification from the Financial Industry Regulatory Authority ("FINRA") was issued to member firms in the financial services industry in December, 2007, noting that "electronic communications", "email", and "electronic correspondence" may be used interchangeably and can include such forms of electronic massaging as *instant massaging* and text massaging. Changes to Federal Rules of Civil Procedure, effective December 1, 2006, created a new category for electronic records which may be requested during discovery in legal proceedings. Most countries around the world also regulate the use of electronic massaging and electronic records retention in similar fashion to the United States. The most common regulations related to IM at work involve the need to produce archived business communications to satisfy government or judicial requests under law. Many instant massaging communications fall into the category of business communications that must be archived and retrievable.

Inappropriate Use

Organizations of all types must protect themselves from the liability of their employees' inappropriate use of IM. The informal, immediate, and ostensibly anonymous nature of instant massaging makes it a candidate for abuse in the workplace. The topic of inappropriate IM use became front page news in October 2006 when Congressman Mark Foley resigned his seat after admitting sending offensive instant messages of a sexual nature to underage former House pages from his Congressional office PC. The Mark Foley Scandal led to media coverage and mainstream newspaper articles warning of the risks of inappropriate IM use in workplaces. In most countries, corporations have a legal responsibility to ensure harassment-free work environment for employees. The use of corporate-owned computers, networks, and software to harass an individual or spread inappropriate jokes or language creates a liability for not only the offender but also the employer. A survey by IM archiving and security provider Akonix Systems, Inc. in March 2007 showed that 31% of respondents had been harassed over IM at work. Companies now include instant massaging as an integral component of their policies on appropriate use of the World Wide Web, email, and other corporate assets.

Intellectual Property Leakage

Within the company there is also the risk of employees using instant massaging to release confidential information and project details to an outside source. This issue is best controlled by a combination of written policy and technology. An organization's policies on use of IM in the workplace could be an integral part of the overall computing and network use policies, and should be published and communicated at least annually. In addition to written policy, organizations should implement "gateways" or IM security products to monitor content of inbound and outbound messages. Products from IM security providers typically allow administrators to set alerts and enforce policy (i.e. allow or block messages) based on keywords and regular expressions within instant messages.

Security and Archiving

In the early 2000s, a new class of IT security provider emerged to provide remedies for the risks and liabilities faced by corporations who chose to use IM for business communications. The IM security providers created new products to be installed in corporate networks for the purpose of archiving, content-scanning, and security-scanning IM traffic moving in and out of the corporation. Similar to the email filtering vendors, the IM security providers focus on the risks and liabilities described above.

With rapid adoption of IM in the workplace, demand for IM security products began to grow in the mid-2000s. By 2007, the preferred platform for the purchase of security software had become the "computer appliance", according to IDC, who estimate that by 2008, 80% of network security products will be delivered via an appliance.

User Base

Note that many of the numbers listed in this section are not directly comparable, and some are speculative. Some instant massaging systems are distributed among many different instances and thus difficult to measure in total (e.g. XMPP). While some numbers are given by the owners of a complete instant massaging system, others are provided by commercial vendors of a part of a distributed system. Some companies may be motivated to inflate their numbers in order to increase advertisement earnings or to attract partners, clients, or customers. Importantly, some numbers are reported as the number of "active" users (without a shared standard of that activity), others indicate total user accounts, while others indicate only the users logged in during an instance of peak usage.

Usenet Newsgroup

A usenet newsgroup is a repository usually within the Usenet system, for messages posted from many users in different locations. The term may be confusing to some, because it is usually a discussion group.

Newsgroups are technically distinct from, but functionally similar to, discussion forums on the World Wide Web. Newsreader software is used to read newsgroups.

Types of Newsgroups

Typically, the newsgroup is focused on a particular topic of interest. Some newsgroups allow the posting of messages on a wide variety of themes, regarding anything a member chooses to discuss as on-topic, while others keep more strictly to their particular subject, frowning on off-topic postings. The news admin (the administrator of a news server) decides how long articles are kept on his server before being expired (deleted). Different servers will have different retention times for the same newsgroup; some may keep articles for as little as one or two weeks, others may hold them for many months. Some admins keep articles in local or technical newsgroups around longer than articles in other newsgroups.

Newsgroups generally come in either of two types, binary or text. There is no technical difference between the two, but the naming differentiation allows users and servers with limited facilities the ability to minimize network bandwidth usage. Generally, Usenet conventions and rules are enacted with the primary intention of minimizing the overall amount of network traffic and resource usage.

Newsgroups are much like the public message boards on old bulletin board systems. For those readers not familiar with this concept, envision an electronic version of the corkboard in the entrance of your local grocery store.

Newsgroups frequently become cliquish and are subject to sporadic flame wars and trolling, but they can also be a valuable source of information, support and friendship, bringing people who are interested in specific subjects together from around the world.

Back when the early community was the pioneering computer society, the common habit seen with many articles was a notice at the end disclosed if the author was free of, or had a conflict of interest, or had any financial motive, or axe to grind, in posting about any product or issue. This is seen much less now, and the reader must read skeptically, just like in society, besides all the privacy or phishing issues.

There are currently well over 100,000 Usenet newsgroups, but only 20,000 or so of those are active. Newsgroups vary in popularity, with some newsgroups only getting a few posts a month while others get several hundred (and in a few cases a couple of thousand) messages a day.

Weblogs have replaced some of the uses of newsgroups (especially because, for a while, they were less prone to spamming).

A website called Deja News began archiving Usenet in the mid-1990s. DejaNews also provided a searchable web interface. Google bought the archive from them and made efforts to buy other Usenet archives to attempt to create a complete archive of Usenet newsgroups and postings from its early beginnings. Like DejaNews, Google has a web search interface to the archive, but Google also allows newsgroup posting.

Non-Usenet newsgroups are possible and do occur, as private individuals or organizations set up their own nntp servers. Examples include the newsgroups Microsoft runs to allow peer-to-peer support of their products and those at news://news.grc.com.

How Newsgroups Work

Newsgroup servers are hosted by various organizations and institutions. Most Internet service providers host their own news servers, or rent access to one, for their subscribers. There are also a number of companies who sell access to premium news servers.

Every host of a news server maintains agreements with other news servers to regularly synchronize. In this way news servers form a network. When a user posts to one news server, the message is stored locally. That server then shares the message with the servers that are connected to it if both carry the newsgroup, and from those servers to servers that they are connected to, and so on. For newsgroups that are not widely carried, sometimes a carrier group is used for crossposting to aid distribution. This is typically only useful for groups that have been removed or newer alt.* *groups. Crossposts between hierarchies, outside of the Big 8 and* alt.* *hierarchies, are failure prone.*

Hierarchies

Newsgroups are often arranged into hierarchies, *theoretically making it simpler to find related groups. The term* top-level hierarchy *refers to the hierarchy defined by the prefix before the first dot.*

The most commonly known hierarchies is the usenet hierarchies. *So for instance newsgroup* rec.arts.sf.starwars.games *would be in the* rec.* *top-level usenet hierarchy, where the asterisk (*) is defined as a wildcard character. There*

were seven original major hierarchies of usenet newsgroups, known as the "Big 7":

- *comp.** — Discussion of computer-related topics
- *news.** — Discussion of Usenet itself
- *sci.** — Discussion of scientific subjects
- *rec.** — Discussion of recreational activities (e.g. games and hobbies)
- *soc.** — Socialising and discussion of social issues.
- *talk.** — Discussion of contentious issues such as religion and politics.
- *misc.** — Miscellaneous discussion—anything which doesn't fit in the other hierarchies.

These were all created in the Great Renaming of 1986–1987, before which all of these newsgroups were in the net.* hierarchy. At that time there was a great controversy over what newsgroups should be allowed. Among those that the usenet cabal (who effectively ran the Big 7 at the time) did not allow were those concerning recipes, drugs, and sex.

This situation resulted in the creation of an *alt.** (short for "alternative") usenet hierarchy, under which these groups would be allowed. Over time, the laxness of rules on newsgroup creation in alt.* compared to the Big 7 meant that many new topics could, given time, gain enough popularity to get a Big 7 newsgroup. There was a rapid growth of alt.* as a result, and the trend continues to this day. Because of the anarchistic nature with which the groups sprung up, some jokingly referred to ALT standing for "Anarchists, Lunatics and Terrorists" (a backronym).

In 1995, *humanities.** was created for the discussion of the humanities (e.g. literature, philosophy), and the Big 7 became the Big 8.

The *alt.** hierarchy has discussion of all kinds of topics, and many hierarchies for discussion specific to a particular geographical area or in a language other than English. Before a new Big 8 newsgroup can be created, an RFD (Request For Discussion) must be posted into the newsgroup news.announce.newgroups, which is then discussed in news.groups.proposals. Once the proposal has been formalized with a name, description, charter, the Big-8 Management Board will vote on whether to create the group. If the proposal is approved by the Big-8 Management Board, the group is created. Groups are removed in a similar manner.

Creating a new group in the alt.* hierarchy is not subject to the same rules; anybody can create a newsgroup, and anybody can remove them, but most news administrators will ignore these requests unless a local user requests the group by name.

Further Hierarchies

There are a number of newsgroup hierarchies outside of the Big 8 (and alt.*) that can be found at many news servers. These include non-English language groups, managed by companies or organizations about their products, geographic/local hierarchies, and even non-internet network boards routed into NNTP. Examples include (alphabetically):

- *aus.** — Australian news groups
- *ba.** — Discussion in the San Francisco Bay area
- *ca.** — Discussion in California
- *can.** — Canadian news groups
- *cn.** — Chinese news groups
- *chi.** — Discussions about the Chicago area
- *de.** — Discussions in German
- *england.** — Discussions (mostly) local to England, see also *uk.**
- *fidonet.** — Discussions routed from FidoNet
- *fr.** — Discussions in French
- *fj.** — "From Japan," discussions in Japanese
- *gnu.** — Discussions about GNU software
- *hawaii.** — Discussions (mostly) local to Hawaii
- *hp.** — Hewlett-Packard internal news groups
- *it.** — Discussions in Italian
- *microsoft.** — Discussions about Microsoft products
- *pl.** — Polish news groups
- *tw.** — Taiwan news groups
- *uk.* — Discussions on matters in the UK*
- *yale.** — Discussions (mostly) local to Yale.

Additionally, there is the free.* hierarchy, which can be considered "more alt than alt.*". There are many local sub-hierarchies within this hierarchy, usually for specific countries or cultures (such as free.it.* for Italy).

Binary Newsgroups

While newsgroups were not created with the intention of distributing binary files, they have proven to be quite effective for this. Because of the way they work, a file uploaded once will be spread and can then be downloaded by an unlimited number of users. More useful is that every user is drawing on the bandwidth of his or her own news server. This means that unlike P2P technology, the user's download speed is under his or her own control, as opposed to under the willingness of other people to share files. In fact, this is another benefit of newsgroups: it is usually not expected that users share. If every user makes uploads then the servers would be flooded; thus it is acceptable and often encouraged for users to just leech.

There were originally a number of obstacles to the transmission of binary files over Usenet. First, Usenet was designed with the transmission of text in mind. Consequently, for a long period of time, it was impossible to send binary data as it was. So, a workaround, Uuencode (and later on Base64 and yEnc), was developed which mapped the binary data from the files to be transmitted (e.g. sound or video files) to text characters which would survive transmission over Usenet. At the receiver's end, the data needed to be decoded by the user's news client.

Additionally, there was a limit on the size of individual posts such that large files could not be sent as single posts. To get around this, Newsreaders were developed which were able to split long files into several posts. Intelligent newsreaders at the other end could then automatically group such split files into single files, allowing the user to easily retrieve the file. These advances have meant that Usenet is used to send and receive many terabytes of files per day.

There are two main issues that pose problems for transmitting binary files over newsgroups. The first is completion rates and the other is retention rates. The business of premium news servers is generated primarily on their ability to offer superior completion and retention rates, as well as their ability to offer very fast connections to users. Completion rates are significant when users wish to download large files that are split into pieces; if any one piece is missing, it is impossible to successfully download and reassemble the desired file. To work around the problem, a redundancy scheme known as PAR is commonly used.

A number of websites exist for the purpose of keeping an index of the files posted to binary newsgroups.

Moderated Newsgroups

A moderated newsgroup has one or more individuals who must approve articles before they are posted at large. A separate address is used for the submission of posts and the moderators then propagate posts which are approved for the readership. The first moderated newsgroups appeared in 1984 under mod.* according to RFC 2235, "Hobbes' Internet Timeline".

Online Shopping

Online shopping is the process consumers go through to purchase products or services over the Internet. An online shop, eshop, e-store, internet shop, webshop, webstore, online store, or virtual store evokes the physical analogy of buying products or services at a bricks-and-mortar retailer or in a shopping mall.

The metaphor of an online catalog is also used, by analogy with mail order catalogues. All types of stores have retail web sites, including those that do and do not also have physical storefronts and paper catalogues. Online shopping is a type of electronic commerce used for business-to-business (B2B) and business-to-consumer (B2C) transactions.

Webshop

The term "Webshop" also refers to a place of business where web development, web hosting and other types of web related activities take place (Web refers to the World Wide Web and "shop" has a colloquial meaning used to describe the place). Buying online introduced new ways of reducing costs by reducing the number of staff needed. It is a more effective way of getting products to people and spreading into different demographics.

Benefits of Online Shopping

1. Bargaining power of consumers. They enjoy a wider choice
2. Supplier power. It is more difficult for consumers to manage a non-digital channel.
3. Internet increases commoditisation
4. Threat of new entrants. Online means it is easier to introduce new services with lower over-heads

5. Threat of substitutes
6. Rivalry among competitors. It is easier to introduce products and services to different markets.

History

Online shopping pre-dates the internet/www, the IBM PC and Microsoft. It was invented in the UK in 1979 by Michael Aldrich of Redifon Computers. Aldrich connected a modified 26" colour television to a real-time transaction processing computer via a domestic telephone line and demonstrated online shopping. From 1980 onwards he sold his systems in the UK with considerable success.

The world's first recorded B2B online shopping system was Thomson Holidays in March 1981. The world's first recorded B2C was Gateshead SIS/Tesco in May 1984. The world's first recorded online home shopper was Mrs Jane Snowball of Gateshead, England in May 1984. During the 1980s online shopping was also used extensively in the UK and some parts of continental Europe by auto makers Peugeot-Talbot, Ford, Nissan and General Motors. All these organizations and others, particularly in Financial Services and manufacturing industry, used the Aldrich systems. These systems operated over the switched public network in dial-up and leased line modes. There was no broadband capability.

In 1990 Tim Berners-Lee created the first World Wide Web server and browser. In 1992 Charles Stack created the first online book store, Book Stacks Unlimited (aka Books.com), two years before Jeff Bezos started Amazon. In 1994 other advances took place, such as online banking and the opening of an online pizza shop by Pizza Hut. During that same year, Netscape introduced SSL encryption of data transferred online, which has become essential for secure online shopping. In 1995 Amazon expanded its online shopping, and in 1996 eBay appeared.

Customers

In general, shopping has always catered to middle class and upper class women. Shopping is fragmented and pyramid-shaped. At the pinnacle are elegant boutiques for the affluent; a huge belt of inelegant but ruthlessly efficient "discounters" flog plenty at the pyramid's precarious middle. According to the analysis of Susan D. Davis, at its base are the world's workers and poor, on whose cheapened labour the rest of the pyramid depends for its incredible abundance. Shopping has evolved from single stores to large malls containing many stores that most often offer attentive service, store credit, delivery, and acceptance of returns. These new additions to shopping have encouraged and targeted middle class women.

In recent years, online shopping has become popular; however, it still caters to the middle and upper class. In order to shop online, one must be able to have access to a computer, a bank account and a debit card. Shopping has evolved with the growth of technology. According to research found in the Journal of Electronic Commerce, if we focus on the demographic characteristics of the in-home shopper, in general, the higher the level of education, income, and occupation of the head of the household, the more favourable the perception of non-store shopping. An influential factor in consumer attitude towards non-store shopping is exposure to technology, since it has been demonstrated that increased exposure to technology increases the probability of developing favourable attitudes towards new shopping channels.

Online shopping widened the target audience to men and women of the middle class. At first, the main users of online shopping were young men with a high level of income and a university education. This profile is changing. For example, in USA in the early years of Internet there were very few women users, but by 2001 women were 52.8% of the online population. Sociocultural pressure has made men generally more independent in their purchase decisions, while women place greater value on personal contact and social relations.

Trends

One third of people that shop online use a search engine to find what they are looking for and about one fourth find websites by word of mouth. Word of mouth has become a leading way by which people find shopping websites. When an online shopper has a good first experience with a certain website, sixty percent of the time they will return to that website to buy more.

Books are one of the things bought most online. However, clothes, shoes, and accessories are all very popular things bought online. Cosmetics, nutrition products, and groceries are increasingly being purchased online. About one fourth of travellers buy their plane tickets online because it is a quick and easy way to compare airline travel and make a purchase. Online shopping provides more freedom and control than shopping in a store.

From a sociological perspective, online shopping is arguably the most predictable way to shop. One knows exactly what website to go to, how much the product will cost, and how long it will take for the product to reach them. Online shopping has become extremely routine and predictable, which is one of its great appeals to the consumer.

Logistics

Consumers find a product of interest by visiting the website of the retailer directly, or do a search across many different vendors using a shopping search engine.

Once a particular product has been found on the web site of the seller, most online retailers use shopping cart software to allow the consumer to accumulate multiple items and to adjust quantities, by analogy with filling a physical shopping cart or basket in a conventional store. A "checkout" process follows (continuing the physical-store analogy) in which payment and delivery information is collected, if necessary. Some stores allow consumers to sign up for a permanent online account so that some or all of this information only needs to be entered once. The consumer often receives an email confirmation once the transaction is complete. Less sophisticated stores may rely on consumers to phone or email their orders (though credit card numbers are not accepted by email, for security reasons).

Payment

Online shoppers commonly use credit card to make payments, however some systems enable users to create accounts and pay by alternative means, such as:

- Debit card
- Various types of electronic money
- Cash on delivery (C.O.D., offered by very few online stores)
- Cheque
- Wire transfer/delivery on payment
- Postal money order
- Reverse SMS billing to mobile phones
- Gift cards
- Direct debit in some countries

Some sites will not allow international credit cards and billing address and shipping address have to be in the same country in which site does its business. Other sites allow customers from anywhere to send gifts anywhere. The financial part of a transaction might be processed in real time (for example, letting the consumer know their credit card was declined before they log off), or might be done later as part of the fulfilment process.

While credit cards are currently the most popular means of paying for online goods and services, alternative online payments will account for 26% of e-commerce volume by 2009 according to Celent.

Product Delivery

Once a payment has been accepted the goods or services can be delivered in the following ways.

- Download: This is the method often used for digital media products such as software, music, movies, or images.
- Shipping: The product is shipped to the customer's address.
- Drop shipping: The order is passed to the manufacturer or third-party distributor, who ships the item directly to the consumer, bypassing the retailer's physical location to save time, money, and space.
- In-store pickup: The customer orders online, finds a local store using locator software and picks the product up at the closest store. This is the method often used in the bricks and clicks business model.
- In the case of buying an admission ticket one may get a code, or a ticket that can be printed out. At the premises it is made sure that the same right of admission is not used twice.

Shopping Cart Systems

- Simple systems allow the offline administration of products and categories. The shop is then generated as HTML files and graphics that can be uploaded to a webspace. These systems do not use an online database.
- A high end solution can be bought or rented as a standalone program or as an addition to an enterprise resource planning program. It is usually installed on the company's own webserver and may integrate into the existing supply chain so that ordering, payment, delivery, accounting and warehousing can be automated to a large extent.

- Other solutions allow the user to register and create an online shop on a portal that hosts multiple shops at the same time.
- Open source shopping cart packages include advanced platforms such as Interchange, and off the shelf solutions as Avactis, Satchmo, osCommerce, Magento, Zen Cart, VirtueMart, Batavi and PrestaShop.
- Commercial systems can also be tailored to ones needs so that the shop does not have to be created from scratch. By using a framework already existing, software modules for different functionalities required by a web shop can be adapted and combined.

Design

Why does electronic shopping exist? For customers it is not only because of the high level of convenience, but also because of the broader selection; competitive pricing and greater access to information.. For organizations it increases their customer value and the building of sustainable capabilities, next to the increased profits.

Information Load

Designers of online shops should consider the effects of information load. Mehrabian and Russel (1974) introduced the concept of information rate (load) as the complex spatial and temporal arrangements of stimuli within a setting.

The notion of information load is directly related to concerns about whether consumers can be given too much information in virtual shopping environments. Compared with conventional retail shopping, computer shopping enriches the information environment of virtual shopping by providing additional product information, such as comparative products and services, as well as various alternatives and attributes of each alternative, etc.

Two major sub-dimensions have been identified for information load: complexity and novelty. Complexity refers to the number of different elements or features of a site, which can be the result of increased information diversity. Novelty involves the unexpected, suppressing, new, or unfamiliar aspects of the site. A research by Huang (2000) showed that the novelty dimension kept consumers exploring the shopping sites, whereas the complexity dimension has the potential to induce impulse purchases.

Consumer Expectations

The main idea of online shopping is not in having a good looking website that could be listed in a lot of search engines and it is not about the art behind the site. It also is not only just about disseminating information, because it is all about building relationships and making money. Mostly, organizations try to adopt techniques of online shopping without understanding these techniques and/or without a sound business model.

Rather than supporting the organization's culture and brand name, the website should satisfy consumer's expectations. Many researchers notify that the uniqueness of the web has dissolved and the need for the design, which will be user centred, is very important. Companies should always remember that there are certain things, such as understanding the customer's wants and needs, living up to promises, never go out of style, because they give reason to come back. And the reason will stay if consumers always get what they expect. McDonaldization theory can be used in terms of online shopping, because online shopping is becoming more and more popular and website that wants to gain more shoppers will use four major principles of McDonaldization: efficiency, calculability, predictability and control.

Organizations, which want people to shop more online for them, should consume extensive amounts of time and money to define, design, develop, test, implement, and maintain website. Also if company wants their website to be popular among online shoppers it should leave the user with a positive impression about the organization, so consumers can get an impression that the company cares about them. The organization that wants to be acceptable in online shopping needs to remember, that it is easier to lose a customer then to gain one.

Lots of researchers state that even when site was a "top-rated", it would go nowhere if the organization failed to live up to common etiquette, such as returning e-mails in a timely fashion, notifying customers of problems, being honest, and being good stewards of the customers' data. Organizations that want to keep their customers or gain new ones try to get rid of all mistakes and be more appealing to be more desirable for online shoppers. And this is why many designers of webshops considered research outcomes concerning consumer expectations. Research conducted by Elliot and Fowell (2000) revealed satisfactory and unsatisfactory customer experiences.

User Interface

It is important to take the country and customers into account. For example, in Japan privacy is very important and emotional involvement is more important on a pension's site than on a shopping site. Next to that, there is a difference in experience: experienced users focus more on the variables that directly influence the task, while novice users are focusing more on understanding the information.

There are several techniques for the inspection of the usability. The ones used in the research of Chen & Macredie (2005) are Heuristic evaluation, cognitive walk through and the user testing. Every technique has its own (dis-)advantages and it is therefore important to check per situation which technique is appropriate.

When the customers went to the online shop, a couple of factors determine whether they will return to the site. The most important factors are the ease of use and the presence of user-friendly features.

Market Share

E-commerce product sales totaled $146.4 billion in the United States in 2006, representing about 6% of retail product sales in the country. The $18.3 billion worth of clothes sold online represented about 10% of the domestic market. For developing countries and low-income households in developed countries, adoption of e-commerce in place of or in addition to conventional methods is limited by a lack of affordable Internet access.

Advantages

Convenience

Online stores are usually available 24 hours a day, and many consumers have Internet access both at work and at home. A visit to a conventional retail store requires travel and must take place during business hours. Searching or browsing an online catalog can be faster than browsing the aisles of a physical store. Consumers with dial-up Internet connections rather than broadband have much longer load times for content-rich web sites and have a considerably slower online shopping experience. Some consumers prefer interacting with people rather than computers sometimes because they find computers hard to use. Not all online retailers have succeeded in making their sites easy to use or reliable.

In most cases, merchandise must be shipped to the consumer, introducing a significant delay and potentially uncertainty about whether or not the item was actually in stock at the time of purchase. Bricks and clicks stores offer the ability to buy online but pick up in a nearby store. Many stores give the consumer the delivery company's tracking number for their package when shipped, so they can check its status online and know exactly when it will arrive. For efficiency reasons, online stores generally do not ship products immediately upon receiving an order. Orders are only filled during warehouse operating hours, and there may be a delay of anywhere from a few minutes to a few days to a few weeks before in-stock items are actually packaged and shipped. Many retailers inform customers how long they can expect to wait before receiving a package, and whether or not they generally have a fulfilment backlog. A quick response time is sometimes an important factor in consumers' choice of merchant. A weakness of online shopping is that, even if a purchase can be made 24 hours a day, the customer must often be at home during normal business hours to accept the delivery. For many professionals this can be difficult, and absence at the time of delivery can result in delays, or in some cases, return of the item to the retailer. Automated delivery booths, such as DHL's Packstation, have tried to address this problem.

In the event of a problem with the item-it is not what the consumer ordered, or it is not what they expected-consumers are concerned with the ease with which they can return an item for the correct one or for a refund. Consumers may need to contact the retailer, visit the post office and pay return shipping, and then wait for a replacement or refund. Some online companies have more generous return policies to compensate for the traditional advantage of physical stores. For example, the online shoe retailer Zappos.com includes labels for free return shipping, and does not charge a restocking fee, even for returns which are not the result of merchant error.

Information and Reviews

Online stores must describe products for sale with text, photos, and multimedia files, whereas in a physical retail store, the actual product and the manufacturer's packaging will be available for direct inspection (which might involve a test drive, fitting, or other experimentation).

Some online stores provide or link to supplemental product information, such as instructions, safety procedures, demonstrations, or manufacturer specifications. Some provide background information, advice, or how-to guides designed to help consumers decide which product to buy.

Some stores even allow customers to comment or rate their items. There are also dedicated review sites that host user reviews for different products.

In a conventional retail store, clerks are generally available to answer questions. Some online stores have real-time chat features, but most rely on email or phone calls to handle customer questions.

Price and Selection

One advantage of shopping online is being able to quickly seek out deals for items or services with many different vendors (though some local search engines do exist to help consumers locate products for sale in nearby stores). Search engines and online price comparison services can be used to look up sellers of a particular product or service.

Shoppers find a greater selection online in certain market segments (for example, computers and consumer electronics) and in some cases lower prices. This is due to a relaxation of certain constraints, such as the size of a "brick-and-mortar" store, lower stocking costs (or none, if drop shipping is used), and lower staffing overhead.

Shipping costs (if applicable) reduce the price advantage of online merchandise, though depending on the jurisdiction, a lack of sales tax may compensate for this.

Shipping a small number of items, especially from another country, is much more expensive than making the larger shipments bricks-and-mortar retailers order. Some retailers (especially those selling small, high-value items like electronics) offer free shipping on sufficiently large orders.

Concerns

Fraud and Security Concerns

Given the lack of ability to inspect merchandise before purchase, consumers are at higher risk of fraud on the part of the merchant than in a physical store. Merchants also risk fraudulent purchases using stolen credit cards or fraudulent repudiation of the online purchase. With a warehouse instead of a retail storefront, merchants face less risk from physical theft.

Secure Sockets Layer (SSL) encryption has generally solved the problem of credit card numbers being intercepted in transit between the consumer and the merchant. Identity theft is still a concern for consumers when hackers break into a merchant's web site and steal names, addresses and credit card numbers. A number of high-profile break-ins in the 2000s has prompted some U.S. states to require disclosure to consumers when this happens. Computer security has thus become a major concern for merchants and e-commerce service providers, who deploy countermeasures such as firewalls and antivirus software to protect their networks.

Phishing is another danger, where consumers are fooled into thinking they are dealing with a reputable retailer, when they have actually been manipulated into feeding private information to a system operated by a malicious party. Denial of service attacks are a minor risk for merchants, as are server and network outages.

Quality seals can be placed on the Shop web page if it has undergone an independent assessment and meets all requirements of the company issuing the seal. The purpose of these seals is to increase the confidence of the online shoppers; the existence of many different seals, or seals unfamiliar to consumers, may foil this effort to a certain extent.

A number of resources offer advice on how consumers can protect themselves when using online retailer services. These include:

- Sticking with known stores, or attempting to find independent consumer reviews of their experiences; also ensuring that there is comprehensive contact information on the website before using the service, and noting if the retailer has enrolled in industry oversight programs such as trust mark or trust seal.
- Before buying from a new company, evaluate the website by considering issues such as: the professionalism and user-friendliness of the site; whether or not the company lists a telephone number and/or street address along with e-contact information; whether a fair and reasonable refund and return policy is clearly stated; and whether there are hidden price inflators, such as excessive shipping and handling charges.
- Ensuring that the retailer has an acceptable privacy policy posted. For example note if the retailer does not explicitly state that it will not share private information with others without consent.

- Ensuring that the vendor address is protected with SSL when entering credit card information. If it does the address on the credit card information entry screen will start with "HTTPS".
- Using strong passwords, without personal information. Another option is a "pass phrase," which might be something along the lines: "I shop 4 good a buy!!" These are difficult to hack, and provides a variety of upper, lower, and special characters and could be site specific and easy to remember.

Although the benefits of online shopping are considerable, when the process goes poorly it can create a thorny situation. A few problems that shoppers potentially face include identity theft, faulty products, and the accumulation of spy ware. Most large online corporations are inventing new ways to make fraud more difficult, however, the criminals are constantly responding to these developments with new ways to manipulate the system. Even though these efforts are making it easier to protect yourself online, it is a constant fight to maintain the lead. It is advisable to be aware of the most current technology and scams out there to fully protect yourself and your finances..

One of the hardest areas to deal with in online shopping is the delivery of the products. Most companies offer shipping insurance in case the product is lost or damaged; however, if the buyer opts not to purchase insurance on their products, they are generally out of luck. Some shipping companies will offer refunds or compensation for the damage, but it is up to their discretion if this will happen. It is important to realize that once the product leaves the hands of the seller, they have no responsibility (provided the product is what the buyer ordered and is in the specified condition).

Privacy

Privacy of personal information is a significant issue for some consumers. Different legal jurisdictions have different laws concerning consumer privacy, and different levels of enforcement. Many consumers wish to avoid spam and telemarketing which could result from supplying contact information to an online merchant. In response, many merchants promise not to use consumer information for these purposes, or provide a mechanism to opt-out of such contacts.

Brick-and-mortar stores also collect consumer information. Some ask for address and phone number at checkout, though consumers may refuse to provide it. Many larger stores use the address information encoded on consumers' credit cards (often without their knowledge) to add them to a catalog mailing list. This information is obviously not accessible to the merchant when paying in cash.

Product Suitability

Category	*U.S. online sales (2006)*
Apparel, accessories and footwear	$18.3 billion
Computer hardware and software	$17.2 billion
Autos and auto parts	$16.7 billion
Home furnishings	$10.0 billion
Total products sales (excluding travel)	$146.4 billion
Travel	$73.5 billion

Many successful purely virtual companies deal with digital products, (including information storage, retrieval, and modification), music, movies, office supplies, education, communication, software, photography, and financial transactions. Other successful marketers use Drop shipping or affiliate marketing techniques to facilitate transactions of tangible goods without maintaining real inventory.

Some non-digital products have been more successful than others for online stores. Profitable items often have a high value-to-weight ratio, they may involve embarrassing purchases, they may typically go to people in remote locations, and they may have shut-ins as their typical purchasers. Items which can fit through a standard letterbox — such as music CDs, DVDs and books — are particularly suitable for a virtual marketer

Products such as spare parts, both for consumer items like washing machines and for industrial equipment like centrifugal pumps, also seem good candidates for selling online. Retailers often need to order spare parts specially, since they typically do not stock them at consumer outlets—in such cases, e-commerce solutions in spares do not compete with retail stores, only with other ordering systems. A factor for success in this niche can consist of providing customers with exact, reliable information about which part number their particular version of a product needs, for example by providing parts lists keyed by serial number.

Products less suitable for e-commerce include products that have a low value-to-weight ratio, products that have a smell, taste, or touch component, products that need trial fittings — most notably clothing — and products where colour integrity appears important. Nonetheless, Tesco.com has had success delivering groceries in the UK, albeit that many of its goods are of a generic quality, and clothing sold through the internet is big business in the U.S. Also, the recycling program Cheapcycle sells goods over the internet, but avoids the low value-to-weight ratio problem by creating different groups for various regions, so that shipping costs remain low.

Aggregation

High-volume websites, such as Yahoo!, Amazon.com and eBay, offer hosting services for online stores to small retailers. These stores are presented within an integrated navigation framework. Collections of online stores are sometimes known as virtual shopping malls or online marketplaces. Become.com is a product price comparison service and discovery shopping search engine with a mission to help shoppers make ideal buying decisions. Dulance was a price engine that specialized in searching for hard-to-find products often sold by small independent online retailers ("The Long Tail").

Online Banking

This article needs additional citations for verification. Please help improve this article by adding reliable references. Unsourced material may be challenged and removed.

Online banking (or Internet banking) allows customers to conduct financial transactions on a secure website operated by their retail or virtual bank, credit union or building society.

Features

Online banking solutions have many features and capabilities in common, but traditionally also have some that are application specific.

The common features fall broadly into several categories :

— Transactional (e.g., performing a financial transaction such as an account to account transfer, paying a bill, wire transfer... and applications... apply for a loan, new account, etc.)

  - Electronic bill presentment and payment-EBPP
  - Funds transfer between a customer's own checking and savings accounts, or to another customer's account
  - Investment purchase or sale
  - Loan applications and transactions, such as repayments

— Non-transactional (e.g., online statements, check links, cobrowsing, chat)
  - Bank statements
  - Financial Institution Administration-
  - Support of multiple users having varying levels of authority
  - Transaction approval process
  - Wire transfer.

Features Commonly Unique to Internet Banking Include

- Personal financial management support, such as importing data into personal accounting software. Some online banking platforms support account aggregation to allow the customers to monitor all of their accounts in one place whether they are with their main bank or with other institutions.

History

The precursor for the modern home online banking services were the distance banking services over electronic media from the early '80s. The term online became popular in the late '80s and referred to the use of a terminal, keyboard and TV (or monitor) to access the banking system using a phone line. 'Home banking' can also refer to the use of a numeric keypad to send tones down a phone line with instructions to the bank. Online services started in New York in 1981 when four of the city's major banks (Citibank, Chase Manhattan, Chemical and Manufacturers Hanover) offered home banking services using the videotex system. Because of the commercial failure of videotex these banking services never became popular except in France where the use of videotex (Minitel) was subsidised by the telecom provider and the UK, where the Prestel system was used.

The UK's first home online banking services was set up by the Nottingham Building Society (NBS) in 1983. The system used was based on the UK's Prestel system and used a computer, such as the BBC Micro, or keyboard (Tandata Td1400) connected to the telephone system and television set. The system (known as 'Homelink') allowed online viewing of statements, bank transfers and bill payments. In order to make bank transfers and bill payments, a written instruction giving details of the intended recipient had to be sent to the NBS who set the details up on the Homelink system. Typical recipients were gas, electricity and telephone companies and accounts with other banks.

Details of payments to be made were input into the NBS system by the account holder via Prestel. A cheque was then sent by NBS to the payee and an advice giving details of the payment was sent to the account holder. BACS was later used to transfer the payment directly.

Stanford Federal Credit Union was the first financial institution to offer online internet banking services to all of its members in Oct, 1994.

Security

Protection through single password authentication, as is the case in most secure Internet shopping sites, is not considered secure enough for personal online banking applications in some countries. Basically there exist two different security methods for online banking.

- The PIN/TAN system where the PIN represents a password, used for the login and TANs representing one-time passwords to authenticate transactions. TANs can be distributed in different ways, the most popular one is to send a list of TANs to the online banking user by postal letter. The most secure way of using TANs is to generate them by need using a security token. These token generated TANs depend on the time and a unique secret, stored in the security token (this is called two-factor authentication or 2FA). Usually online banking with PIN/TAN is done via a web browser using SSL secured connections, so that there is no additional encryption needed.
- Signature based online banking where all transactions are signed and encrypted digitally. The Keys for the signature generation and encryption can be stored on smartcards or any memory medium, depending on the concrete implementation.

Attacks

Most of the attacks on online banking used today are based on deceiving the user to steal login data and valid TANs. Two well known examples for those attacks are phishing and pharming. Cross-site scripting and keylogger/Trojan horses can also be used to steal login information.

A method to attack signature based online banking methods is to manipulate the used software in a way, that correct transactions are shown on the screen and faked transactions are signed in the background.

A recent FDIC Technology Incident Report, compiled from suspicious activity reports banks file quarterly, lists 536 cases of computer intrusion, with an average loss per incident of $30,000. That adds up to a nearly $16-million loss in the second quarter of 2007. Computer intrusions increased by 150 percent between the first quarter of 2007 and the second. In 80 percent of the cases, the source of the intrusion is unknown but it occurred during online banking, the report states.

The most recent kind of attack is the so-called Man in the Browser attack, where a Trojan horses permits a remote attacker to modify the destination account number and also the amount.

Countermeasures

There exist several countermeasures which try to avoid attacks. Digital certificates are used against phishing and pharming, the use of class-3 card readers is a measure to avoid manipulation of transactions by the software in signature based online banking variants. To protect their systems against Trojan horses, users should use virus scanners and be careful with downloaded software or email attachments.

In 2001 the FFIEC issued guidance for multifactor authentication (MFA) and then required to be in place by the end of 2006.

Online Office Suites

An online office suite or online productivity suite is a type of office suite offered by websites in the form of software as a service. They can be accessed online from any Internet-enabled device running any operating system. This allows people to work together worldwide and at any time, thereby leading to international web-based collaboration and virtual teamwork. Usually, the basic versions are offered for free and for more advanced versions one is required to pay a nominal subscription fee.

Applications are often developed on the Web 2.0 paradigms with leverage on the existing developer community. Players come from both the commercial software market and from the open source, free software communities.

Office 2.0

The term Office 2.0, which is sometimes used to refer to online office suites, originated with Ismael Ghalimi in an experimental effort to test whether he could perform all of his computer based work in online applications. It is a marketing neologism representing the concepts of office productivity applications as published applications rather than stand-alone programs, leveraging the Web 2.0 concept to conjure imagery of collaborative, community based and centralised effort rather than the more traditional application running on a platform locally. It is also the focus of the annual Office 2.0 Conference.

Examples

Examples of where the term may apply include:

- The centralized administration of office productivity software, installation, licensing and version control;
- Collaborative applications which improve personal and organizational productivity;
- Centralized storage of data, rather than traditional personal data responsibility;
- Applications which focus on collaborative data sharing, document review and document resource management;
- Office applications which are able to be run from multiple independent platforms with a suitable back-end framework to present the application in a uniform manner.

Advantages

- The cost is low. In most cases, there is no specific charge for using the service for users who already have access to a computer with a web browser and a connection to the Internet.
- There is no need to download or install software outside of the office suite's web page, including the ongoing upgrade chores of adding new features to or eliminating bugs from the office suite.
- Online office suites can run out of thin clients with minimal hardware requirements.
- Online office suites provide the ability for a group of people to share a document without the need to run their own server.
- There is no need to purchase or upgrade a software license. Instead, the online office suite is available as software as a service.
- Online office suites are portable. Users can access their documents from almost any computer with a connection to the Internet, regardless of which operating system they use.
- If the user's computer fails, the documents are still safely stored on the remote server. Online service providers' backup

processes and overall stability will generally be superior to that of most home systems.

Disadvantages

- Access requires connectivity—if the remote server or network is unavailable, the content will also be unavailable. However, in many cases, the online suite will allow the user to regularly backup data or even provide synchronization of documents between the server and the local computer.
- There are speed and accessibility issues. Most of the currently available online office suites require a high speed (broadband) Internet connection. That can be a problem for users who are limited by a slower connection to the Internet.
- The number of features available is an issue. Online office suites lack the more advanced features available on their offline counterparts.
- There may be a subscription charge to use the service. In that case, in the long run, the ongoing subscription cost may be more expensive than purchasing offline software upfront.

Criticism

As with most marketing neologisms which later become accepted public trends, technologists contend that these technologies have existed for some time, particularly in the form of Microsoft Terminal Services based applications and Citrix XenApp published application frameworks. The term itself is likely to only be used as a reference to a group of selling points.

There are also questions as to how businesses will be affected by storing all of their documents in online environments. For example, the search and seizures provisions offered by the Fourth Amendment do not apply to online service providers storing third-party data.

Components

An online office suite normally includes a broad set of the following applications:

Document Creation and Editing Applications

- Word processor
- Spreadsheet
- Presentation program

- Flowchart
- Raster image processor.

Publishing Applications

- CMS
- Web portal
- Wiki
- Blog
- Forums.

Collaborative Applications

- Email
- Instant massaging (VoIP)
- Calendar.

Management Applications

- Data management
- Project management
- CRM
- ERP
- Accounting
- Domestic and international payment systems.

Payment System

A payment system is a system (including physical or electronic infrastructure and associated procedures and protocols) used to settle financial transactions in Automated teller machine networks, Stored-value card networks, bond markets, currency markets, and futures, derivatives, or options markets, or to transfer funds between financial institutions. Due to the backing of modern fiat currencies with government bonds, payment systems are a core part of modern monetary systems.

Also, Electronic Payment is a subset of an e-commerce transaction to include electronic payment for buying and selling goods or services offered through the Internet.

Shopping Cart Software

"Electronic shopping cart" redirects here. For the wheelchair-like shopping cart used by disabled persons, see Motorized shopping cart.

Shopping cart software is software used in e-commerce to assist people making purchases online, analogous to the American English term 'shopping cart'. In British English it is generally known as a shopping basket, almost exclusively shortened on websites to 'basket'.

The software allows online shopping customers to accumulate a list of items for purchase, described metaphorically as "placing items in the shopping cart". Upon checkout, the software typically calculates a total for the order, including shipping and handling (i.e. postage and packing) charges and the associated taxes, as applicable.

Technical Definition

These applications typically provide a means of capturing a client's payment information, but in the case of a credit card they rely on the software module of the secure gateway provider, in conjunction with the secure payment gateway, in order to conduct secure credit card transactions online.

Some setup must be done in the HTML code of the website, and the shopping cart software must be installed on the server which hosts the site, or on the secure server which accepts sensitive ordering information. E-shopping carts are usually implemented using HTTP cookies or query strings. In most server based implementations however, data related to the shopping cart is kept in the Session object and is accessed and manipulated on the fly, as the user selects different items from the cart. Later at the process of commit, the information is accessed and an order is generated against the selected item thus clearing the shopping cart.

Although the most simple shopping carts strictly allow for an item to be added to a basket to start a checkout process (e.g. the free PayPal shopping cart), most shopping cart software actually provides additional features that an Internet merchant uses to fully manage an online store. Data (products, categories, discounts, orders, customers, etc.) is normally stored in a database and accessed in real time by the software.

Shopping Cart Software is also known as e-commerce software, e-store software, online store software or storefront software.

Components

Shopping cart software typically consists of two components:

- *Storefront:* the area of the Web store that is accessed by visitors to the online shop. Category, product, and other pages (e.g.

search, best sellers, etc.) are dynamically generated by the software based on the information saved in the store database. The look of the storefront can normally be changed by the store owner so that it merges with the rest of the Web site (i.e. with the pages not controlled by the shopping cart software in use on the store).

- *Administration:* the area of the Web store that is accessed by the merchant to manage the online shop. The amount of store management features changes depending on the sophistication of the shopping cart software chosen by the merchant, but in general a store manager is able to add and edit products, categories, discounts, shipping and payment settings, etc. Order management features are also included in many shopping cart programs. The administration area can be:
- Web-based (accessed through a Web browser)
- Desktop-based (a desktop application that runs on the user's computer and then transfers changes to the storefront component).

Licensed vs. Hosted Shopping Carts

Shopping cart software can be generally categorized into two main categories.

- *Licensed Software:* The software is downloaded and then installed on a Web server. This is most often associated with a one-time fee, although there are many free products available as well. The main advantages of this option are that the merchant owns a license and therefore can host it on any Web server that meets the server requirements, and that the source code can often be accessed and edited to customize the application.
- Hosted service: The software is never downloaded, but rather is provided by a hosted service provider and is generally paid for on a monthly/annual basis; also known as the application service provider (ASP) software model. Some of these services also charge a percentage of sales in addition to the monthly fee. This model often has predefined templates that a user can choose from to customize their look and feel. In this model users typically have less ability to modify or customize the software with the advantage of having the vendor continuously

keep the software up to date for security patches as well as adding new features added.

Teleconference

A teleconference or teleseminar is the live exchange and mass articulation of information among several persons and machines remote from one another but linked by a telecommunications system. Terms as audio conferencing, telephone conferencing and phone conferencing are also sometimes used to refer to teleconferencing.

The telecommunications system may support the teleconference by providing one or more of the following audio, video, and/or data services by one or more means, such as telephone, computer, telegraph, teletype, radio, and television.

Internet Teleconferencing

Internet teleconferencing includes internet telephone conferencing, video conferencing, and Augmented Reality conferencing.

Internet telephony involves conducting a teleconference over the Internet or a Wide Area Network. One key technology in this area is Voice over Internet Protocol (VOIP). Popular software for personal use includes Skype, Google Talk, Windows Live Messenger and Yahoo Messenger.

A working example of a Augmented Reality conferencing was demonstrated at the Salone di Mobile in Milano by AR+RFID Lab. TELEPORT is another AR teleconferencing tool.

Electronic Ticket

"E-ticket" redirects here. For the former Disneyland and Disney World tickets, see E ticket.

An electronic ticket or e-ticket is used to represent the purchase of a seat on a passenger airline, usually through a website or by telephone. This form of airline ticket has rapidly replaced the old multi-layered paper tickets (from close to zero to 100% in about 10 years) and became mandatory for IATA members as of June 1, 2008. During the last few years, where paper tickets were still available, airlines frequently charged extra for issuing them. E-tickets are also available for certain entertainment venues.

Once a reservation is made, an e-ticket exists only as a digital record in the airline computers. Customers usually print out a copy of their receipt which contains the record locator or reservation number and the e-ticket number.

According to critical acclaim, Joel R. Goheen is recognized as the Inventor of Electronic Ticketing in the Airline Industry, an industry where global electronic ticket sales (the industry standard) accounts for over $400 Billion (US) a year (2007).

Electronic tickets have been introduced in road, urban or rail public transport as well.

Checking in with an e-ticket

To check in with an e-ticket, the passenger usually comes to the check-in counter and presents the e-ticket itinerary receipt which contains a confirmation or reservation code. In some airports and airlines it's not even necessary to present this document or quote the confirmation code or e-ticket number as the reservation is confirmed solely on the basis of the passenger's identity, which may be proven by a passport or the matching credit card. After confirming the reservation, the passenger checks-in his/her luggage and is given a boarding pass which usually says "Electronic Ticket" or "E-ticket."

Self-service and Remote Check-in

The option to check-in online is available on some airlines. A passenger enters their confirmation number at the airline's website, and the passenger prints the boarding pass on their home printer. Online check-in is typically permitted up to twenty-four hours before the flight's scheduled departure time, though this may vary by airline. On airlines without assigned seating such as Southwest, it typically guarantees a passenger early boarding and a better seat. Besides identification, the boarding pass that has been printed is all that needs to be presented upon arriving at the airport. On airlines without online check-in, the check in may take place at a self-service kiosk in the airport, or at the check-in counter.

A boarding pass is required to board an aircraft; in some countries, such as the United States, it is also needed to pass through airport security checkpoints.

E-tickets are very popular because they allow extra services like:

- online/telephone/self-service kiosk check-in
- early check-in

- printing boarding passes at airport kiosks and at locations other than an airport
- automated refunds and exchanges online, by telephone and at kiosks

Several web sites exist to help people holding e-tickets accomplish online check-ins in advance of the twenty-four-hour airline restriction. These sites store a passenger's flight information and then when the airline opens up for online check-in the data is transferred to the airline and the boarding pass is emailed back to the customer.

E-ticket Limitations

This section does not cite any references or sources. Please help improve this article by adding citations to reliable sources. Unsourced material may be challenged and removed.

E-tickets are sometimes not available for some flights from an airline which usually offers them. This can be due to a number of reasons, the most common being software incompatibility. If an airline issues tickets for a codeshare flight with another company, and there is no e-ticket interlining agreement, the operating carrier would not be able to see the issuing carrier's ticket. Therefore, the carrier that books the flight needs to provide hard copy versions of the tickets so that the ticket can be processed. Similarly, if the destination airport does not have access to the airline who booked the flight, a paper ticket needs to be issued.

Industry discount (ID) tickets also tend to be issued on paper if they are valid for more than one airline, and if the airlines that the tickets are valid for do not have an interlining agreement. Since e-ticket interlining is still the exception rather than the rule, tickets valid for more than one airline are usually issued on paper.

Currently the ticketing systems of most airlines are only able to produce e-tickets for itineraries of no more than 16 segments, including surface segments.

IATA Mandated Transition

As part of the IATA Simplifying the Business initiative, the association instituted a program to switch the industry to 100% electronic ticketing. The program concluded on June 1, 2008, with the association saying that the resulting industry savings were approximately US$3 billion.

In 2004, IATA Board of Governors set the end of 2007 as the deadline for airlines to make the transition to 100% electronic ticketing for tickets processed through the IATA billing and settlement plan; in June 2007, the deadline was extended to May 31, 2008.

As of June 1, 2008 paper tickets can no longer be issued on neutral stock by agencies reporting to their local BSP. Agents reporting to the ARC, using company-provided stock or issuing tickets on behalf of an airline (GSAs and ticketing offices) are not subject to that restriction.

Except the industry was unable to comply with the IATA mandate and paper tickets remain in circulation as of February 2009.

Government Regulations

In the United States, some electronic commerce activities are regulated by the Federal Trade Commission (FTC). These activities include the use of commercial e-mails, online advertising and consumer privacy. The CAN-SPAM Act of 2003 establishes national standards for direct marketing over email. The Federal Trade Commission Act regulates all forms of advertising, including online advertising, and states that advertising must be truthful and non-deceptive. Using its authority under Section 5 of the FTC Act, which prohibits unfair or deceptive practices, the FTC has brought a number of cases to enforce the promises in corporate privacy statements, including promises about the security of consumers' personal information. As result, any corporate privacy policy related to e-commerce activity may be subject to enforcement by the FTC.

The Ryan Haight Online Pharmacy Consumer Protection Act of 2008, which came into law in 2008, amends the Controlled Substances Act to address online pharmacies.

Forms

Contemporary electronic commerce involves everything from ordering "digital" content for immediate online consumption, to ordering conventional goods and services, to "meta" services to facilitate other types of electronic commerce.

On the consumer level, electronic commerce is mostly conducted on the World Wide Web. An individual can go online to purchase anything from books or groceries, to expensive items like real estate. Another example would be online banking, i.e. online bill payments, buying stocks, transferring funds from one account to another, and initiating wire payment to another country. All of these activities can be done with a few strokes of the keyboard.

On the institutional level, big corporations and financial institutions use the internet to exchange financial data to facilitate domestic and international business. Data integrity and security are very hot and pressing issues for electronic commerce today.

Technical Support for Business

Technical support (also *tech support*) is a range of services providing assistance with technology products such as mobile phones, televisions, computers, or other electronic or mechanical goods. In general, technical support services attempt to help the user solve specific problems with a product—rather than providing training, customization, or other support services.

Most companies offer technical support for the products they sell, either freely available or for a fee. Technical support may be delivered over the telephone or online by email or a web site. Larger organizations frequently have internal technical support available to their staff for computer related problems. The internet is also a good source for freely available tech support, where experienced users may provide advice and assistance with problems. In addition, some fee-based service companies charge for premium technical support services.

Coverage of Support

Technical support may be delivered by different technologies depending on the situation. For example, direct questions can be addressed using SMS, Online chat, Email or Fax; basic software problems can be addressed over the telephone or, increasingly, by using remote access repair services; while more complicated problems with hardware may need to be dealt with in person.

Outsourcing Technical Support

With the increasing use of technology in modern times, there is a growing requirement to provide technical support. Many organizations locate their technical support departments or call centres in countries with lower costs. There has also been a growth in companies specializing in providing technical support to other organizations. These are often referred to as MSP's (Managed Service Providers)

For businesses needing to provide technical support, outsourcing provides them with the ability to maintain a high availability of service.

This comes as a result of peaks in call volumes during the day, periods of high activity due to the introduction of new products and maintenance service packs, and the necessity to provide consumers with a high level of service at a low cost to the business. For businesses needing technical support assets, outsourcing enables their core employees to focus more on their work in order to maintain productivity. It also enables them to utilize specialized personnel whose technical knowledge base and experience may exceed the scope of the business, thus providing a higher level of technical support to their employees.

Multi-tiered Technical Support

Technical support is often subdivided into tiers, or levels, in order to better serve a business or customer base. The number of levels a business uses to organize their technical support group is dependent on a business' need, want, or desire as it revolves around their ability to sufficiently serve their customers or users. The reason for providing a multi-tiered support system instead of one general support group is to provide the best possible service in the most efficient possible manner. Success of the organizational structure is dependent on the technicians' understanding of their level of responsibility and commitments, their customer response time commitments, and when to appropriately escalate an issue and to which level. A common support structure revolves around a three-tiered technical support system.

Tier I

This is the initial support level responsible for basic customer issues. It is synonymous with first-line support, level 1 support, front-end support, line 1, and various other headings denoting basic level technical support functions. The first job of a Tier I specialist is to gather the customer's information and to determine the customer's issue by analysing the symptoms and figuring out the underlying problem. When analysing the symptoms, it is important for the technician to identify what the customer is trying to accomplish so that time is not wasted on "attempting to solve a symptom instead of a problem." Once identification of the underlying problem is established, the specialist can begin sorting through the possible solutions available. Technical support specialists in this group typically handle straightforward and simple problems while "possibly using some kind of knowledge management tool." This includes troubleshooting methods such as verifying physical layer issues, resolving username and password problems, uninstalling/

reinstalling basic software applications, verification of proper hardware and software set up, and assistance with navigating around application menus. Personnel at this level have a basic to general understanding of the product or service and may not always contain the competency required for solving complex issues. Nevertheless, the goal for this group is to handle 70%-80% of the user problems before finding it necessary to escalate the issue to a higher level.

Tier II

This is a more in-depth technical support level than Tier I containing experienced and more knowledgeable personnel on a particular product or service. It is synonymous with level 2 support, support line 2, administrative level support, and various other headings denoting advanced technical troubleshooting and analysis methods. Technicians in this realm of knowledge are responsible for assisting Tier I personnel solve basic technical problems and for investigating elevated issues by confirming the validity of the problem and seeking for known solutions related to these more complex issues. However, prior to the troubleshooting process, it is important that the technician review the work order to see what has already been accomplished by the Tier I technician and how long the technician has been working with the particular customer. This is a key element in meeting both the customer and business needs as it allows the technician to prioritize the troubleshooting process and properly manage his or her time. If a problem is new and/or personnel from this group cannot determine a solution, they are responsible for raising this issue to the Tier III technical support group. In addition, many companies may specify that certain troubleshooting solutions be performed by this group to help ensure the intricacies of a challenging issue are solved by providing experienced and knowledgeable technicians. This may include, but is not limited to onsite installations or replacements of various hardware components, software repair, diagnostic testing, and the utilization of remote control tools used to take over the user's machine for the sole purpose of troubleshooting and finding a solution to the problem.

Tier III

This is the highest level of support in a three-tiered technical support model responsible for handling the most difficult or advanced problems. It is synonymous with level 3 support, back-end support, support line 3, high-end support, and various other headings denoting expert level troubleshooting and analysis methods. These individuals are experts in their fields and are responsible for not only assisting both Tier I and Tier II personnel, but with the research and development of solutions to new or unknown issues. Note that Tier III technicians have the same responsibility as Tier II technicians in reviewing the work order and assessing the time already spent with the customer so that the work is prioritized and time management is sufficiently utilized. If it is at all possible, the technician will work to solve the problem with the customer as it may become apparent that the Tier I and/or Tier II technicians simply failed to discover the proper solution. Upon encountering new problems; however, Tier III personnel must first determine whether or not to solve the problem and may require the customer's contact information so that the technician can have adequate time to troubleshoot the issue and find a solution. In some instances, an issue may be so problematic to the point where the product cannot be salvaged and must be replaced. Such extreme problems are also sent to the original developers for in-depth analysis. If it is determined that a problem can be solved, this group is responsible for designing and developing one or more courses of action, evaluating each of these courses in a test case environment, and implementing the best solution to the problem. Once the solution is verified, it is delivered to the customer and made available for future troubleshooting and analysis.

Tier IV

While not universally used, a fourth level often represents an escalation point beyond the organization. This is generally a hardware or software vendor. Within a corporate incident management system it is important to continue to track incidents even when they are being actioned by a vendor and the Service Level Agreement (or SLA) may have specific provision for this.

Remote PC Repair or Remote Computer Repair

Remote PC repair or Remote Computer Repair is a method for troubleshooting software related problems via remote desktop connections. Technicians use software that allows the technician to access the user's desktop via the Internet. With the user's permission, the technician can take control of the user's mouse and keyboard, transfer various diagnostic and repair applications to the user's desktop, run scans, install antivirus programs, etc. If the remote service permits it, the technician can even reboot the PC and reconnect remotely to continue his work without the user needing to assist. Common repairs available with online computer support providers are computer virus and spyware removal, computer optimization, registry repair, device driver issues, Web related issues, and Windows security updates.

Generally, only software can be "repaired" remotely; a computer with a broken hardware component such as a motherboard or hard disk can in some cases be diagnosed, but must be repaired in person.

Technical Support Centre Certification

Technical support centres can be certified to help ensure a particular business is maintaining a high level of information technology service and support standards. Of the certifications available for support centres and technicians, there are two internationally recognized certifications geared specifically towards support centres as a whole – The Help Desk Institute (HDI) Support Centre Certification and the Service Strategies Service Capability and Performance (SCP) Standards. Both certifications were developed by experts and organizations from around the world and both were developed under the premise of enhancing the quality of customer service and support.

Call Centre

A very large collections call centre in Lakeland, Florida.

A call centre or call centre is a centralised office used for the purpose of receiving and transmitting a large volume of requests by telephone. A call centre is operated by a company to administer incoming product support or information inquiries from consumers. Outgoing calls for telemarketing, clientele, product services, and debt collection are also made. In addition to a call centre, collective handling of letters, faxes, live chat, and e-mails at one location is known as a contact centre.

A call centre is often operated through an extensive open workspace for call centre agents, with work stations that include a computer for each agent, a telephone set/headset connected to a telecom switch, and one or more supervisor stations. It can be independently operated or networked with additional centres, often linked to a corporate computer network, including main frames, microcomputers and LANs. Increasingly, the voice and data pathways into the centre are linked through a set of new technologies called computer telephony integration (CTI).

Most major businesses use call centres to interact with their customers. Examples include utility companies, mail order catalogue retailers, and customer support for computer hardware and software. Some businesses even service internal functions through call centres. Examples of this include help desks, retail financial support, and sales support.

A contact centre, also known as customer interaction centre is a central point of any organization from which all customer contacts are managed. Through contact centres, valuable information about company are routed to appropriate people, contacts to be tracked and data to be gathered. It is generally a part of company's customer relationship management (CRM). Today, customers contact companies by calling, emailing, chatting online, visiting websites, faxing and even instant massaging.

Technology

Call centre technology is subject to improvements and innovations. Some of these technologies include speech recognition software to allow computers to handle first level of customer support, text mining and natural language processing to allow better customer handling, agent training by automatic mining of best practices from past interactions, support automation and many other technologies to improve agent productivity and customer satisfaction. Automatic lead selection or lead steering is also intended to improve efficiencies, both for inbound and outbound campaigns, whereby inbound calls are intended to quickly land with the appropriate agent to handle the task, whilst minimising wait times and long lists of irrelevant options for people calling in, as well as for outbound calls, where lead selection allows management to designate what type of leads go to which agent based on factors including skill, socioeconomic factors and past performance and percentage likelihood of closing a sale per lead. The concept of the Universal Queue standardises the processing of communications across multiple technologies such as fax, phone, and email whilst the concept of a Virtual queue provides callers with an alternative to waiting on hold when no agents are available to handle inbound call demand.

Premise-based Call Centre Technology Historically, call centres have been built on PBX equipment that is owned and hosted by the call centre operator. The PBX might provide functions such as Automatic Call Distribution, Interactive Voice Response, and skills-based routing. The call centre operator would be responsible for the maintenance of the equipment and necessary software upgrades as released by the vendor. Virtual Call Centre Technology With the advent of the Software as a service technology delivery model, the virtual call centre has emerged. In a virtual call centre model, the call centre operator does not own, operate or host the equipment that the call centre runs on. Instead, they subscribe to a service for a monthly or annual fee with a service provider that hosts the call centre telephony equipment in their own data centre. Such a vendor may host many call centres on their equipment. Agents connect to the vendor's equipment through traditional PSTN telephone lines, or over Voice over IP. Calls to and from prospects or contacts originate from or terminate at the vendor's data centre, rather than at the call centre operator's premise. The vendor's telephony equipment then connects the calls to the call centre operator's agents.

Patents

Call Centre Floor During Shift.

There are a large number of patents covering various aspects of call centre operation, automation, and technology. One of the early inventors in this field, Ronald A. Katz, personally holds over 50 patents covering inventions related to toll free numbers, automated attendant, automated call distribution, voice response unit, computer telephone integration and speech recognition.

Dynamics

Types of calls are often divided into outbound *and* inbound. *Inbound calls are calls that are made by the consumer to obtain information, report a malfunction, or ask for help. These calls are substantially different from outbound calls, where agents place calls to potential customers mostly with intentions of selling or service to the individual. It is possible to combine inbound and outbound campaigns.*

Call centre staff are often organised into a multi-tier support system for a more efficient handling of calls. The first tier in such a model consists of operators, who direct inquiries to the appropriate department and provide general directory information. If a caller requires more assistance, the call is forwarded to the second tier, where most issues can be resolved. In some cases, there may be three or more tiers of support staff. If a caller requires more assistance, the caller is forwarded to the third tier of support; typically the third tier of support is formed by product engineers/developers or highly skilled technical support staff of the product.

Call centres have their critics, some of which argue that the work atmosphere in such an environment is de-humanising. Others point to the low rates of pay and restrictive working practices of some employers. There has been much controversy over such things as restricting the amount of time that an employee can spend in the toilet. Furthermore, call centres have been the subject of complaints by callers who find the staff often do not have enough skill or authority to resolve problems, while the dehumanised workers very often exhibit an attitude of apathy to even the most abusive customer.

Owing to the highly technological nature of the operations in such offices, the close monitoring of staff activities is easy and widespread. This can be argued to be beneficial, to enable the company to better plan the workload and time of its employees. Some people have argued that such close monitoring breaches human rights to privacy.

Varieties

Some variations of call centre models are listed below:

- *Contact centre* – Supports interaction with customers over a variety of media, including but not necessarily limited to telephony, email and internet chat.
- *Inbound call centre*-Exclusively or predominantly handles inbound calls (calls initiated by the customer).
- *Outbound call centre*-One in which call centre agents make outbound calls to customers or sales leads.
- *Blended call centre*-Combining automatic call distribution for incoming calls with predictive dialling for outbound calls, it makes more efficient use of agent time as each type of agent (inbound or outbound) can handle the overflow of the other.

Criticism and Performance

This article's *Criticism* or *Controversy* section(s) may mean the article does not present a neutral point of view of the subject. It may be better to integrate the material in those sections into the article as a whole.

Criticisms of call centres generally follow a number of common themes, from both callers and call centre staff. From callers, common criticisms include:

- Operators working from a script
- Non-expert operators (call screening)

- Incompetent or untrained operators incapable of processing customers' requests effectively
- Overseas location, with language and accent problems
- Touch tone menu systems and automated queuing systems
- Excessive waiting times to be connected to an operator
- Complaints that departments of companies do not engage in communication with one another
- Deceit over location of call centre (such as allocating overseas workers false English names)
- Requiring the caller to repeat the same information multiple times

Common Criticisms from Staff Include

- Close scrutiny by management (e.g. frequent random call monitoring)
- Low compensation (pay and bonuses)
- Restrictive working practices (some operators are required to follow a pre-written script)
- High stress: a common problem associated with front-end jobs where employees deal directly with customers
- Repetitive job task
- Poor working conditions (e.g. poor facilities, poor maintenance and cleaning, cramped working conditions, management interference, lack of privacy and noisy)
- Impaired vision and hearing problems
- Rude and abusive customers—especially callers who ask, "Is this the answering service?" (Most operators are not allowed to disclose this.)

The net-net of these concerns is that call centres as a business process exhibit stratospheric levels of variability. The experience a customer gets and the results a company achieves on a given call are almost totally dependent on the quality of the agent answering that call. Call centres are beginning to address this by using agent-assisted voice solutions to standardise the process all agents use. Anton and Phelps have provided a detailed HOWTO to conduct the performance evaluation of the business, whereas others are using various scientific technologies to do the jobs. However more popular alternatives are using personality and skill based approaches. The various challenges encountered by call operators are discussed by several authors.

Unionisation

Unions in North America have made some effort to gain members from this sector, including the Communications Workers of America and the United Steelworkers. In Australia, the Call Centre Workers Union represents unionised workers; their activities form part of the Australian labour movement. In Europe, Uni Global Union of Switzerland is involved in assisting unionisation in this realm.

Standardisation

Currently, there are no universally bracketable international standards, other than ISO 9000 series, available for the industry to follow up. However, some of the relevant standards are loosely published by ISO with the division of ICS 33.040.35. Most of the standards under this division have not been reviewed thoroughly, but there are some guidelines and standing operating procedures available on the internet.

Mathematical Theory

Queuing theory is a branch of mathematics in which models of queuing systems have been developed. A call centre can be seen as a queuing network. The models can be applied to answer queueing questions for call centres.

Call centre operations have been supported by mathematical models beyond queueing, with operations research, which considers a wide range of optimisation problems.

Customer Service

Customer service is the provision of service to customers before, during and after a purchase.

According to Jamier L. Scott. (2002), "Customer service is a series of activities designed to enhance the level of customer satisfaction – that is, the feeling that a product or service has met the customer expectation."

Its importance varies by product, industry and customer; defective or broken merchandise can be exchanged/swapped, often only with a receipt and within a specified time frame. Retail stores will often have a desk or counter devoted to dealing with returns, exchanges and complaints, or will perform related functions at the point of sale.

Customer service may be provided by a person (e.g., sales and service representative), or by automated means called self-service. Examples of self service are Internet sites. The experience a customer has of a product also affect the total service experience, but this is more of a product direct feature than what is included in the definition of customer service.

Customer service is normally an integral part of a company's customer value proposition. In their book *Rules to Break and Laws to Follow,* Don Peppers and Martha Rogers, Ph.D. write that "customers have memories. They will remember you, whether you remember them or not." Further, "customer trust can be destroyed at once by a major service problem, or it can be undermined one day at a time, with a thousand small demonstrations of incompetence."

From the point of view of an overall sales process engineering effort, customer service plays an important role in an organization's ability to generate income and revenue. From that perspective, customer service should be included as part of an overall approach to systematic improvement.

Some have argued that the quality and level of customer service has decreased in recent years, and that this can be attributed to a lack of support or understanding at the executive and middle management levels of a corporation and/or a customer service policy.

Instant Feedback

Recently, many organizations have implemented feedback loops that allow them to capture feedback at the point of experience. For example, National Express, one of the UK's leading travel companies invites passengers to send text messages whilst riding the bus. This has been shown to be useful as it allows companies to improve their customer service before the customer defects, thus making it far more likely that the customer will return next time.

Setting the Right KPIs

This section contains instructions, advice, or how-to content. The purpose of Wikipedia is to present facts, not to train. Please help improve this article either by rewriting the how-to content or by moving it to Wikiversity or Wikibooks. *(August 2009)*

A challenge working with Customer Service is to ensure that you have focused your attention on the right key areas, measured by the right Key Performance Indicator. There is no challenge to come up with a lot of meaningful KPIs, but the challenge is to select a few which reflects your overall strategy. In addition to reflecting your strategy it should also enable staff to limit their focus to the areas that really matter. The focus must be of those KPIs, which will deliver the most value to the overall objective, e.g. cost saving, service improving etc. It must also be done in such a way that staff sincerly believe that they can make a difference with the effort.

One of the most important aspects of a customer service KPI is that of what is often referred to as the "Feel Good Factor". Basically the goal is to not only help the customer have a good experience, but to offer them an experience that exceeds their expectations. Several key points are listed as follows:

1. Know your product-Know what products/service you are offering back to front. In other words be an information expert. It is okay to say "I don't know", but it should always be followed up by... "but let me find out" or possibly " but my friend knows!" Whatever the situation may be, make sure that you don't leave your customer with an unanswered question.
2. Body Language/Communication-Most of the communication that we relay to others is done through body language. If we have a negative body language when we interact with others it can show our lack of care. Two of the most important parts of positive body language are smiling, and eye contact. Make sure to look your customers in the eye. It shows that we are listening to them, not at them. And then of course smiling is just more inviting than someone who has a blank look on their face.
3. Anticipate Guest Needs-Nothing surprises your customer more than an employee going the extra mile to help them. Always look for ways to serve your customer more than they expect. In doing so it helps them to know that you care and it will leave them with the "Feel Good Factor" that we are searching for.

Standardization

There are few standards on this topic. ISO and The International Customer Service Institute (TICSI) have published the following ones:

- ISO 9004:2000, on performance improvement

- ISO 10001:2007, on customer service conduct
- ISO 10002:2004, on quality management in handling customer complaints
- ISO 10003:2007, on dispute resolution
- The International Customer Service Standard (TICSS).

There is also an Information Technology service management standard: ISO/IEC 20000:2005. Its first part concerns specifications and its second part the code of practice.

Help Desk

This article needs additional citations for verification. Please help improve this article by adding reliable references. Unsourced material may be challenged and removed. *(September 2008).*

A help desk is an information and assistance resource that troubleshoots problems with computers or similar products. Corporations often provide help desk support to their customers via a toll-free number, website and/or email. There are also in-house help desks geared toward providing the same kind of help for employees only. Some schools offer classes in which they perform similar tasks as a help desk. In the Information Technology Infrastructure Library, within companies adhering to ISO/IEC 20000 or seeking to implement IT Service Management best practice, a help desk may offer a wider range of user centric services and be part of a larger Service Desk.

Functions

A typical help desk has several functions. It provides the users a central point to receive help on various computer issues. The help desk typically manages its requests via help desk software, such as an incident tracking system, that allows them to track user requests with a unique ticket number. This can also be called a "Local Bug Tracker" or LBT. The help desk software can often be an extremely beneficial tool when used to find, analyze, and eliminate common problems in an organization's computing environment. There are many software applications available to support the help desk function. Some are targeting enterprise level help desk (rather large) and some are targeting departmental needs.

In the mid 1990s, Middleton at Robert Gordon University found through his research that many organizations had begun to recognize that the real value of their help desk(s) derives not solely from their reactive response to users' issues but from the help desk's unique position where it communicates daily with numerous customers or employees. This gives the help desk the ability to monitor the user environment for issues from technical problems to user preferences and satisfaction. Such information gathered at the help desk can be valuable for use in planning and preparation for other units in IT.

Organization

Large help desks have different levels to handle different types of questions. The first-level help desk is prepared to answer the most commonly asked questions, or provide resolutions that often belong in an FAQ or knowledge base. Typically, an incident tracking system has been implemented that allows a logging process to take place at the onset of a call. If the issue isn't resolved at the first-level, the ticket is escalated to a second, higher, level that has the necessary resources to handle more difficult calls. Also note that some organizations have a third, higher again, line of support which often deals with software specific needs, such as updates and bug-fixes that affect the client directly.

Larger help desks have a person or team responsible for managing the tickets and are commonly called queue managers or queue supervisors. The queue manager is responsible for the ticket queues, which can be setup in various ways depending on the help desk size or structure. Typically, larger help desks have several teams that are experienced in working on different issues. The queue manager will assign a ticket to one of the specialized teams based on the type of issue. Some help desks may have phone systems with ACD splits that ensure that calls about specific topics are put through to analysts with experience or knowledge on that topic.

Many help desks are also strictly rostered. Time is set aside for analysts to perform tasks such as following up problems, returning phone calls, and answering questions via email. The roster system ensures that all analysts get time to follow up on calls, and also ensures that analysts are always available to take incoming phone calls. As the incoming phone calls are random in nature, help desk agent schedules are often maintained using an Erlang C calculation.

Deskside Team

The deskside team (sometimes known as "desktop support") is responsible for the desktops, laptops, and peripherals, such as PDAs.

The help desk will assign the desktop team the second level deskside issues that the first level was not able to solve. They set up and configure computers for new users and are typically responsible for any physical work relating to the computers such as repairing software or hardware issues and moving workstations to another location.

Network Team

The network team is responsible for the network software, hardware and infrastructure such as servers, switches, backup systems and firewalls. They are responsible for the network services such as email, file, and security. The help desk will assign the network team issues that are in their field of responsibility.

Other Teams

Some companies have a telecom team that is responsible for the phone infrastructure such as PBX, voicemail, VOIP, telephone sets, modems and fax machines. They are responsible for configuring and moving telephone numbers, voicemail setup and configuration and are assigned these types of issues from the help desk.

Companies with custom application software may also have an applications team, who are responsible for development of any in-house software. The Applications team may be assigned problems such as software bugs from the help desk. Requests for new features or capabilities to in-house software that come through the help desk are also assigned to applications groups.

Not all of the help desk staff and supporting IT staff are in the same location. With remote access applications, technicians are able to solve many help desk issues from another location or their home office. There is a need for onsite support to physically work on some help desk issues; however, help desks are able to be more flexible with their remote support. They can also audit workstations.

Help desk is a broadly applied term referring to a staffed resource—often, an actual desk, or a telephone service—that can help persons answer questions or to use resources such as audiovisual or computer resources.

Support Automation

This article does not cite any references or sources. Please help improve this article by adding citations to reliable sources. Unsourced material may be challenged and removed. Support automation-is the name given to software platforms designed for technical support and service organizations to address problems and to achieve lower mean time to repair (MTTR) by automating problem prevention and resolution processes.

Support automation involves the building of a knowledge base of known issues and their resolutions to support incidents with delivery mechanisms. A service automation platform includes a suite of support solutions including proactive support, assisted support and self support.

With automated support, service organizations can deliver 24x7 availability to their customers by monitoring alarms, identifying problems at an early stage and resolving issues before they become problems. Automated assisted support enables remote access to sites that need instant problem solving. By automating the collection of information of devices and applications coexisting with the supported application, problems can be quickly detected and fixed.

Automated self support, automates the self support process, freeing users from self-help diagnostics and troubleshooting from online libraries or knowledge bases. Support automation solutions can be integrated with customer relationship management (CRM) systems and network management systems (NMS), and provide full customer reports to management tallying problems and incidents that were solved mechanically ensuring compliance to industry regulations like Sarbanes Oxley, 21 CFR part 11, and HIPAA.

Proactive Support Automation

Proactive Support Automation refers to support automation solutions that minimize downtime and enable 24x7 availability. This is achieved by constant health check tracking with diagnostic procedures to enable issue monitoring and problem solving.

Pre-emptive Support Automation

Pre-emptive Support Automation refers to a support solution that utilizes information that is either generated or culled from an application or service, e.g. log files, database queries, configuration changes, etc. This information can then be exploited to predict service degradations or interruptions. The upshot of this is a higher level of service/ application availability for the underlying application

Self Support Automation

Self support automation is the term organizations give to their support structures that provide online libraries and tools for self-help and easy troubleshooting solutions to automatically and precisely diagnose and resolve problems and incidents.

Assisted Support Automation

Assisted support automation is the software that enables support personnel to remotely access their customers desktop or server for diagnostics and trouble ticket resolution.

Internet

The Internet is a global system of interconnected computer networks that use the standard Internet Protocol Suite (TCP/IP) to serve billions of users worldwide. It is a *network of networks* that consists of millions of private and public, academic, business, and government networks of local to global scope that are linked by a broad array of electronic and optical networking technologies. The Internet carries a vast array of information resources and services, most notably the inter-linked hypertext documents of the World Wide Web (WWW) and the infrastructure to support electronic mail.

Most traditional communications media, such as telephone and television services, are reshaped or redefined using the technologies of the Internet, giving rise to services such as Voice over Internet Protocol (VoIP) and IPTV. Newspaper publishing has been reshaped into Web sites, blogging, and web feeds. The Internet has enabled or accelerated the creation of new forms of human interactions through instant massaging, Internet forums, and social networking sites.

The origins of the Internet reach back to the 1960s when the United States funded research projects of its military agencies to build robust, fault-tolerant and distributed computer networks. This research and a period of civilian funding of a new U.S. backbone by the National Science Foundation spawned worldwide participation in the development of new networking technologies and led to the commercialization of an international network in the mid 1990s, and resulted in the following popularization of countless applications in virtually every aspect of modern human life. As of 2009, an estimated quarter of Earth's population uses the services of the Internet.

The Internet has no centralized governance in either technological implementation or policies for access and usage; each constituent network sets its own standards. Only the overreaching definitions of the two principal name spaces in the Internet, the Internet Protocol address space and the Domain Name System, are directed by a maintainer organization, the Internet Corporation for Assigned Names and Numbers (ICANN). The technical underpinning and standardization of the core protocols (IPv4 and IPv6) is an activity of the Internet Engineering Task Force (IETF), a non-profit organization of loosely-affiliated international participants that anyone may associate with by contributing technical expertise.

Terminology

The terms Internet *and* World Wide Web *are often used in everyday speech without much distinction. However, the Internet and the World Wide Web are not one and the same. The Internet is a global data communications system. It is a hardware and software infrastructure that provides connectivity between computers. In contrast, the Web is one of the services communicated via the Internet. It is a collection of interconnected documents and other resources, linked by hyperlinks and URLs. The term* the Internet, *when referring to* the *Internet, has traditionally been treated as a proper noun and written with an initial capital letter. There is a trend to regard it as a generic term or common noun and thus write it as "the internet", without the capital.*

History

The USSR's launch of Sputnik spurred the United States to create the Advanced Research Projects Agency, known as ARPA, in February 1958 to regain a technological lead. ARPA created the Information Processing Technology Office (IPTO) to further the research of the Semi Automatic Ground Environment (SAGE) program, which had networked country-wide radar systems together for the first time. J. C. R. Licklider was selected to head the IPTO. Licklider moved from the Psycho-Acoustic Laboratory at Harvard University to MIT in 1950, after becoming interested in information technology. At MIT, he served on a committee that established Lincoln Laboratory and worked on the SAGE project. In 1957 he became a Vice President at BBN, where he bought the first production PDP-1 computer and conducted the first public demonstration of time-sharing.

Professor Leonard Kleinrock with one of the first ARPANET Interface Message Processors at UCLA.

At the IPTO, Licklider got Lawrence Roberts to start a project to make a network, and Roberts based the technology on the work of Paul Baran, who had written an exhaustive study for the United States Air Force that recommended packet switching (opposed to circuit switching) to achieve better network robustness and disaster survivability. UCLA professor Leonard Kleinrock had provided the theoretical foundations for packet networks in 1962, and later, in the 1970s, for hierarchical routing, concepts which have been the underpinning of the development towards today's Internet.

After much work, the first two nodes of what would become the ARPANET were interconnected between UCLA's School of Engineering and Applied Science and SRI International (SRI) in Menlo Park, California, on October 29, 1969. The ARPANET was one of the "eve" networks of today's Internet. Following on from the demonstration that packet switching worked on the ARPANET, the British Post Office, Telenet, DATAPAC and TRANSPAC collaborated to create the first international packet-switched network service. In the UK, this was referred to as the International Packet Switched Service (IPSS), in 1978. The collection of X.25-based networks grew from Europe and the US to cover Canada, Hong Kong and Australia by 1981. The X.25 packet switching standard was developed in the CCITT (now called ITU-T) around 1976.

X.25 was independent of the TCP/IP protocols that arose from the experimental work of DARPA on the ARPANET, Packet Radio Net and Packet Satellite Net during the same time period. Vinton Cerf and Robert Kahn developed the first description of the TCP protocols during 1973 and published a paper on the subject in May 1974. Use of the term "Internet" to describe a single global TCP/IP network originated in December 1974 with the publication of RFC 675, the first full specification of TCP that was written by Vinton Cerf, Yogen Dalal and Carl Sunshine, then at Stanford University. During the next nine years, work proceeded to refine the protocols and to implement them on a wide range of operating systems. The first TCP/IP-based wide-area network was operational by January 1, 1983 when all hosts on the ARPANET were switched over from the older NCP protocols. In 1985, the United States' National Science Foundation (NSF) commissioned the construction of the NSFNET, a university 56 kilobit/second network backbone using computers called "fuzzballs" by their inventor, David L. Mills. The following year, NSF sponsored the conversion to a higher-speed 1.5 megabit/second network. A key decision to use the DARPA TCP/IP protocols was made by Dennis Jennings, then in charge of the Supercomputer program at NSF.

The opening of the network to commercial interests began in 1988. The US Federal Networking Council approved the interconnection of the NSFNET to the commercial MCI Mail system in that year and the link was made in the summer of 1989. Other commercial electronic email services were soon connected, including OnTyme, Telemail and Compuserve. In that same year, three commercial Internet service providers (ISPs) were created: UUNET, PSINet and CERFNET. Important, separate networks that offered gateways into, then later merged with, the Internet include Usenet and BITNET. Various other commercial and educational networks, such as Telenet, Tymnet, Compuserve and JANET were interconnected with the growing Internet. Telenet (later called Sprintnet) was a large privately funded national computer network with free dial-up access in cities throughout the U.S. that had been in operation since the 1970s. This network was eventually interconnected with the others in the 1980s as the TCP/IP protocol became increasingly popular. The ability of TCP/IP to work over virtually any pre-existing communication networks allowed for a great ease of growth, although the rapid growth of the Internet was due primarily to the availability of an array of standardized commercial routers from many companies, the availability of commercial Ethernet equipment for local-area networking, and the widespread implementation and rigorous standardization of TCP/IP on UNIX and virtually every other common operating system.

Although the basic applications and guidelines that make the Internet possible had existed for almost two decades, the network did not gain a public face until the 1990s. On 6 August 1991, CERN, a pan European organisation for particle research, publicized the new World Wide Web project. The Web was invented by English scientist Tim Berners-Lee in 1989. An early popular web browser was ViolaWWW, patterned after HyperCard and built using the X Window System. It was eventually replaced in popularity by the Mosaic web browser. In 1993, the National Centre for Supercomputing Applications at the University of Illinois released version 1.0 of Mosaic, and by late 1994 there was growing public interest in the previously academic, technical Internet. By 1996 usage of the word *Internet* had become commonplace, and consequently, so had its use as a synecdoche in reference to the World Wide Web.

Meanwhile, over the course of the decade, the Internet successfully accommodated the majority of previously existing public computer networks (although some networks, such as FidoNet, have remained separate). During the 1990s, it was estimated that the Internet grew by 100 percent per year, with a brief period of explosive growth in 1996 and 1997. This growth is often attributed to the lack of central administration, which allows organic growth of the network, as well as the non-proprietary open nature of the Internet protocols, which encourages vendor interoperability and prevents any one company from exerting too much control over the network. The estimated the population of Internet users is 1.67 billion as of June 30, 2009.

Technology

Protocols

The complex communications infrastructure of the Internet consists of its hardware components and a system of software layers that control various aspects of the architecture. While the hardware can often be used to support other software systems, it is the design and the rigorous standardization process of the software architecture that characterizes the Internet and provides the foundation for its scalability and success. The responsibility for the architectural design of the Internet software systems has been delegated to the Internet Engineering Task Force (IETF). The IETF conducts standard-setting work groups, open to any individual, about the various aspects of Internet architecture. Resulting discussions and final standards are published in a series of publications, called Request for Comments (RFCs), freely available on the IETF web site. The principal methods of networking that enable the Internet are contained in specially designated RFCs that constitute the Internet Standards.

These standards describe a framework known as the Internet Protocol Suite. This is a model architecture that divides methods into a layered system of protocols (RFC 1122, RFC 1123). The layers correspond to the environment or scope in which their services operate. At the top is the Application Layer, the space for the application-specific networking methods used in software applications, e.g., a web browser program. Below this top layer, the Transport Layer connects applications on *different hosts* via the network (e.g., client-server model) with appropriate data exchange methods. Underlying these layers are the core networking technologies, consisting of two layers. The Internet

Layer enables computers to identify and locate each other via Internet Protocol (IP) addresses, and allows them to connect to one-another via intermediate (transit) networks. Lastly, at the bottom of the architecture, is a software layer, the Link Layer, that provides connectivity between hosts on the same local network link, such as a local area network (LAN) or a dial-up connection. The model, also known as TCP/IP, is designed to be independent of the underlying hardware which the model therefore does not concern itself with in any detail. Other models have been developed, such as the Open Systems Interconnection (OSI) model, but they are not compatible in the details of description, nor implementation, but many similarities exist and the TCP/IP protocols are usually included in the discussion of OSI networking.

The most prominent component of the Internet model is the Internet Protocol (IP) which provides addressing systems (IP addresses) for computers on the Internet. IP enables internet working and essentially establishes the Internet itself. IP Version 4 (IPv4) is the initial version used on the first generation of the today's Internet and is still in dominant use. It was designed to address up to ~4.3 billion (10^9) Internet hosts. However, the explosive growth of the Internet has led to IPv4 address exhaustion which is estimated to enter its final stage in approximately 2011. A new protocol version, IPv6, was developed in the mid 1990s which provides vastly larger addressing capabilities and more efficient routing of Internet traffic. IPv6 is currently in commercial deployment phase around the world and Internet address registries (RIRs) have begun to urge all resource managers to plan rapid adoption and conversion.

IPv6 is not interoperable with IPv4. It essentially establishes a "parallel" version of the Internet not directly accessible with IPv4 software. This means software upgrades or translator facilities are necessary for every networking device that needs to communicate on the IPv6 Internet. Most modern computer operating systems are already converted to operate with both versions of the Internet Protocol. Network infrastructures, however, are still lagging in this development. Aside from the complex physical connections that make up its infrastructure, the Internet is facilitated by bi-or multi-lateral commercial contracts (e.g., peering agreements), and by technical specifications or protocols that describe how to exchange data over the network. Indeed, the Internet is defined by its interconnections and routing policies.

Structure

The Internet structure and its usage characteristics have been studied extensively. It has been determined that both the Internet IP routing structure and hypertext links of the World Wide Web are examples of scale-free networks. Similar to the way the commercial Internet providers connect via Internet exchange points, research networks tend to interconnect into large subnetworks such as GEANT, GLORIAD, Internet (successor of the Abilene Network), and the UK's national research and education network JANET. These in turn are built around smaller networks.

Many computer scientists describe the Internet as a "prime example of a large-scale, highly engineered, yet highly complex system". The Internet is extremely heterogeneous; for instance, data transfer rates and physical characteristics of connections vary widely. The Internet exhibits "emergent phenomena" that depend on its large-scale organization. For example, data transfer rates exhibit temporal self-similarity. The principles of the routing and addressing methods for traffic in the Internet reach back to their origins the 1960s when the eventual scale and popularity of the network could not be anticipated. Thus, the possibility of developing alternative structures is investigated.

Governance

The Internet is a globally distributed network comprising many voluntarily interconnected autonomous networks. It operates without a central governing body. However, to maintain interoperability, all technical and policy aspects of the underlying core infrastructure and the principal name spaces are administered by the Internet Corporation for Assigned Names and Numbers (ICANN), headquartered in Marina del Rey, California. ICANN is the authority that coordinates the assignment of unique identifiers for use on the Internet, including domain names, Internet Protocol (IP) addresses, application port numbers in the transport protocols, and many other parameters. Globally unified name spaces, in which names and numbers are uniquely assigned, are essential for the global reach of the Internet. ICANN is governed by an international board of directors drawn from across the Internet technical, business, academic, and other non-commercial communities. The US government continues to have the primary role in approving changes to the DNS root zone that lies at the heart of the domain name system. ICANN's role in coordinating the assignment of unique identifiers distinguishes it as perhaps the only central coordinating body on the global Internet. On November 16, 2005, the World Summit on the Information Society, held in Tunis, established the Internet Governance Forum (IGF) to discuss Internet-related issues.

Modern Uses

The Internet is allowing greater flexibility in working hours and location, especially with the spread of unmetered high-speed connections and web applications.

The Internet can now be accessed almost anywhere by numerous means, especially through mobile Internet devices. Mobile phones, datacards, handheld game consoles and cellular routers allow users to connect to the Internet from anywhere there is a wireless network supporting that device's technology. Within the limitations imposed by small screens and other limited facilities of such pocket-sized devices, services of the Internet, including email and the web, may be available. Service providers may restrict the services offered and wireless data transmission charges may be significantly higher than other access methods.

The Internet has also become a large market for companies; some of the biggest companies today have grown by taking advantage of the efficient nature of low-cost advertising and commerce through the Internet, also known as e-commerce. It is the fastest way to spread information to a vast number of people simultaneously. The Internet has also subsequently revolutionized shopping—for example; a person can order a CD online and receive it in the mail within a couple of days, or download it directly in some cases.

The Internet has also greatly facilitated personalized marketing which allows a company to market a product to a specific person or a specific group of people more so than any other advertising medium. Examples of personalized marketing include online communities such as MySpace, Friendster, Orkut, Facebook and others which thousands of Internet users join to advertise themselves and make friends online.

Many of these users are young teens and adolescents ranging from 13 to 25 years old. In turn, when they advertise themselves they advertise interests and hobbies, which online marketing companies can use as information as to what those users will purchase online, and advertise their own companies' products to those users.

The low cost and nearly instantaneous sharing of ideas, knowledge, and skills has made collaborative work dramatically easier, with the help of collaborative software. Not only can a group cheaply communicate and share ideas, but the wide reach of the Internet allows such groups to easily form in the first place. An example of this is the free software movement, which has produced, among other programs, Linux, Mozilla Firefox, and OpenOffice.org. Internet "chat", whether in the form of IRC chat rooms or channels, or via instant massaging systems, allow colleagues to stay in touch in a very convenient way when working at their computers during the day. Messages can be exchanged even more quickly and conveniently than via email. Extensions to these systems may allow files to be exchanged, "whiteboard" drawings to be shared or voice and video contact between team members.

Version control systems allow collaborating teams to work on shared sets of documents without either accidentally overwriting each other's work or having members wait until they get "sent" documents to be able to make their contributions. Business and project teams can share calendars as well as documents and other information. Such collaboration occurs in a wide variety of areas including scientific research, software development, conference planning, political activism and creative writing. Social and political collaboration is also becoming more widespread as both Internet access and computer literacy grow. From the flash mob 'events' of the early 2000s to the use of social networking in the 2009 Iranian election protests, the Internet allows people to work together more effectively and in many more ways than was possible without it.

The Internet allows computer users to remotely access other computers and information stores easily, wherever they may be across the world. They may do this with or without the use of security, authentication and encryption technologies, depending on the requirements. This is encouraging new ways of working from home, collaboration and information sharing in many industries. An accountant sitting at home can audit the books of a company based in another country, on a server situated in a third country that is remotely maintained by IT specialists in a fourth. These accounts could have been created by home-working bookkeepers, in other remote locations, based on information e-mailed to them from offices all over the world. Some of these things were possible before the widespread use of the Internet, but the cost of private leased lines would have made many of them infeasible in practice. An office worker away from their desk, perhaps on the other side of the world on a business trip or a holiday, can open a remote desktop session into his normal office PC using a secure Virtual Private Network (VPN) connection via the Internet. This gives the worker complete access to all of his or her normal files and data, including email and other applications, while away from the office. This concept is also referred to by some network security people as the Virtual Private Nightmare, because it extends the secure perimeter of a corporate network into its employees' homes.

Services

Information

Many people use the terms *Internet* and *World Wide Web* (or just the *Web*) interchangeably, but, as discussed earlier, the two terms are not synonymous. The World Wide Web is a global set of documents, images and other resources, referenced and interconnected by Uniform Resource Locators (URLs) and hyperlinks. These URLs allow users to address the web servers and other devices that store these resources and access them as required using the Hypertext Transfer Protocol (HTTP). HTTP is only one of the communication protocols used on the Internet. Web services may also use HTTP to allow software systems to communicate in order to share and exchange business logic and data.

Software products that can access the resources of the Web are often called *user agents*. In normal use, web browsers, such as Internet Explorer, Firefox, Opera, Apple Safari, and Google Chrome, let users navigate from one web page to another via hyperlinks. Documents on the web may contain any combination of computer data, including graphics, sounds, text, video, multimedia and interactive content including games, office applications and scientific demonstrations. Through keyword-driven Internet research using search engines like Yahoo! and Google, users worldwide have easy, instant access to a vast and diverse amount of online information. Compared to printed encyclopedias and traditional libraries, the World Wide Web has enabled a sudden and extreme decentralization of information and data.

Using the Web, it is also easier than ever before for individuals and organizations to publish ideas and information to a potentially large audience. Publishing a web page, a blog, or building a website involves little initial cost and many cost-free services are available. Publishing and maintaining large, professional web sites with attractive, diverse and up-to-date information is still a difficult and expensive proposition, however. Many individuals and some companies and groups use *web logs* or blogs, which are largely used as easily updatable online diaries. Some commercial organizations encourage staff to communicate advice in their areas of specialization in the hope that visitors will be impressed by the expert knowledge and free information, and be attracted to the corporation as a result. One example of this practice is Microsoft, whose product developers publish their personal blogs in order to pique the public's interest in their work. Collections of personal web pages published by large service providers remain popular, and have become increasingly sophisticated. Whereas operations such as Angelfire and GeoCities have existed since the early days of the Web, newer offerings from, for example, Facebook and MySpace currently have large followings. These operations often brand themselves as social network services rather than simply as web page hosts.

Advertising on popular web pages can be lucrative, and e-commerce or the sale of products and services directly via the Web continues to grow. In the early days, web pages were usually created as sets of complete and isolated HTML text files stored on a web server. More recently, websites are more often created using content management or wiki software with, initially, very little content. Contributors to these systems, who may be paid staff, members of a club or other organization or members of the public, fill underlying databases with content using editing pages designed for that purpose, while casual visitors view and read this content in its final HTML form. There may or may not be editorial, approval and security systems built into the process of taking newly entered content and making it available to the target visitors.

Communication

Email is an important communications service available on the Internet. The concept of sending electronic text messages between parties in a way analogous to mailing letters or memos predates the creation of the Internet. Today it can be important to distinguish between internet and internal email systems. Internet email may travel and be stored unencrypted on many other networks and machines out of both the sender's and the recipient's control. During this time it is quite possible for the content to be read and even tampered with by third parties, if anyone considers it important enough. Purely internal or intranet mail systems, where the information never leaves the corporate or organization's network, are much more secure, although in any organization there will be IT and other personnel whose job may involve monitoring, and occasionally accessing, the email of other employees not addressed to them. Pictures, documents and other files can be sent as email attachments. E-mails can be cc-ed to multiple email addresses.

Internet telephony is another common communications service made possible by the creation of the Internet. VoIP stands for Voice-over-Internet Protocol, referring to the protocol that underlies all Internet communication. The idea began in the early 1990s with walkie-talkie-like voice applications for personal computers. In recent years many VoIP systems have become as easy to use and as convenient as a normal telephone. The benefit is that, as the Internet carries the voice traffic, VoIP can be free or cost much less than a traditional telephone call, especially over long distances and especially for those with always-on Internet connections such as cable or ADSL. VoIP is maturing into a competitive alternative to traditional telephone service. Interoperability between different providers has improved and the ability to call or receive a call from a traditional telephone is available. Simple, inexpensive VoIP network adapters are available that eliminate the need for a personal computer.

Voice quality can still vary from call to call but is often equal to and can even exceed that of traditional calls. Remaining problems for VoIP include emergency telephone number dialling and reliability. Currently, a few VoIP providers provide an emergency service, but it is not universally available. Traditional phones are line-powered and operate during a power failure; VoIP does not do so without a backup power source for the phone equipment and the Internet access devices. VoIP has also become increasingly popular for gaming applications, as a form of communication between players. Popular VoIP clients for gaming include Ventrilo and Teamspeak. Wii, PlayStation 3, and Xbox 360 also offer VoIP chat features.

Data Transfer

File sharing is an example of transferring large amounts of data across the Internet. A computer file can be e-mailed to customers, colleagues and friends as an attachment. It can be uploaded to a website or FTP server for easy download by others. It can be put into a "shared location" or onto a file server for instant use by colleagues. The load of bulk downloads to many users can be eased by the use of "mirror" servers or peer-to-peer networks. In any of these cases, access to the file may be controlled by user authentication, the transit of the file over the Internet may be obscured by encryption, and money may change hands for access to the file. The price can be paid by the remote charging of funds from, for example, a credit card whose details are also passed—usually fully encrypted—across the Internet. The origin and authenticity of the file received may be checked by digital signatures or by MD5 or other message digests. These simple features of the Internet, over a worldwide basis, are changing the production, sale, and distribution of anything that can be reduced to a computer file for transmission. This includes all manner of print publications, software products, news, music, film, video, photography, graphics and the other arts. This in turn has caused seismic shifts in each of the existing industries that previously controlled the production and distribution of these products.

Streaming media refers to the act that many existing radio and television broadcasters promote Internet "feeds" of their live audio and video streams (for example, the BBC). They may also allow time-shift viewing or listening such as Preview, Classic Clips and Listen Again features. These providers have been joined by a range of pure Internet "broadcasters" who never had on-air licenses. This means that an Internet-connected device, such as a computer or something more specific, can be used to access online media in much the same way as was previously possible only with a television or radio receiver. The range of material is much wider, from pornography to highly specialized, technical webcasts. Podcasting is a variation on this theme, where—usually audio—material is downloaded and played back on a computer or shifted to a portable media player to be listened to on the move. These techniques using simple equipment allow anybody, with little censorship or licensing control, to broadcast audiovisual material worldwide.

Webcams can be seen as an even lower-budget extension of this phenomenon. While some webcams can give full-frame-rate video, the picture is usually either small or updates slowly. Internet users can watch animals around an African waterhole, ships in the Panama Canal, traffic at a local roundabout or monitor their own premises, live and in real time. Video chat rooms and video conferencing are also popular with many uses being found for personal webcams, with and without two-way sound. You Tube was founded on 15 February 2005 and is now the leading website for free streaming video with a vast number of users. It uses a flash-based web player to stream and show video files. Registered users may upload an unlimited amount of video and build their own personal profile. You Tube claims that its users watch hundreds of millions, and upload hundreds of thousands, of videos daily.

Accessibility

The prevalent language for communication on the Internet is English. This may be a result of the origin of the Internet, as well as English's role as a lingua franca. It may also be related to the poor capability of early computers, largely originating in the United States, to handle characters other than those in the English variant of the Latin alphabet. After English (29% of Web visitors) the most requested languages on the World Wide Web are Chinese (22%), Spanish (8%), Japanese (6%), French (5%), Portuguese and German (4% each), Arabic (3%) and Russian and Korean (2% each). By region, 42% of the world's Internet users are based in Asia, 24% in Europe, 15% in North America, 11% in Latin America and the Caribbean taken together, 4% in Africa, 3% in the Middle East and 1% in Australia/Oceania. The Internet's technologies have developed enough in recent years, especially in the use of Unicode, that good facilities are available for development and communication in most widely used languages. However, some glitches such as *mojibake* (incorrect display of foreign language characters, also known as *kryakozyabry*) still remain.

Common methods of Internet access in homes include dial-up, landline broadband (over coaxial cable, fiber optic or copper wires), Wi-Fi, satellite and 3G technology cell phones. Public places to use the Internet include libraries and Internet cafes, where computers with Internet connections are available. There are also Internet access points in many public places such as airport halls and coffee shops, in some cases just for brief use while standing. Various terms are used, such as "public Internet kiosk", "public access terminal", and "Web payphone". Many hotels now also have public terminals, though these are usually fee-based. These terminals are widely accessed for various usage like ticket booking, bank deposit, online payment etc. Wi-Fi provides wireless access to computer networks, and therefore can do so to the Internet itself. Hotspots providing such access include Wi-Fi cafes, where would-be users need to bring their own wireless-enabled devices such as a laptop or PDA. These services may be free to all, free to customers only, or fee-based. A hotspot need not be limited to a confined location. A whole campus or park, or even an entire city can be enabled. Grassroots efforts have led to wireless community networks. Commercial Wi-Fi services covering large city areas are in place in London, Vienna, Toronto, San Francisco, Philadelphia, Chicago and Pittsburgh. The Internet can then be accessed from such places as a park bench. Apart from Wi-Fi, there have been experiments with proprietary mobile wireless networks like Ricochet, various high-speed data services over cellular phone networks, and fixed wireless services. High-end mobile phones such as smartphones generally come with Internet access through the phone network. Web browsers such as Opera are available on these advanced handsets, which can also run a wide variety of other Internet software. More mobile phones have Internet access than PCs, though this is not as widely used. An Internet access provider and protocol matrix differentiates the methods used to get online.

Social Impact

The Internet has made possible entirely new forms of social interaction, activities and organizing, thanks to its basic features such as widespread usability and access. Social networking websites such as Facebook and MySpace have created a new form of socialization and interaction. Users of these sites are able to add a wide variety of items to their personal pages, to indicate common interests, and to connect with others. It is also possible to find a large circle of existing acquaintances, especially if a site allows users to utilize their real names, and to allow communication among large existing groups of people. Sites like meetup.com exist to allow wider announcement of groups which may exist mainly for face-to-face meetings, but which may have a variety of minor interactions over their group's site at meetup.org, or other similar sites.

The first generation is now being raised with widespread availability of Internet connectivity, with consequences for privacy, identity, and copyright concerns. These "Digital natives" face a variety of concerns that were not present for prior generations.

In democratic societies, the Internet has achieved new relevance as a political tool, leading to Internet censorship by some states. The presidential campaign of Howard Dean in 2004 in the United States became famous for its ability to generate donations via the Internet. Many political groups use the Internet to achieve a whole new method of organizing, in order to carry out Internet activism. Some governments, such as those of Iran, North Korea, Myanmar, the People's Republic of China, and Saudi Arabia, restrict what people in their countries can access on the Internet, especially political and religious content. This is accomplished through software that filters domains and content so that they may not be easily accessed or obtained without elaborate circumvention.

In Norway, Denmark, Finland and Sweden, major Internet service providers have voluntarily (possibly to avoid such an arrangement being turned into law) agreed to restrict access to sites listed by police. While this list of forbidden URLs is only supposed to contain addresses of known child pornography sites, the content of the list is secret. Many countries, including the United States, have enacted laws making the possession or distribution of certain material, such as child pornography, illegal, but do not use filtering software. There are many free and commercially available software programs, called content-control software, with which a user can choose to block offensive websites on individual computers or networks, such as to limit a child's access to pornography or violence.

The Internet has been a major source of leisure since before the World Wide Web, with entertaining social experiments such as MUDs and MOOs being conducted on university servers, and humour-related Usenet groups receiving much of the main traffic. Today, many Internet forums have sections devoted to games and funny videos; short cartoons in the form of Flash movies are also popular. Over 6 million people use blogs or message boards as a means of communication and for the sharing of ideas. The pornography and gambling industries have both taken full advantage of the World Wide Web, and often provide a significant source of advertising revenue for other websites. Although many governments have attempted to put restrictions on both industries' use of the Internet, this has generally failed to stop their widespread popularity.

One main area of leisure on the Internet is multiplayer gaming. This form of leisure creates communities, bringing people of all ages and origins to enjoy the fast-paced world of multiplayer games. These range from MMORPG to first-person shooters, from role-playing games to online gambling. This has revolutionized the way many people interact and spend their free time on the Internet. While online gaming has been around since the 1970s, modern modes of online gaming began with services such as GameSpy and MPlayer, to which players of games would typically subscribe. Non-subscribers were limited to certain types of game play or certain games. Many use the Internet to access and download music, movies and other works for their enjoyment and relaxation. As discussed above, there are paid and unpaid sources for all of these, using centralized servers and distributed peer-to-peer technologies. Some of these sources take more care over the original artists' rights and over copyright laws than others.

Many use the World Wide Web to access news, weather and sports reports, to plan and book holidays and to find out more about their random ideas and casual interests. People use chat, massaging and email to make and stay in touch with friends worldwide, sometimes in the same way as some previously had pen pals. Social networking websites like MySpace, Facebook and many others like them also put and keep people in contact for their enjoyment. The Internet has seen a growing number of Web desktops, where users can access their files, folders, and settings via the Internet. Cyberslacking can become a serious drain on corporate resources; the average UK employee spent 57 minutes a day surfing the Web while at work, according to a 2003 study by Peninsula Business Services.

How to Use the Internet to Promote Your Business

Are you a company that has a low advertising budget? If so, there are a variety of fairly new low-cost advertising and promotional tools that you can use.

If you are a business that wants to expand your territory but cannot afford to plant stores all around, you can take advantage of the Internet. Nearly everyone is on the Internet now, and they enjoy the convenience and ease of buying online. Give your customers what they want.

Steps

1. Set up your own website. You can either set up your own website or you can pay someone to set it up for you. You can usually have a nice website designed by yourself for as little as $5.00 per month plus yearly registration of your domain name, the website address.

2. Use pay per click advertising. You can set a price that you would be willing to pay every time someone clicks on an ad that you write. You only have to pay this when someone clicks on your ad. If no one clicks on your ad you do not have to pay. They allow you to set up a daily advertising budget and you have the freedom to cancel and restart your ads any time you want.
3. Submit your name to many website directories. You can search the Internet for free website directories and you will find quite a few links to places where you can advertise.
4. Participate in forums and blogs. This is one way to help promote your product or services. Often you can do this for free. Be sure to post in the ones that are website promotion friendly, however. Not all blog sites or forums allow promotion blog or forum posts. In some cases you may have to pay a fee to advertise on their sites but usually you do not.
5. Use email marketing. You can create lists of customers, or potential customers that you can keep in touch with on a regular basis. Some people do not recommend this, and some people find this annoying. Also you have to beware of Spamming Laws. That means that you are not allowed to send people information they do not want. Usually it is best to only send information to people who want your products or services and not to those who do not. These e-mailings can all be sent out in bulk, as if you were sending them through postal mail.

Tips

- Usually in order to set up your own website for your business you need to purchase both a web hosting program, which mentioned above can be purchased for as cheap as 5.00 a month. Usually a great package deal for a website can be purchased for about 10.00-15.00 a month. Also, you can purchase online store sites, also called e-commerce sites, which usually average in price of about 60.00 a month.
- Even though advertising on the Internet can still cost money, the beauty of advertising and have your store stationed on the Internet is that you do not have to spend large amounts of money on paper advertising. Furthermore, you do not waste

as much natural resources such as trees and plastic when you promote over the Internet.

- You can also keep business cards in local stores, mail out flyers to residents when you are having a sale, get listed in a business directory if your town has one, and more. Be creative with your marketing, and you will save time and money. Another way is to visit workshops associated with your business. There you can network with others in your business and get ideas on what works and what doesn't. Studying your competition is a great way to see what you are up against, and even learn from their mistakes!
- Remember your business basics. The best form of advertising is free – word of mouth. If you are an excellent business with superior customer service, your customers will tell everyone they know about their experience. That makes their friends and family remember your business name when they are in need of your products and/or services.

Business Can Use the Internet

Reach a worldwide audience The Internet is a worldwide network allowing you to reach people even very expensive advertising could not.

Provide product information Give customers direct access to information about your products. Some people prefer to learn about products on their own. The Internet has an unsurpassed ability to make information about your company's products or services available to potential customers. It also provides the information when the customer wants it (now).

Save on literature costs Providing the information online reduces the need to print and mail product literature, thereby resulting in significant cost reductions.

Augment/replace phone banks Often people staffing phone banks are serving merely as interfaces to computer databases. In an age of graphical, networked computing, this function is less necessary. Simple graphical interfaces can be designed to allow customers to find the information they want quickly and inexpensively.

Provide easy access to customer service representatives Human interaction cannot be totally replaced by even the best graphical interface. When customers have a question, or would like to speak with a person, provide a list of contacts and phone numbers or allow them to send email directly to a customer service representative, requesting that they be contacted.

Level your customer service load How many customers are turned away unsatisfied when your customer service lines are busy? How often do you have slack times when customer support personnel are not handling calls but still cost your business money? Email provides "asynchronous communication" that can help level the load. Customers with problems that do not require immediate attention can send an email message through your Web site which can be handled when support people are not busy. Telephone-tag is eliminated for your customers, and you.

Inexpensively create/augment your corporate image It is easy and inexpensive to define your image on the Internet, whether you are a one-person-company or a large corporation. If your company information changes rapidly due to market forces, there is no easier way to change your image than electronically.

Recruit new employees Many companies (now nearly all), provide current information about job openings and attract talented people from places they could not reach otherwise.

Provide useful information to attract customers Ski shops often have a board listing local snow conditions. Search sites like " yahoo " and " Lycos " provide useful search services for the Web. Providing useful information to potential customers is a good way to get them to come to your site and return again and again (a property now called "stickiness"). Provide your service online Many products and services can be delivered over the Internet. Online services will become an even brighter option for many businesses. Since the transaction is electronic, billing and inventory control can be automated, increasing accuracy and reducing your accounting and product storage costs.

Give customers access to searchable information Computers on the Internet allow companies to post information in the form of static Web pages. But, with some of the latest software (or some clever programming), these computers can also help your customers find the information you are providing quickly. Federal Express created an award winning Web site that allows customers to track their packages. In doing this, Fed-Ex is providing a useful customer service while also promoting their product (service).

Help customers understand why they need you Another thing computers do well is provide artificial intelligence, expertise, or analysis. The Internet allows you to deliver custom software applications and extend your expertise virtually. Suppose you manufacture thermopane windows. A spreadsheet application could allow potential customers to determine how much money they would save in energy costs if they installed your windows. A financial services company could allow potential customers to analyze their investments in light of a financial service the company offers.

Let customers try a sample of your product or service Many new Web tools are becoming available that will allow consumers to try out a sample of what you have to offer before they buy. Gain a competitive advantage by offering a "test drive" of your product or service.

Eliminate the middleman Middlemen exist in some industries where there are barriers to direct contact between producers and consumers. The Internet is a vehicle for removing these barriers. This lowers prices for consumers and increases profits for producers.

Online commerce This has been much touted in the popular press. Some products and services are well suited for sales online. Rapid growth in this area will occur as secure credit card transactions become (are now) standardized. Efficiency of shipping and delivery methods for hard goods is important for typically impatient internet shoppers.

Consider an Intranet Use the same Internet technology within your company to help workers communicate better and work more productively. Many companies are finding an Intranet to be a much more cost effective solution to their network information needs than proprietary software.

Reach a worldwide audience The Internet is a worldwide network allowing you to reach people even very expensive advertising could not.

Provide product information Give customers direct access to information about your products. Some people prefer to learn about products on their own. The Internet has an unsurpassed ability to make information about your company's products or services available to potential customers. It also provides the information when the customer wants it (now).

Save on literature costs Providing the information online reduces the need to print and mail product literature, thereby resulting in significant cost reductions.

Augment/replace phone banks Often people staffing phone banks are serving merely as interfaces to computer databases. In an age of graphical, networked computing, this function is less necessary. Simple graphical interfaces can be designed to allow customers to find the information they want quickly and inexpensively.

Provide easy access to customer service representatives Human interaction cannot be totally replaced by even the best graphical interface. When customers have a question, or would like to speak with a person, provide a list of contacts and phone numbers or allow them to send email directly to a customer service representative, requesting that they be contacted.

Level your customer service load How many customers are turned away unsatisfied when your customer service lines are busy? How often do you have slack times when customer support personnel are not handling calls but still cost your business money? Email provides "asynchronous communication" that can help level the load. Customers with problems that do not require immediate attention can send an email message through your Web site which can be handled when support people are not busy. Telephone-tag is eliminated for your customers, and you.

Inexpensively create/augment your corporate image It is easy and inexpensive to define your image on the Internet, whether you are a one-person-company or a large corporation. If your company information changes rapidly due to market forces, there is no easier way to change your image than electronically.

Recruit new employees Many companies (now nearly all), provide current information about job openings and attract talented people from places they could not reach otherwise.

Provide useful information to attract customers Ski shops often have a board listing local snow conditions. Search sites like " yahoo " and " Lycos " provide useful search services for the Web. Providing useful information to potential customers is a good way to get them to come to your site and return again and again (a property now called "stickiness").

Provide your service online Many products and services can be delivered over the Internet. Online services will become an even brighter option for many businesses. Since the transaction is electronic, billing and inventory control can be automated, increasing accuracy and reducing your accounting and product storage costs. Give customers access to searchable information Computers on the Internet allow companies to post information in the form of static Web pages. But, with some of the latest software (or some clever programming), these computers can also help your customers find the information you are providing quickly. Federal Express created an award winning Web site that allows customers to track their packages. In doing this, Fed-Ex is providing a useful customer service while also promoting their product (service).

Help customers understand why they need you Another thing computers do well is provide artificial intelligence, expertise, or analysis. The Internet allows you to deliver custom software applications and extend your expertise virtually. Suppose you manufacture thermopane windows. A spreadsheet application could allow potential customers to determine how much money they would save in energy costs if they installed your windows. A financial services company could allow potential customers to analyze their investments in light of a financial service the company offers.

Let customers try a sample of your product or service Many new Web tools are becoming available that will allow consumers to try out a sample of what you have to offer before they buy. Gain a competitive advantage by offering a "test drive" of your product or service.

Eliminate the middleman Middlemen exist in some industries where there are barriers to direct contact between producers and consumers. The Internet is a vehicle for removing these barriers. This lowers prices for consumers and increases profits for producers.

Online commerce This has been much touted in the popular press. Some products and services are well suited for sales online. Rapid growth in this area will occur as secure credit card transactions become (are now) standardized. Efficiency of shipping and delivery methods for hard goods is important for typically impatient internet shoppers.

Consider an Intranet Use the same Internet technology within your company to help workers communicate better and work more productively. Many companies are finding an Intranet to be a much more cost effective solution to their network information needs than proprietary software

What is Internet Marketing

Online Businesses have gained popularity because they help business owners to place their businesses in front of thousands of users across time zones in one instant. Web based businesses rely heavily on online marketing One of the biggest advantages of online marketing that it facilitates quick and easy sharing of information amongst consumers. This reduces an organization's marketing costs to a large extent.

Unlike the olden days when users had to spend money to transmit information by a telephone call or a letter; these days the same can be done free of cost through email. Online marketing also helps in eliciting a quicker response from users. Users no longer need to post business reply envelopes or make expensive telephone calls. All it needs is a few mouse clicks to obtain all the desired information about a company's product or service.

Online marketing quickens the two-way communication process between a company and its customer. It also offers a company an unobtrusive way to communicate with its potential customers. It means that online marketing diminishes the role of intermediaries allowing companies to pass on the incumbent benefits to their customers.

Affiliates benefit a lot through online marketing. Their marketing initiatives get a boost as they get an inexpensive way to target overseas clients. Another advantage of online marketing is that it helps companies to close deals without incurring much expenditure. Deals can be closed via email or telephone without the need for an executive to visit the prospect personally. Online marketing can help start-ups save a lot on infrastructure costs. It eliminates the need to rent a separate office as start up owners can work from home. Other associated costs like electricity, water, heating, communication costs can also be eliminated.

With Online Marketing, the astronomical costs associated with television, print or radio advertising can be side stepped. Unlike traditional advertising where users have to accept the rates offered by the publishers; online marketing allows users to design campaigns according to their budget with no upper or lower limits attached to their marketing expenditure.

The interactivity inherent in an online marketing campaign is simply unmatched. If you are looking for a cost-effective way to target your audience the online marketing is the best option.

2

Computer Networking

Introduction

A computer network allows computers to communicate with many other computers and to share resources and information. The Advanced Research Projects Agency (ARPA) funded the design of the "Advanced Research Projects Agency Network" (ARPANET) for the United States Department of Defence. It was the first operational computer network in the world. Development of the network began in 1969, based on designs begun in the 1960s.

Network Classification

The following list presents categories used for classifying networks.

Connection Method

Computer networks can also be classified according to the hardware and software technology that is used to interconnect the individual devices in the network, such as Optical fiber, Ethernet, Wireless LAN, HomePNA, Power line communication or G.hn. Ethernet uses physical wiring to connect devices. Frequently deployed devices include hubs, switches, bridges and/or routers.

Wireless LAN technology is designed to connect devices without wiring. These devices use radio waves or infrared signals as a transmission medium. ITU-T G.hn technology uses existing home wiring (coaxial cable, phone lines and power lines) to create a high-speed (up to 1 Gigabit/s) local area network.

Wired Technologies

Twisted-Pair Wire: This is the most widely used medium for telecommunication. Twisted-pair wires are ordinary telephone wires which consist of two insulated copper wires twisted into pairs and are used for both voice and data transmission. The use of two wires twisted together helps to reduce crosstalk and electromagnetic induction. The transmission speed range from 2 million bits per second to 100 million bits per second.

Coaxial Cable: These cables are widely used for cable television systems, office buildings, and other worksites for local area networks. The cables consist of copper or aluminum wire wrapped with insulating layer typically of a flexible material with a high dielectric constant, all of which are surrounded by a conductive layer. The layers of insulation help minimize interference and distortion. Transmission speed range from 200 million to more than 500 million bits per second.

Fiber Optics: These cables consist of one or more thin filaments of glass fiber wrapped in a protective layer. It transmits light which can travel over long distance and higher bandwidths. Fiber-optic cables are not affected by electromagnetic radiation. Transmission speed could go up to as high as trillions of bits per second. The speed of fiber optics is hundreds of times faster than coaxial cables and thousands of times faster than twisted-pair wire.

Wireless Technologies

Terrestrial Microwave: Terrestrial microwaves use Earth-based transmitter and receiver. The equipment look similar to satellite dishes. Terrestrial microwaves use low-gigahertz range, which limits all communications to line-of-sight. Path between relay stations spaced approx. 30 miles apart. Microwave antennas are usually placed on top of buildings, towers, hills, and mountain peaks.

Communications Satellites: The satellites use microwave radio as their telecommunications medium which are not deflected by the Earth's atmosphere. The satellites are stationed in space, typically 22,000 miles above the equator. These Earth-orbiting systems are capable of receiving and relaying voice, data, and TV signals.

Cellular and PCS Systems: Use several radio communications technologies. The systems are divided to different geographic area. Each area has low-power transmitter or radio relay antenna device to relay calls from one area to the next area.

Wireless LANs: Wireless local area network use a high-frequency radio technology similar to digital cellular and a low-frequency radio technology. Wireless LANS use spread spectrum technology to enable communication between multiple devices in a limited area. Example of open-standard wireless radio-wave technology is IEEE 802.11b.

Bluetooth: A short range wireless technology. Operate at approx. 1Mbps with range from 10 to 100 meters. Bluetooth is an open wireless protocol for data exchange over short distances.

The Wireless Web: The wireless web refers to the use of the World Wide Web through equipments like cellular phones, pagers, PDAs, and other portable communications devices. The wireless web service offers anytime/anywhere connection.

Scale

Networks are often classified as Local Area Network (LAN), Wide Area Network (WAN), Metropolitan Area Network (MAN), Personal Area Network (PAN), Virtual Private Network (VPN), Campus Area Network (CAN), Storage Area Network (SAN), etc. depending on their scale, scope and purpose. Usage, trust levels and access rights often differ between these types of network-for example, LANs tend to be designed for internal use by an organization's internal systems and employees in individual physical locations (such as a building), while WANs may connect physically separate parts of an organization to each other and may include connections to third parties.

Why You Need a Computer Network

If your business has more than one computer, chances are you could benefit from networking them. A local area network (LAN) connects your company's computers, allowing them to share and exchange a variety of information. While one computer can be useful on its own, several networked computers can be much more useful.

Here are some of the Ways a Computer Network can help Your Business:

- *File sharing:* Have you ever needed to access a file stored on another computer? A network makes it easy for everyone to access the same file and prevents people from accidentally creating different versions.
- *Printer Sharing:* If you use a computer, chances are you also use a printer. With a network, several computers can share the same printer. Although you might need a more expensive printer to handle the added workload, it's still cheaper to use

a network printer than to connect a separate printer to every computer in your office.

- *Communication and collaboration:* It's hard for people to work together if no one knows what anyone else is doing. A network allows employees to share files, view other people's work, and exchange ideas more efficiently. In a larger office, you can use email and instant massaging tools to communicate quickly and to store messages for future reference.
- *Organization:* A variety of scheduling software is available that makes it possible to arrange meetings without constantly checking everyone's schedules. This software usually includes other helpful features, such as shared address books and to-do lists.
- *Remote access:* Having your own network allows greater mobility while maintaining the same level of productivity. With remote access in place, users are able to access the same files, data, and messages even when they're not in the office. This access can even be given to mobile handheld devices.
- *Data protection:* You should know by now that it's vital to back up your computer data regularly. A network makes it easier to back up all of your company's data on an offsite server, a set of tapes, CDs, or other backup systems. (Of course, another aspect of data protection is data *security*. In our article, What Is a Firewall? you can read more about how a network can protect the data it transmits.)

Of course, this isn't a complete list; once you have a network, you'll probably find many other uses for it. And once you get used to the benefits of a network, you'll never look at your computer the same way again.

When you're ready to network your computers, one of the first choices you'll encounter is the speed of connection. You might also wonder whether to spring for a wireless LAN.

Networking for Business

Even the smallest businesses can take advantage of networking to share the cost of peripherals such as printers and scanners and provide access to shared data.

However, the growth of wireless networks and the increasing use of virtual private networks, which allow a user to access a business' network via the internet, have not only resulted in a wider choice of solutions for the business owner, but also a number of additional business benefits.

This guide will explain the basics of computer networking, outline the potential business benefits of the different solutions available and highlight the need for effective security measures whatever network is used.

Benefits of Using Networks

As your business grows, good communication between employees is essential. You can improve efficiency by sharing information such as common files, databases and business application software over a computer network.

With improvements in network capacity and the ability to work wirelessly or remotely, successful businesses should regularly re-evaluate their needs and their IT infrastructure. Properly planned, an efficient network brings a wide range of benefits to a company.

You can Improve Communication by Connecting Your Computers and Working on Standardised Systems, so that:

- staff, suppliers and customers are able to share information and get in touch more easily
- sharing information can make your business more efficient-eg networked access to a common database can avoid the same data being keyed multiple times, which would waste time and could result in errors
- staff are better equipped to deal with queries and deliver a better standard of service as a result of sharing customer data

You can reduce costs and improve efficiency by storing information in one centralised database and streamlining working practices, so that:

- staff can deal with more customers at the same time by accessing customer and product databases
- network administration can be centralised, less IT support is required
- costs are cut through sharing of peripherals such as printers, scanners, external discs, tape drives and internet access.

You can reduce errors and improve consistency by having all staff work from a single source of information, so that standard versions of manuals and directories can be made available, and data can be backed up from a single point on a scheduled basis, ensuring consistency.

Office Networks

For many businesses, the first computer network they need will be confined to a single building. This type of network is called a local area network (LAN). There are two common kinds of LAN-peer-to-peer and client/server.

Peer-to-peer networks connect two or more computers directly, allowing them to share files or programs. They are particularly suitable for collaborative work, fairly straightforward and relatively cheap to create.

However, peer-to-peer networks can be much slower than server-based networks and are unsuitable for very complex networks. Also, peer-to-peer systems connect users through other users' computers, so a failure at one point in the network will affect every computer connected to that network.

Client/server networks use one computer as a server-where shared files and programs are kept-which other PCs connect to. This central machine can be a normal PC, although it is best to use a powerful computer or a purpose-built server computer.

Client/server networks have a number of advantages. As files are stored centrally, these systems are more efficient at backing up and handling data. For example, users cannot modify files simultaneously. You can also link to different types of computer, and support more users more reliably than you can with a peer-to-peer network.

Unlike peer-to-peer systems, a failure at a single point in a client/server network will not affect other computers on the network, as long as the server remains intact.

Choosing Cable or Wireless

Local area networks (LANs) were traditionally implemented using cabling. However, wireless LANs have become easier and often cheaper to create and maintain and are now providing flexible networking options for many businesses.

As with most technology solutions there are pros and cons for both approaches.

Wireless networking frees the user from being physically attached to a network. It also offers much greater flexibility and mobility-office-based wireless workers can be networked without sitting at dedicated computers, and can continue to work while off-site.

In most cases, a wireless network costs less to install and maintain than a cabled network. It eliminates cabling, so you don't need to drill holes through walls and floors to lay cables, and you don't need to rewire the office if, for instance, a department moves.

Occasional difficulties with signal quality may be experienced with wireless networks-for example where neighbours in the same building use the same wireless channels, or where other sources of radio interference are present. In addition, it can be difficult to get consistent coverage in some buildings, leading to 'black spots' where no signal is available.

Wireless networks are generally slower than cabled networks, and so in larger wireless networks the 'backbone' network will usually be cabled.

Other Types of Computer Network

As your business develops, you might wish to consider other networks such as wide area networks (WANs), virtual private networks (VPNs), intranets and extranets. These networks each offer different business benefits, such as linking together systems in different offices, allowing remote workers to access your office systems securely, or providing up-to-date information for your staff and business partners.

WANs are used by companies with offices at different locations. The WAN connects different local area networks together, into a more complex network. You will need to use client/server networks, which are based around central server computers, so that you can connect the various servers over a telecommunications network. WANs use cables/ lines that are leased from a telecoms company.

A VPN allows the user to connect across the internet to the business' private network. It creates a secure link between the remote worker's computer and the central system. A VPN can be cheaper to use than leased lines or domestic-type broadband connections.

Many businesses now build internal networks more commonly known as an intranet. These intranets store information on a central system at a private internet address. Employees can access business information by connecting to the internet, making it particularly useful for employees who travel or work from home. You will need to invest in the design and management of the intranet. The information in it must be accurate and up-to-date so users will have confidence in it. One way of ensuring this is to use a content management system to update information on the intranet.

Businesses can also open up certain areas of their intranets to partners, such as suppliers and customers, typically with a password. This is an extranet. For example, a business can let clients track the progress of their orders, and the payment of suppliers online can be linked directly to the business accounts system.

Assess your Networking Needs

Consider what you want the system to do and what results you want. Express your requirements in business terms, not computer terms-for example, you might consider the value remote workers can provide customers by having immediate access to stock levels.

Consider the following issues to help assess your needs:

Analyse your System

- Consider your business processes. Do any depend on producing or accessing information-could you benefit from storing this centrally and letting staff access it via individual PCs?
- Consider which processes networking could support, eg staff might need access to centralised customer records to create sales quotations.
- Estimate your future computing requirements. If your business takes on more staff your IT system will need to expand to support them-this is called scalability.
- Audit your existing equipment.
- Consider how many people will use the network-staff, suppliers and customers.
- Assess your printing requirements and the best locations for equipment such as scanners and disk drives.
- Decide how much you can spend on computer networks.
- Calculate costs-include purchase, installation, support, maintenance and training as well as lost business due to staff involvement. Consult your local Chamber of Commerce or

Business Link, or similar-sized businesses that you deal with. Find your local Business Link through our Contacts Directory.
- Calculate potential savings-replacing manual and paper-based processes, reducing hardware costs by sharing facilities, and capital allowances.

Consider Security

- Consider who will use the network.
- Identify what access controls you will require, such as passwords.
- Outline backup procedures-eg take regular backups of your data in case your system crashes.

Select Products

- Research the available technology through networking suppliers' websites, specialist exhibitions, or discussing your requirements with PC and networking companies. Networking magazines-often online-include features on the latest developments.
- Do you want a peer-to-peer network-which you could install in-house-or do you need an expert to help set up a client/server system?
- Prepare a shortlist of suitable products from different vendors.
- Talk to people using these products or read magazine reviews.
- Consider the support facilities for each product.

Networking Administration, Support and Maintenance

For your network to benefit your business it must be run effectively. This means careful planning of how it will be maintained and developed.

For a small network, it is worth appointing a network administrator and supporting that person with additional training. Ideally, the administrator would have some technical knowledge, but expertise can be brought in where necessary- although this can be costly. Choose someone who is methodical and good at keeping records and monitoring tasks.

The Administrator's Basic Responsibilities Include:

- security, including password monitoring
- designing and implementing backup procedures-see our guide on keeping your systems and data secure
- disaster recovery planning.

As the network grows the network administrator will need further training. At this point you will need their expertise to also cover the installation, configuration and maintenance of PCs, networking equipment and network operating systems.

It is a good idea to define exactly what type of emergency support and after-sales services your technology providers should supply, as they can be an important point of contact for any queries or problems you may have. If they cannot provide these services, consider another supplier who can.

You need to maintain your network. You'll need to monitor software compatibility. This doesn't necessarily mean automatically getting the latest release available. Compatibility needs to extend across the network, so an upgrade strategy must be carefully planned and budgeted.

Make rules for file naming to ensure that changes take place to the right files at the right time. Multiple file copies will be created as employees download central files to work on whilst off-site and upload them later. Naming rules prevent overwriting of any changes made to the original files.

Network Security Issues

The increase in businesses connecting their systems and using the internet has its drawbacks. When all computers are networked, one user's problems may affect everyone. You should consider the greater potential for data loss, security breaches and viruses when creating a network.

It is important to ensure data security through regular housekeeping such as backing up files, password routines and system logs. It is important to remove access from employees who leave, otherwise they may still be able to access customer records.

As your data will be stored in one location on the server, physical security is very important.

You should enhance your system security to protect your business from potential virus attacks and hacking. This should include antivirus software and a firewall or software barrier.

Keep this up to date and download relevant patches-updates to software that fix security threats-because new viruses are frequently released. If you are affected by a virus your employees could lose data and have difficulties using their computers, and your business could come to a standstill. If your staff need to access the network while off-site, consider a virtual private network. This creates a secure link and protects information sent and received.

If you opt for a wireless networking solution then be aware that they can be insecure unless you take appropriate precautions. Typical threats include people being able to eavesdrop on your business activities or a hacker using a wireless connection to gain access to your key business systems.

Irrespective of the technology solution you select, you should seek expert advice when your system is installed-from your internet service provider, system provider, installer or an adviser. As when seeking any type of professional guidance, you should find out whether any adviser is familiar with businesses of your size or in your sector, or follow personal recommendations. Consult your local Chamber of Commerce or Business Link.

Here's how I used the right technology to make my business more efficient

Newcastle-based building restoration and renovation business MGM Ltd has introduced technology into many of its day-to-day operations to help streamline processes and manage costs. Managing director Steve Gray explains how he did it and outlines the improvements in customer satisfaction, time management and cost control that the technology has delivered.

What I did

Ask for Advice

"I talked to our accountants as I wanted to use an IT system which would easily integrate with theirs. I also discussed workloads with staff. We decided that the most efficient way of progressing was to take on someone who had already worked on accounting packages. This would save time and cost on training, and we simply didn't have enough people in the office to handle the extra workload."

Put Technology Into Action in Stages

"First of all we introduced an accounting package, so we could invoice customers and make and receive payments through BACS. This is the automated clearance system where you can transfer money directly into recipients' accounts, rather than write cheques and have to wait for them to clear. This made our financial control much tighter so we didn't miss any payments.

"We then put the payroll onto the accounts system to pay staff monthly salaries direct into their bank accounts. This has cut down on paperwork and reduced manual errors. Next we introduced job costings and programming of workloads so we could guarantee that the right people are in the right place, doing the right work, at the right time. This has greatly increased customer satisfaction."

Use Technology to Provide cost Savings Through Efficiency

"The latest change is the introduction of a tracker system in each of our 21 vehicles. I researched the available systems on the market and opted for the one best suited to our needs. I explained to everyone that the tracker system would streamline our efficiency as we would be able to plan routes more effectively. This meant they arrived to jobs on time, and had an easy to follow, reasonable schedule every day. The tracker system has resulted in a number of cost savings, including reducing our insurance premiums and petrol costs."

What I'd do Differently

Network our IT Systems Earlier

"It's only during 2004 that we've finally networked all our technology together. It's made a huge difference to our efficiency. We can all see the same IT files and can access information as soon as we need to. We can keep our invoicing up-to-date and respond to customer queries immediately."

Produce Detailed Management Accounts Straight Away

"Now we have our monthly management accounts, we can control the business better, knowing what our profitability is at regular intervals, and making adjustments if needed."

Keeping Your Systems and data Secure

Most businesses store information in both computer and paper-based systems.

Whatever storage method you use, keeping your data secure and confidential will help safeguard the information you need to run your business successfully and ensure you comply with relevant legislation.

If your business data is lost, misused or accessed without

authorisation, it can be difficult to make informed business decisions. This can also put you at a competitive disadvantage. Serious data loss can put your whole business at risk.

This guide sets out the benefits of looking after your data, the principles of business continuity and the risks associated with using technology for storage.

Why data Security is Important

Data security is important to most businesses. Financial information-eg accounts and tax details-or employee information-eg payroll and personnel files-could be very difficult to replace. This could expose you to certain risks that need managing carefully. If you lost data through human error, fire, theft or for some other reason, you would at the very least have to spend time and effort collecting and reproducing the information.

More seriously, your sales, distribution and the reputation of your business could be directly affected. Projects in progress-eg new product designs-could be delayed as the work is redone.

Losing data in a customer database-such as customer names, contact details and information on their buying habits-could stop you targeting customers with appropriate mail shots or informing them of new products. This could mean you lose potential sales, and revenue.

A virus can damage your business by making documents stored on computers unusable. As more and more business is conducted via email, a virus can also make getting in contact with suppliers and customers more difficult. This can mean delays in making purchase orders and taking customer orders.

Risk Management

Risk management is a process whereby risks are identified, assessed for their impact and likelihood and then, depending on their seriousness, reduced to an acceptable level.

Risk assessment can help you identify what risks your business faces and what would happen if you lost valuable data or your systems failed.

Carrying out a Risk Assessment

Firstly, you need to identify potential hazards to your data and systems. This will include looking at:

- physical threats-eg an office fire, power cuts, malicious damage and theft
- human error-eg input error, mistaken processing of data and careless disposal of data
- threats from corporate espionage and malicious damage.

You can then consider how you currently secure data and information systems and identify areas where you are vulnerable. Consider:

- who has access to what information
- who uses the internet, emails, data and how they do so
- whether access is restricted to those who need data for their work
- whether passwords are used and how they are kept
- what antivirus software and firewalls you have in place to protect systems
- your level of staff training.

Once this is done, you can prioritise the data and systems that are the most critical to your business, and decide which require additional security safeguards.

It is worthwhile drawing up a business continuity plan that employees can follow if systems fail. You should review your risks and security safeguards regularly to allow for changes in your business' circumstances or working methods. See our guide on business continuity planning in IT.

You may want to consider using the services of a professional risk consultant.

IT Security Policy

Data security is only one aspect of the wider issue of IT security in a small business. It is good practice to write an IT security policy, setting out the general rules that will be followed to minimise IT security risks. This can then be used by management and employees to help ensure good practice.

You should develop a clear policy that takes account of common risks to your data. This will allow staff to understand and adopt appropriate security measures, and help create a security-conscious culture. The policy does not need to be lengthy or complicated, but should provide a reference point for all staff.

An IT security policy should cover both external threats such as viruses and internal threats such as the theft of data.

Your IT Security Policy might Include

- Secure login identification for using IT systems
- Logical access controls-limiting access to information and restricting access to the level needed for each job
- Confidentiality rules for customer and business information
- Plans for business continuity management

You also need a clear policy on what you consider acceptable use of the internet and email, as these are usually the means by which viruses get into systems. Such a policy will normally prohibit the browsing of websites likely to contain offensive material. Similarly, you should prohibit the use of email to send or receive such material.

You should have a clear policy about the transmission of sensitive commercial information via email. In addition, you should clearly state your policy on the use of business email and web facilities for private use.

Types of Threay Virus

Computer viruses are created to cause a nuisance or damage computer systems. Viruses are programs that can replicate themselves, spreading from computer to computer, and often damage files. They are usually activated by opening a program or document and are often passed on to unsuspecting users.

There are Several Variants of the Virus idea that you may see:

- Trojan-a program that appears to do something useful, but actually has a hidden destructive capability.
- Worm-a program that spreads itself over a network, reproducing itself as it goes. Worms can cause problems by creating a lot of useless traffic on your network.

You can be Infected by:

- email
- clicking on website advertisements
- using infected CDs
- attaching a corrupted removable media storage device via a USB port.

- clicking on a link in a social networking site message, which then takes you to a malicious website that can steal your details or potentially take over your computer as part of a botnet, ie a network of computers acquired by hackers for malicious intent.

Viruses can spread rapidly through your business network via internal email, an intranet, a shared disk, or an infected media storage device. They can overload or crash your computers and network.

They can capture keystrokes-everything you type, such as confidential passwords and credit card details-and they can destroy files.

Tools for Combating the Problem Include the Following:

- Install antivirus software to detect viruses, stop them running, help you delete them and repair the damage. Remember to update the software regularly.
- Use the surfing security functions available with your web browser to restrict specific high-risk sites.
- Have a clear IT policy for acceptable use of business systems and email. Refer to this policy in employment contracts and provide training for the procedures.

Using and regularly updating antivirus software to scan emails is good practice and can be invaluable for protecting your systems. Ensure employees are warned not to open attachments from unknown or suspicious senders. Restricting email and internet access to those who need it can lower the risks of your systems being infected by a virus.

Computer Misuse and Hacking

Unauthorised access, known as hacking, involves someone breaking into your IT systems without consent. The threat can come from inside or outside your business. There are various legal penalties for hackers, but you should not rely on these to act as a deterrent.

If your IT systems connect to the internet then you need to take special precautions against hacking, including the following:

- Firewall-this checks what goes into and out of your systems and blocks things that could be a threat according to a set of rules.
- Intrusion detection systems-these look for the signs of a hacking attempt on your systems and warn you if such an attempt is

seen. Intrusion detection systems software can be obtained from a number of suppliers. You can find one using a web search. However, you will need some understanding of networks-or external support-to install and use them effectively. You might take action based on the warning, eg shutting down systems at risk.

Just as important as these tools is to keep your software up-to-date, as hackers will try to take advantage of older software that contains known weaknesses.

It is an offence to gain unauthorised access to a computer, even if no damage is done and no files are deleted or changed. It is also an offence to purposefully change files on a computer with intent and without authorisation, eg deleting files or even changing computer settings. If there is the intent to commit a further offence, eg access your bank account online to transfer money, then an individual could face five years imprisonment and/or a fine.

Don't rely on the law to protect your IT systems. It is a deterrent to hackers, but you must also take your own precautions. You must also ensure that your employees do not use your system to hack other organisations.

Internet and email Issues

The inappropriate use of email and the internet, eg using the internet for non-work purposes, can have significant consequences for your business. This could be in terms of:

- damage to your business' reputation
- loss of productivity
- increased risk of liability and legal action, eg as a result of sexist or racist emails
- increased risk of virus attack

To avoid inappropriate usage, it is a good idea to clarify exactly what is and is not permitted at your business in a written record. You could ask employees to sign to confirm that they have understood the email and internet policy.

You may also wish to consider putting guidelines in place regarding the use of online diaries, detailing the kinds of comments that are acceptable.

You certainly should prohibit the use of your business' IT systems for the distribution of information (perhaps via a website) that has no relevance to your business. For example, the distribution of music and video tracks might well result in civil action against your business.

It is also worth introducing electronic safeguards. You should ensure that all email that enters or leaves your business passes through virus checking. You can install filtering software that searches emails for specific words or phrases, normally obscene or discriminatory, or monitors which websites your employees are accessing, or filters the type of websites they can access. You can extend this filtering to block access to sites that are known to carry obscene or racist material.

These measures are not infallible. You should not rely on filters alone to protect your business.

Before monitoring your employees' email and web usage it may be worthwhile seeking legal advice as there are data protection issues to consider.

Data backup and Disaster Recovery

The extensive use of computer systems makes business operations vulnerable to major problems, ranging from the accidental loss of data to deliberate sabotage. Storage systems, whether computer or paper-based, can be at risk of theft or physical damage through a fire or flood.

If computer systems are out of action due to any of these reasons, you may face problems in paying staff, complying with data protection law, taking customer orders, or having deliveries cancelled because you have not paid your suppliers.

Backups can allow you to continue trading even if computer data has been lost. Backups consist of data copied from your key systems. These copies are made to portable media such as magnetic tapes, DVD ROMS, external hard disks, or to offsite media provided by online backup services that allow data back up over the internet. You should have a backup routine (often done every day) as part of your IT security policy and you should check that this is being correctly carried out.

Best Practice for Backing-up Data Includes

- giving one person the main responsibility for backing up, and designating a second to cover for absence
- using a different tape or disk to back up each day of the week and have a schedule for rotating them

- keeping backups secure-preferably off-site from the main business premises, eg in a bank box
- periodically testing your backups to ensure that your data can be successfully restored

Disaster recovery is intended to provide cover for really serious incidents such as fire or flood. It is good security practice to work out in advance how your business could survive and recover from such an incident, recording this in the form of a disaster recovery plan. Good data security and data backups are essential requirements for disaster recovery.

You should train your staff in business continuity methods-safeguarding essential functions. You should also consider IT security-see the page in this guide on IT security policy.

Staff Training and Data Security Awareness

Communicating security policies and procedures to employees, and getting their commitment to adopting such methods, is an important way of lowering the risk of loss or damage to your data and systems.

If your staff regularly use and process data, make them aware of data security and protection principles, and what actions might infringe on security or confidentiality.

Staff who use IT for their work need to know how to use systems and how to be security-conscious. If staff know the procedures to follow when systems fail, it will be easier for them to get back to work in such an event.

To create awareness about data security issues, it may be helpful to consider the following:

- Train staff to use systems correctly and give responsibility for backups.
- Communicate data security procedures and principles-consider obtaining signed declarations from anyone handling sensitive information.
- Plan how particular tasks will be carried out manually if technology breaks down.
- Set out IT good practice, including use of email, software and the internet, and the use of passwords. Draw staff attention to it by referring to it in employment contracts.

- Involve staff in a risk assessment and in regular reviews of your procedures.

Here's how Anti-Virus Security Protected my Business

In 2001 London-based financial adviser Trinity Financial Limited was hit by a computer virus that erased its client-records database. Now, says managing director Jeff Moores, email downtime is a thing of the past for the business, which has realised the benefits of protecting against virus attacks.

What I did

Assess our Options

"It was devastating when we lost our client database as a result of a computer virus. Luckily we were able to restore most of the data promptly and use our hard-copy backups for a couple of days. But this process cost a considerable amount of money-so we couldn't afford to let it happen again.

"So we assessed the options for antivirus protection. Most of our ideas came from speaking to our clients and finding out about the services they used. We decided we also needed something to counter the increased virus threat that stems from staff working remotely - something we were keen to introduce."

Install Firewalls and Anti-Virus Software

"We installed antivirus software to detect and delete computer viruses as soon as they enter our IT network. We went for a solution that is monitored and updated by our IT supplier, which means we don't have to worry about it on a day-to-day basis. We also configured a managed firewall to monitor and protect the network from people trying to illegally gain access to our database from outside the business.

"Now our IT system is fast, stable and secure. And because of the extra security we can allow staff to work remotely, which in turn has boosted our productivity levels."

Monitor Progress

"It's been a huge benefit to be able to demonstrate to clients that their data is safer than ever. But we do remain alert and continue to review the quality of our antivirus protection. In fact, this ongoing review has even helped us revamp our staff IT policy and complete our company audit.

"But most of all, thanks to our antivirus measures, email downtime is a problem of the past, leaving us free to concentrate on winning new business."

What I'd do Differently

Speak to Other Small Businesses

"As we began our search for a solution we started talking to some software consultants. But this process ultimately wasted valuable time because once we started contacting some of our clients, we got ideas which were a lot more suited to our needs."

Introduce a staff IT Usage Policy

"Looking back, if everyone knew the limits of what was acceptable then we might have averted a virus attack. But as a growing business it was difficult to know how we should have restricted staff internet use."

Online Networking

The connections you and your business make are of paramount importance today. Developing strategic relationships via networking events has been the traditional means of making new business contacts.

Today, the internet is becoming a meeting place in its own right. With advanced communications technology now available, face-to-face meetings can be just as rewarding and productive when conducted online.

Traditional networking events are increasingly giving way to online alternatives, as business leaders realise that cost and efficiency gains can be made by avoiding a physical networking event.

How Online Networks Work

Online networking has become a reality because of two key technologies. The first is the availability of fast broadband access to the internet. The second is the continued development of computers that can handle full-motion video and graphics. Text, audio and video have come together to offer online networking as a practical proposition for even the smallest enterprise.

Word of Mouse

As an owner/manager you understand that the connections you make in business are essential for the long-term profits of your enterprise.

Networking events had long been the way that business relationships have been built. The internet has provided yet another way for businesses to communicate with each other.

There are a number of different online networks that your business can participate in, including:

- email lists
- chat rooms and forums
- video conferencing
- virtual world online networks.

Each of the different types of online network has its pros and cons. It is vital that you think through what you want to achieve by taking part in an online network. This will guide you to the networking format that is right for your business.

Building Business Relationships

Online networks enable you and your business to maintain close relationships with other enterprises over long geographical distances. Physical networking events often only take place once a month. You can communicate with other businesses via online networks on a daily basis.

This close connection fosters a much more intimate working relationship that you can build on over time. The commercial aspect being that a business looking to buy goods or services will instinctively look for partners that they already know via the online networks they are members.

Business Benefits of Online Networking

Online networks give your business an opportunity to gain new contacts from the comfort of your office. Don't underestimate the savings in cost, time and other resources such as travel that not having to attend a physical networking event can bring to your enterprise. With nothing more than your computer and an internet connection you can be networking with hundreds of other businesses in minutes.

Business Benefits

Online networks can offer an enterprise the chance to improve their businesses in a number of key areas:

- recruitment
- marketing

- brand building
- customer interaction
- locating strategic commercial partners
- gathering business intelligence.

It is important that you understand your business' motivation for joining one or more online networks. Think about what you want to gain from building a relationship with other businesses. If you focus your needs the type of online network that is ideal for you will become clear.

Targeted Advertising

Online networks are now becoming a hotbed for advertising space. Businesses have been quick to realise that the captive audience of online networks are ideal for focused marketing messages for goods or services.

Placing advertising within online networks is gathering pace. As with your business' other marketing spend, carefully consider which online networks to use and the marketing message you want to get across. This will ensure a good return on your investment.

Find practical information about advertising on the Advertising Association website.-Opens in a new window

Social networking sites such as Facebook and MySpace offer a number of different advertising options including pay per click, pay per view, banner ads, Flash ads and classified notices. Advertising can be targeted against a variety of demographic criteria (eg age, marital status, location) relating to network members. Some sites have tools that can be used for research giving your business valuable customer profile information. This will allow you to make informed decisions about whether a particular social networking site is appropriate to your marketing strategy.

How to Choose and Join Online Networks

With so many different online networks available, from simple email lists to complete virtual worlds, it can be difficult to choose the right network for your business. Joining several networks is an option, but it is still important to spend your time and resources with online networks that actually deliver real benefits to your business.

How to Choose the Right Network

The criteria you use to make a decision about which online network(s)

are ideal for your business will ultimately depend on what motivates you to join the network initially. Ask yourself the following questions to help you identify the right kind of online network that will deliver the benefits you are looking for:

- What is your key reason for joining the network?
- What level of return do you expect?
- What kind of businesses are already members of the network?
- Do you have the time and resources to commit to your network membership?

The internet is now awash with networking websites that cover just about every conceivable business sector. You may already be aware of the high profile business networks like LinkedIn, but there are a great number of smaller networks that may be a better fit with your business. This is especially true if your business operates in a niche market.

Online Networks Explained

There are many different types of online network your business could join. However, they do fall into distinct categories that include:

- profile/market building networks-BT Tradespace, Network 2012
- social information exchange-Facebook, MySpace, bebo
- microblogging-Twitter
- referral and connection building-LinkedIn, Plaxo, Ecademy
- book marking and reviewing -Digg, Stumbleupon
- email connection and network building-Yahoo! Groups, MSN Groups
- self perpetuating groups-flickr, iStockphoto.

Before you become active on any of these networks, it is vitally important that you understand the profile of the other people and businesses already using the network. Posting inappropriate messages, or worse still placing advertising that is not welcome by the members will damage your business' brand and reputation. Spend some time researching the networks you think are ideal for your business. This is time well spent, and will deliver the results you are looking for.

How to Choose and Join Online Networks

With so many different online networks available, from simple email lists to complete virtual worlds, it can be difficult to choose the right network for your business. Joining several networks is an option, but it is still important to spend your time and resources with online networks that actually deliver real benefits to your business.

How to Choose the Right Network

The criteria you use to make a decision about which online network(s) are ideal for your business will ultimately depend on what motivates you to join the network initially. Ask yourself the following questions to help you identify the right kind of online network that will deliver the benefits you are looking for:

- What is your key reason for joining the network?
- What level of return do you expect?
- What kind of businesses are already members of the network?
- Do you have the time and resources to commit to your network membership?

The internet is now awash with networking websites that cover just about every conceivable business sector. You may already be aware of the high profile business networks like LinkedIn, but there are a great number of smaller networks that may be a better fit with your business. This is especially true if your business operates in a niche market.

Before you become active on any of these networks, it is vitally important that you understand the profile of the other people and businesses already using the network. Posting inappropriate messages, or worse still placing advertising that is not welcome by the members will damage your business' brand and reputation. Spend some time researching the networks you think are ideal for your business. This is time well spent, and will deliver the results you are looking for.

Etiquette and Online Networks

Online networks have their own rules that should be followed, just like face-to-face networking events. Whether you are joining a network as a member or starting your own-which means that you become the moderator of the network-you must ensure you abide by the etiquette that has been developed since online networks first appeared.

When Using Online Networks, Try to Apply the Following Principles

- Don't make each of your posts on a network an advertisement for your business' services or products. Blatant self-promotion is usually frowned upon by other network users.

- Always read the network's guidelines before you make any posts. This will ensure you don't make any beginner's mistakes.
- Don't post inappropriate or off-topic questions or comments. If in doubt contact the network's moderator.
- Never make personal criticisms of other network users or their businesses. This is very bad etiquette and could result in your business being thrown off the network entirely. In the most serious cases, it could even lead to legal action against you, eg for libel or defamation.
- Think about privacy. Some email lists are read by thousands of people. If you want a private conversation with someone you have met via a network, exchange private email address and continue the conversation through that channel.
- Carefully read the terms and conditions for any network that you participate in.

Security and Online Networking

Whether you intend to join one or a number of online networks, security should be at the top of your agenda. With the rise of identity theft, fake emails and security threats to small and large companies, ensuring you are using online networks safely is essential.

Security in a Web 2.0 World

Each time you login to use an online network you expose yourself and your business to a level of attack from hackers and other malicious groups. However, you are not powerless in the face of what may seem like an unstoppable wave of identity theft and threats to your security. Follow the guidelines below to ensure you use online networks safely:

- Keep your login details secure and regularly change your password.
- Be suspicious of anyone who contacts you out of the blue claiming to be part of one of the networks you are a member of. This could be a phishing attack. Phishing is where legitimate looking emails seemingly from a reliable source, eg a bank, are used with the aim of obtaining personal details.
- Watch out for corporate identity theft. Your business name could be used within online networks without your knowledge or permission. Contact Companies House Contact Centre on Tel 0303 1234 500 for more information about this type of

security threat. Find out about using the Protected Online Filing Scheme (PROOF) on the Companies House website- Opens in a new window.

- Never reveal any sensitive information about yourself or your business without first checking the credentials of the enquirer.
- If you use email-based online networks, use filtering software to reduce the instances of spam and phishing attacks.
- If you access online networks via wireless internet access ensure you have adequate security to protect your wireless network from eavesdropping and hacker attack.
- Avoid opening email attachments from unknown sources-or if known-eg from a fellow employee, check with the sender first if the attachment isn't something you expected. Don't open attachments such as those ending with '.exe' (an executable file) or those with the '.scr' which is the file extension used for Windows screensavers, as these can also be Trojans that can infect your computer.
- Avoid clicking on links added to messages in any social networking websites that you use. These include links to current events, entertainment news or other links to high traffic sites. These links can take you to phishing websites and have the potential to infect your computer. If clicking on a link always check the website address you have been taken to, in order to ensure you are where you believe you should be.
- Avoid clicking on advertising emails and popup boxes and be cautious of any application that wants to install itself on your computer.

Checklist: Online Networking

Whether you are looking for one or more online networks to join, or are thinking about starting your own network, there are a lot of factors to consider. Planning is vitally important to ensure you join the right network(s) that will deliver the business benefits you are looking for.

When Joining a Network, Ensure That You:

- Choose the right network for your business goals. Ask yourself why you are joining an online network. What do you want to get out of this activity?

- Develop your user profile. Networking is all about relationships. The more people and businesses know about you, the closer that relationship. However, be careful when exposing information about yourself and your business. Always check your data is being held securely.
- Avoid the hard sell. Your core motivation for joining an online network may be to sell your business' goods or products. Try to avoid hard sales pitches on your networks as these are usually rejected.
- Obey the network rules. Every network has its own rules. Ensure you are aware of the etiquette that is in place.
- Commit enough resources. When joining one or more online networks that support your sector, think about how much time and resources you have available. You and your business need to maintain these network connections, which can take more time and resources than you might initially think.
- Enhance your business brand. Joining a network can have a great positive impact on your business' brand. The close working relationships you can build via networks is now an essential component of modern branding practice.
- Include online networking within your marketing mix. Online networks may have marketing at their heart, but don't forget the other forms of promotion your business is using. It's easy to disproportionately assign resources to online networking. Don't forget your other forms of advertising and promotion, as they are effective as well.
- Create new, original and engaging content. No one wants to read boring posts on the networks you are a member of. Try to write relevant and engaging content each time you contribute to a network.
- Place advertising on carefully chosen networks. The online networks that have developed over the last few years are clearly a great location for your business' advertising. Banner ads are now appearing on network websites. Careful consideration must be given to what kind of advertising is placed on these networks and what messages they contain. Research the profile of network members to help you design an engaging advertising message they will positively respond to.

3

Business Application

Introduction

Maintaining accounts can be challenging for any business. Many businesses entrust everything to an accountant. Others aim to save time and money by using specialist accounting software.

If you choose the right package, good accounting software can help your business manage accounts more efficiently. It can make the process quicker and more straightforward. The growing emphasis on e-filing-or submitting records electronically-means that the use of accounts software is even more attractive because many packages can make this process very simple.

However, not all businesses will benefit from accounting software. This guide will help you to decide whether your business needs an accounts package and, if so, help you select the right type of product. The guide will also help you plan your implementation effectively.

An Overview of the Different Ways to Keep Business Accounts

In order to run any business you need to keep accounts or pay someone to do this for you. Keeping accounts is a legal obligation, but keeping good records is vital to run your business effectively. There are many ways of keeping accounts.

Traditionally, accounts were kept on paper with handwritten entries. Many small businesses still use the traditional methods of bookkeeping, often using specially printed books to organise records. However, handwritten accounts can take a significant amount of your business' time and it is easy to make mistakes.

Computing spreadsheets can be set up to keep accounts. They can do the sums for you and update all data in a series of spreadsheets simultaneously. However, designing and maintaining a spreadsheet accounts system can be a significant task. Mistakes made in a spreadsheet may go unnoticed and not get corrected until the end of the year.

Computer Based Accounts Packages Can:

- save time by only requiring you to enter information once
- keep track of your business' debtors and creditors
- reduce delays between making a sale and generating an invoice
- automatically calculate VAT
- facilitate more accurate forecasting
- allow you to add payroll modules to calculate pay and produce pay slips

However, a computer accounts package can have some drawbacks:

- The package cost, although small in relation to your other costs, is higher than a paper-based system.
- You may need to purchase yearly maintenance and support for your package.
- An accounts package is designed to suit most types of business. However, if your business is very unusual you may find that you need to change the way you operate to suit the package.
- You will probably need some initial help setting up an accounts package. This will usually be a chargeable service, perhaps obtained from your accountant.

Choosing the Right Accounting Package

Accounting packages can be used for all the important financial transactions in your business and you will rely on it to give you critical information about the health of your business. In order to make the right choice, you need to consider a number of different issues.

To get the right package for your business, you need to define your business requirements and then match them to the available packages. A good way to do this is to decide on the overall requirements first, then consider the more detailed requirements within that framework.

Your package must meet all the statutory (legal) requirements that apply to your business and must continue to do so in the future, by, for example, submitting annual accounts that meet defined accountancy standards. Some requirements apply equally to all businesses, but others are specific to particular businesses and the way they operate. For example, a business that deals mostly in cash will keep accounts in a different way to a business that does not. If you have been running your business with manual accounts then you will probably be familiar with these requirements, but if not, your accountant will be able to help.

You need to consider what help you will need to set up, install and maintain your accounts package. For example, if you need to send in your VAT return, but a problem occurs with your accounts package, you need to be able to solve the problem very quickly to avoid penalties for a late return. You need a person or support organisation that you can rely on to sort out this type of problem. Understanding and defining your support requirements is a major part of choosing the right package.

Assessing your Business' Overall Needs for an Accounts Package

In order to assess what your overall requirements for an accounts package could be, you need to gather some information together on your business. It may be helpful to consider the following:

- Is your business a limited company or do you operate as a sole trader? If the latter then you may be able to use a personal accounts package rather than one designed for a business, as you are unlikely to need payroll processing in this case.
- How many transactions-ie changes that you need to record in your accounts-will you have in a month? If the number is less than about ten, then you may find that a manual accounts system will be the best choice. If you have a high level of transactions per month, then you need to select a package that is designed for this level of activity.
- How many people will be using the accounts package at the same time? If you only have one person who does all the accounts work then you can use a simple low-cost package. If you need to have several people entering transactions at the same time then you will need something more sophisticated.
- What computer systems do you use? Personal computers with a Windows Operating System such as Windows XP are the most popular for business use, and there is a wide range of accounts software for this platform. If you use Macintosh or

Linux then you may have a more restricted choice available. You may need to consider using a Windows based PC just for the accounts package in these cases.

Assessing your Detailed Requirements for an Accounts Package

Your detailed requirements for an accounts package depend on the type of business you have and how you run it. Ideally, you should look for an accounts package that can meet all your overall and detailed requirements. However, you may find that there is no available or affordable package and you may have to consider changing the way you operate your business in order to suit the available packages.

To make sure you don't buy an overly complicated system, involve the people who will use it in defining their requirements. They will know what is necessary and what isn't and are likely to be happy to use something they helped to choose.

Requirements you may want to Consider for Your Accounts Package Include:

- Basic bookkeeping-for example sales and purchase ledgers, nominal ledger and invoicing.
- VAT calculations-your accounts system should be able to keep track of VAT and calculate your VAT payment at the end of each VAT period.
- Payroll processing-if you have more than two or three employees, consider a payroll function that calculates PAYE (Pay As You Earn) and National Insurance contributions weekly or monthly.
- The production of management information and decision support reports-you may need to prepare internal management reports periodically.
- Invoicing-any accounts package needs to be able to produce invoices, but you will probably want to be able to tailor the appearance of these and you may want to be able to send them by email.
- Credit control-an accounts package can help by highlighting where customers have exceeded their limits and provide statements to chase them.
- Compatibility with other accounts systems-including the one used by your accountant.

- Industry accreditation-from an independent industry body such as the Business Application Software Developers Association (BASDA).
- Stock control.

Prioritising your Requirements for an Accounts Package

Once you have a list of your overall and detailed requirements you should put them in order of priority.

Your overall requirements should have the highest priority since these generally reflect aspects of your business that are very important and will not change-eg whether you operate as a limited company or are a sole trader.

To Prioritise your Detailed Requirements Consider

- how much time and cost a particular feature will save you
- what would be the consequences of omitting the feature
- how your requirements are likely to change in the future

You could give each Detailed Requirement a Rating, for Example

- must have-without this feature the package is not usable
- advantageous-the feature would save a lot of time
- nice to have-useful, but not essential

You can now compare your list of requirements to the information that you have about each package.

To carry out the comparison, reject all accounts packages that cannot meet your outline requirements or any of your 'must have' detailed requirements. From the remainder select the one that delivers the greatest number of your advantageous and 'nice to have' features at a price your business can afford.

Issues to Consider when Making your Accounts Package Selection

The market place for accounts packages is more complex than for typical office packages. You will probably require continuing support and maintenance to ensure that you have someone to call to solve problems if and when they occur.

You may want to work with your accountant to submit your business accounts. To make this process easier for both your business and the accountant, it is important that you can exchange accounts data electronically.

You may want to use some special stationery with your accounts package-eg standard or specially printed invoices, statements, remittance advice or credit notes. You may need these in multi-part or laser printer forms. Laser printer stationery is designed for use with a laser printer. Some businesses still prefer to use an impact printer such as a dot-matrix printer for accounts. In this case multi-part forms can be used so that several copies are printed at the same time.

For some purposes, it is very important that your accounts package is properly accredited as compliant to a standard or code. The HM Revenue & Customs (HMRC) Payroll Accreditation Scheme, for example, shows that the package correctly carries out the PAYE functions. You can read about the Payroll Standard Accreditation Scheme at the HMRC website-Opens in a new window.

The number of different accounts packages typically used by small businesses in the UK is fairly limited. You can easily obtain information about all these packages from the internet.

Specialised Requirements for your Accounts Package

There are a number of more specialised requirements that you may need to consider when deciding on your accounts package. You can obtain accounts packages with all of these features if you need them, but the cost is likely to be higher.

VAT schemes-there are a number of these, the most familiar of which is the Cash Accounting Scheme where you pay VAT when your invoices have been paid. There are others such as the Flat Rate and Retail Schemes. If you use any of these schemes then you should look for a package that supports them.

Foreign currency-if you need to buy and sell in foreign currencies then your accounts may need to be more complex. You can purchase accounts packages that fully support foreign currencies, but these tend to be designed and priced for larger businesses. You can still operate with a cheaper package, but you will have to do more of the work manually. You can read foreign currency accountancy rules at the Financial Reporting Council (FRC) website-Opens in a new window.

Stock control-if your business sells products rather than services and you have a high turnover of sales, then you may benefit from a stock control function integrated with your accounts. Retail point-of-sale-if you have a high volume of small value sales, eg if you have a shop, then you should look for an accounts systems that supports this type of operation appropriately.

Electronic payments-there are significant benefits in paying invoices online using electronic funds transfer. Some accounts packages support this capability in an integrated fashion. If this would deliver significant benefits for your business then it is worth investigating how the packages work and the costs that might apply to this type of service.

Implementing your Accounts Package

Implementation is much more than just installing some software. Your implementation plan should consider the following.

Package installation-this will usually be in the form of a CD-Rom and may require you to register the package with the supplier so that it is fully licensed and works correctly.

Initial company setup-you will need to enter details of your business including the year-end' date, the form of VAT accounting you use and other details. Your accounts package may have several different Charts of Accounts-ie the headings that you use in your accounts-so you can choose to suit your type of business. However, you may need to tailor this to your requirements. Your accountant should be able to advise you on this work, or undertake it for you.

Parallel running-you may find it useful to run your old accounts and the new package alongside each other for a while to ensure that you are getting correct results. However, it is difficult to maintain parallel running for very long because of the duplication of effort.

Training-the staff who work with the accounts package on a day-to-day basis should ideally have some formal training in the use of the package. You should time this training so that it is done shortly before the installation of the software.

Support-it is a good idea to purchase a support agreement from your supplier for your new accounts package, at least for the first year of operation so that you have a readily available contact to help sort out queries and problems. Many small businesses find that a support agreement is a good investment even after this initial period.

Here's how accounting software brought efficiency savings to my business

Anne Herbert is managing director of PhotoArtistry, a digital printing service for artists and photographers based in Northampton. After a few years of keeping manual accounts, Anne realised there would be business benefits in introducing accounting software. Here Anne explains how she chose the right package for her business and what she is now able to do at the touch of a button.

What I did

Go Electric

"PhotoArtistry had been running for three years before I decided to introduce an accounting software package. Until then I had run the business as a hobby alongside my full-time job, so the accounts were manageable by hand. It just required keeping a copy of each invoice sent out and each payment made.

"When I decided to run the business full-time, I knew that an accounting package would make things easier and quicker. I wanted it to calculate VAT, run reports to see how much I was spending with each supplier, and to be able to easily compare how much the business was spending compared with how much it was bringing in."

Upgrade When Necessary

"I started off with a basic package from a well-known supplier, but as the business grew I realised I needed something that would link with our online orders, so I upgraded to another version. Using software from the same supplier meant I could easily migrate all customer and supplier records from one package to the other. This was something I took into consideration when choosing the package. I also know there is another version I can upgrade to if necessary in the future.

"I was attracted to the particular supplier because it has a good reputation and is widely known. I also knew that other businesses I had worked for used its software and found it reliable."

Utilise Support Services

"When buying the package, I decided it would be beneficial to pay for the telephone support service. As a small-business owner, if accounting or computing is not your speciality, you don't want to spend half your day under the desk trying to work out which wire connects where.

"Although the support package makes up a fair proportion of our total spend, we benefit from it. When we were installing the package, we had a few problems-the helpline was able to guide us towards a solution over the telephone."

What I'd do Differently

Upgrade Sooner

"If I had the money, I might have upgraded our accounting package sooner. As we got more online orders I was spending a lot of time printing out people's details and inputting them into our accounting package. It is also difficult trying to make changes to the business while you are very busy, so it is worth planning what you will need and when in the early stages."

Customer Relationship Management

Introduction

The better a business can manage the relationships it has with its customers the more successful it will become. Therefore IT systems that specifically address the problems of dealing with customers on a day-to-day basis are growing in popularity.

Customer relationship management (CRM) is not just the application of technology, but is a strategy to learn more about customers' needs and behaviours in order to develop stronger relationships with them. As such, it is more of a business philosophy than a technical solution to assist in dealing with customers effectively and efficiently. Nevertheless, successful CRM relies on the use of technology.

This guide will outline the business benefits and the potential drawbacks of implementing CRM. It will also offer help on the types of solution you could choose and how to implement them.

Why CRM?

In the commercial world the importance of retaining existing customers and expanding business is paramount. The costs associated with finding new customers mean that every existing customer could be important.

The more opportunities that a customer has to conduct business with your company the better, and one way of achieving this is by opening up channels such as direct sales, online sales, franchises, use of agents, etc. However, the more channels you have, the greater the need to manage your interaction with your customer base. Customer relationship management (CRM) helps businesses to gain an insight into the behaviour of their customers and modify their business operations to ensure that customers are served in the best possible way. In essence, CRM helps a business to recognise the value of its customers and to capitalise on improved customer relations. The better you understand your customers, the more responsive you can be to their needs.

CRM can be Achieved by:

- finding out about your customers' purchasing habits, opinions and preferences
- profiling individuals and groups to market more effectively and increase sales
- changing the way you operate to improve customer service and marketing

Benefiting from CRM is not just a question of buying the right software. You must also adapt your business to the needs of your customers.

Business Benefits of CRM

Implementing a customer relationship management (CRM) solution might involve considerable time and expense. However, there are many potential benefits.

A major benefit can be the development of better relations with your existing customers, which can lead to:

- increased sales through better timing by anticipating needs based on historic trends
- identifying needs more effectively by understanding specific customer requirements
- cross-selling of other products by highlighting and suggesting alternatives or enhancements
- identifying which of your customers are profitable and which are not

This can lead to better marketing of your products or services by focusing on:

- effective targeted marketing communications aimed specifically at customer needs

- a more personal approach and the development of new or improved products and services in order to win more business in the future.

Ultimately this could lead to:

- enhanced customer satisfaction and retention, ensuring that your good reputation in the marketplace continues to grow
- increased value from your existing customers and reduced costs associated with supporting and servicing them, increasing your overall efficiency and reducing total cost of sales
- improved profitability by focusing on the most profitable customers and dealing with the unprofitable in more cost effective ways.

Once your business starts to look after its existing customers effectively, efforts can be concentrated on finding new customers and expanding your market. The more you know about your customers, the easier it is to identify new prospects and increase your customer base.

Even with years of accumulated knowledge, there's always room for improvement. Customer needs change over time, and technology can make it easier to find out more about customers and ensure that everyone in an organisation can exploit this information.

Types of CRM Solution

Customer relationship management (CRM) is important in running a successful business. The better the relationship, the easier it is to conduct business and generate revenue. Therefore using technology to improve CRM makes good business sense.

CRM solutions fall into the following four broad categories.

Outsourced Solutions

Application service providers can provide web-based CRM solutions for your business. This approach is ideal if you need to implement a solution quickly and your company does not have the in-house skills necessary to tackle the job from scratch. It is also a good solution if you are already geared towards online e-commerce.

Off-the-shelf Solutions

Several software companies offer CRM applications that integrate with existing packages. Cut-down versions of such software may be suitable for smaller businesses. This approach is generally the cheapest option as you are investing in standard software components. The downside is that the software may not always do precisely what you want and you may have to trade off functionality for convenience and price. The key to success is to be flexible without compromising too much.

Bespoke Software

For the ultimate in tailored CRM solutions, consultants and software engineers will customise or create a CRM system and integrate it with your existing software. However, this can be expensive and time consuming. If you choose this option, make sure you carefully specify exactly what you want. This will usually be the most expensive option and costs will vary depending on what your software designer quotes.

Managed Solutions

A half-way house between bespoke and outsourced solutions, this involves renting a customised suite of CRM applications as a bespoke package. This can be cost effective but it may mean that you have to compromise in terms of functionality.

How to Implement CRM

The implementation of a customer relationship management (CRM) solution is best treated as a six-stage process, moving from collecting information about your customers and processing it to using that information to improve your marketing and the customer experience.

Stage 1-Collecting Information

The priority should be to capture the information you need to identify your customers and categorise their behaviour. Those businesses with a website and online customer service have an advantage as customers can enter and maintain their own details when they buy.

Stage 2-Storing Information

The most effective way to store and manage your customer information is in a relational database-a centralised customer database that will allow you to run all your systems from the same source, ensuring that everyone uses up-to-date information.

Stage 3-Accessing Information

With information collected and stored centrally, the next stage is to make this information available to staff in the most useful format.

Stage 4-Analysing Customer Behaviour

Using data mining tools in spreadsheet programs, which analyse data to identify patterns or relationships, you can begin to profile customers and develop sales strategies.

Stage 5-Marketing More Effectively

Many businesses find that a small percentage of their customers generate a high percentage of their profits. Using CRM to gain a better understanding of your customers' needs, desires and self-perception, you can reward and target your most valuable customers.

Stage 6-Enhancing the Customer Experience

Just as a small group of customers are the most profitable, a small number of complaining customers often take up a disproportionate amount of staff time. If their problems can be identified and resolved quickly, your staff will have more time

Potential Drawbacks of CRM

There are several reasons why implementing a customer relationship management (CRM) solution might not have the desired results.

There could be a lack of commitment from people within the company to the implementation of a CRM solution. Adapting to a customer-focused approach may require a cultural change. There is a danger that relationships with customers will break down somewhere along the line, unless everyone in the business is committed to viewing their operations from the customers' perspective. The result is customer dissatisfaction and eventual loss of revenue.

Poor communication can prevent buy-in. In order to make CRM work, all the relevant people in your business must know what information you need and how to use it.

Weak leadership could cause problems for any CRM implementation plan. The onus is on management to lead by example and push for a customer focus on every project. If a proposed plan isn't right for your customers, don't do it. Send your teams back to the drawing board to come up with a solution that will work.

Trying to implement CRM as a complete solution in one go is a tempting but risky strategy. It is better to break your CRM project down into manageable pieces by setting up pilot programs and short-term milestones. Consider starting with a pilot project that incorporates all the necessary departments and groups but is small and flexible enough to allow adjustments along the way.

Don't underestimate how much data you will require, and make sure that you can expand your systems if necessary. You need to carefully consider what data is collected and stored to ensure that only useful data is kept.

You must also ensure you comply with the eight principles of the Data Protection Act that govern the processing of information on living, identifiable individuals.

Avoid adopting rigid rules which cannot be changed. Rules should be flexible to allow the needs of individual customers to be met.

Questions for CRM Suppliers

For many businesses customer relationship management (CRM) can be a large investment. Therefore it is vital to choose your supplier carefully. Making the wrong choice could be expensive and even jeopardise your business. Before implementing a solution based on CRM technology, you might want to ask any potential suppliers the following questions:

- How long has the supplier been established?
- What are the specific costs associated with the product, ie a one-off purchase price, an annual renewable license, a charge per user etc?
- Does the supplier offer any form of evaluation software so that you can try before you buy?
- How much is charged for technical support?
- Does the supplier provide consultancy and, if so, at what rates?
- Is the system scalable? If your customer base grows will the system expand to cope?
- Can the supplier recommend any third-party developers that make use of their core CRM products?
- Is there an active independent user group where experience and ideas can be freely exchanged?
- Can the supplier provide references for businesses in your industry sector that use their software?
- Does it offer training in the CRM solution and, if so, at what typical cost?

Here's how CRM Software Improved my Business

Based in Runcorn, Cheshire, with 60 employees, Chance & Hunt specialises in supply chain management for the international chemical industry. Here managing director Joan Traynor describes the benefits that Customer Relationship Management (CRM) software has brought to the business.

What I did

Define Objectives

"Four years ago we began looking at new ways to manage our existing databases, which were largely running in isolation from each other.

"Our key objectives in selecting a solution were to enhance customer relationships, cut costs and grow sales. With the help of a student working with us in a Knowledge Transfer Partnership we researched CRM systems and selected the right software package for us.

"Our decision was partly based on the fact that the new software would work with our existing platform, so we wouldn't have to start completely from scratch."

Implement and Monitor the Solution

"The software was relatively easy to install, although we were lucky that we had the expertise in-house. The process involved training for all staff, since user buy-in is crucial. If employees aren't motivated to keep records up to date, you won't get anywhere. In that respect, it's important that everyone knows the project has management commitment too.

"We monitored success using key performance indicators, such as the number of customer complaints, and by conducting customer surveys. Complaints are down and customers report improved responsiveness. It's definitely had an impact on sales as well, since our team now has all the customer information they need at the touch of a button. We also monitor employee usage of the system during staff appraisals."

Keep Evolving

"One thing we've learnt about CRM software is that it's about evolution rather than revolution. We developed our system in bite-sized chunks, learning as we went along.

"When we started, we captured fairly basic information like customer details, buying history and sales visits. The system has since been adapted to include a range of additional functions. For example, we are now able to access the system from a handheld PDA or call up a list of customers located en-route to a sales call.

"The great thing is that most of the improvements have been suggested by users. Because they can see the advantages of the system and that it's easy to use, they're keen to take ownership."

What I'd do Differently

Structure the Data

"Early on, we were mostly searching for individual customer records, so it didn't seem to matter how records were grouped. As things developed we wanted to be able to search a variety of indexes, for example by product name, location and so on. Structuring data by defined 'headings' from the start would have helped us when we came to refine the system later."

Benefits of Databases

The gathering, processing and use of information relating to the operations of a business are vital to its success. Even something as simple as a customer mailing list needs to be managed appropriately if it is to be kept up to date and accurate. Therefore, any tools or applications that can make the tasks involved easier and more efficient need to be given serious consideration.

The database is one of the cornerstones of information technology, and its ability to organise, process and manage information in a structured and controlled manner is key to many aspects of modern business efficiency. This guide describes the various types of database tools and systems available and provides guidance on how to choose the best solution for your business needs.

What is a Database?

A database is a collection of data which has been organised so that a computer program can quickly select desired items. This could be something as straightforward as a list of names in alphabetical order or an ascending list of numeric stock codes. The secret to the successful use of database technology is the way in which data or information is structured to enable efficient processing.

Manual filing systems have drawbacks that make them inefficient. Take as an example a simple card file index of customer information. This depends on consistent use to be effective. For example, if the card always has the surname in the top left-hand corner then they are easy to put in alphabetical order. However, if some cards have the postcode in this position instead, the task becomes more complicated.

Database tools and applications are designed to help you store and manage data in a controlled and structured manner.

Single-card file indexes can be simple, but it is more complex to cross-reference information held in two separate files. The relational database management system (RDBMS) makes use of common 'keys' to tie related information together. For example, a customer ID number could be used to identify an individual customer in a large list of customers, or to link a customer with an order for specific goods.

Types of Database System

Databases generally have one of two basic forms-the single-file database or the multi-file relational database. Single-file databases are often called 'flat file' systems and relational databases are frequently known as 'structured' databases.

The type of database system or tool that you require depends on a number of factors, such as:

- the complexity of the data involved, eg plain text, images, sound files
- the quantity of data to be stored and processed
- whether the data needs to be accessed and amended by more than one person simultaneously
- whether data needs to be imported from, or exported to, other IT systems.

If your requirements are simple, eg monitoring the names and addresses of around 100 customers, you might find that standard office tools such as a spreadsheet might be all you need.

However, if your needs become more complicated you will need to look at more sophisticated and capable packages such as Microsoft Access, FileMaker Pro, Oracle, Sybase, Informix or MySQL. These are specifically designed to sort and search large amounts of data of a variety of types, for instance allowing you to manage customer names, goods orders and payment histories.

Certain business processes are often managed using specialist database products or applications. Contact management packages such as ACT, Maximiser or Time and Chaos are specifically designed for managing and manipulating contact information within a business.

Similarly, many business types such as manufacturing, publishing, insurance, etc will have database solutions specifically targeted at their precise needs and requirements. It is worth seeking out any products which address the particular needs of your business sector. You might find them by asking your industry or trade association or trading partners. You can use the internet to research popular database products.

Deciding What Type of Database you Need

Whether your business would benefit from database technology largely depends on volume.

A small business with half a dozen customers, fewer than a hundred product lines and five suppliers will not need a sophisticated relational database management system (RDBMS) to manage its data. Many small businesses manage very well with the limited database capabilities in a standard spreadsheet package.

However, a larger business with hundreds of customers and products, and dozens of suppliers, may find that an RDBMS is the only option. A modern RDBMS is capable of handling millions of records and is designed to cope with very large processing requirements.

The other major factor affecting your decision is the number of people you need to be able to share information with simultaneously. While a spreadsheet may be viewed by several people at once, generally only one person at a time can make amendments to it. With an RDBMS several people can access and amend different individual records at the same time. This makes the data store more of a shared resource.

Small flat file database packages are generally inexpensive, but they are limited in their capabilities. Usually only one person can access and amend the data at a time. In addition, while it is possible to store data in multiple files, a simple database system is unlikely to offer sophisticated data processing or manipulation. Therefore, if you need a large or powerful database application, you should consider an RDBMS.

RDBMS packages range in price from a few hundred pounds to several thousand pounds, often with licensing fees based on the number of simultaneous users that are able to access the data. The larger the system and the more users accessing it, the more you will have to pay. Most packages allow you to start off quite modestly with, for example, a licence for five users which you can increase as your requirements grow. Open source software may provide your business with more cost-effective alternatives to proprietary software. Common database solutions such as MySQL and Ingres will provide your business with RDBMS solutions that you can change to meet your business requirements.

Systems Development

Databases can benefit practically any business that needs to process large amounts of information. Many database products are actually tools that are used to develop specific applications, such as sales ordering systems, ticket reservation systems, inventory management, etc.

Unlike conventional programming languages, database development tools make maintaining and managing structured data files easier. They also impose strict design parameters on developers to ensure that data retains its integrity and accuracy.

For example, most database development systems operate on a commit basis. This means that any changes to data are made in such a way that the data will not be corrupted if the system fails. Similarly, professional database development tools allow multiple users to view and use data simultaneously, which greatly improves the efficiency of these systems.

The primary advantage of using a database development system is that your applications can be specifically tailored to meet your precise requirements. This avoids accepting any compromises by using 'off-the-shelf' packages. Specifying your requirements is a specialist task, so you may need to consult a professional system developer.

Most modern database development systems use structured query language (SQL) processing, which allows data to be analysed and reports to be generated in a wide variety of different ways. Using SQL you can make enquiries of its data and often ask highly specific questions. Generating a report that shows all customers who have ordered products on a Friday afternoon, for example, can then be used to gauge the demand for weekend deliveries.

SQL requires expertise to be used effectively-you may need to consult a professional systems developer. Alternatively, the supplier of your database software may offer consultancy as an add-on.

Potential Drawbacks of Database Development

One of the main benefits of relational database management system (RDBMS) technology is the ability to build applications that are tailored to your business requirements. However, the development of RDBMS applications can be expensive and time-consuming.

You can develop your own applications in-house. However, the skills required are often quite extensive. You may not have the necessary skills available to undertake your own systems development and will have to consider employing outside help.

The Basic Tasks Required to Build an RDBMS Solution Include:

- initial consultancy
- analysis of requirements
- system specification
- database design
- programming
- testing
- implementation
- training
- ongoing maintenance.

Building an RDBMS solution is unlikely to be a quick process and because there are so many steps involved, the costs can escalate.

You should also consider the risk to your business operations if the RDBMS solution fails to meet your specific requirements. The risks are especially high if the solution is intended to be used for your core day-to-day business operations.

You should avoid committing yourself to a system which looks good on paper but which is totally unproven in practice. You could make use of an off-the-shelf solution to provide the core functions of your system, for example the standard financial accounting needs, and build on your own specific requirements in the form of extra modules for functions such as sales order processing or supply chain management. That way you are minimising the overall risk to your business.

Questions to ask a Database Supplier

For many businesses a relational database management system (RDBMS) can be a large investment. Therefore, it is important to choose your supplier carefully as choosing the wrong one could be very expensive and might even jeopardise your business. Before implementing a solution based on RDBMS technology, you might find it useful to ask any potential suppliers the following key questions:

- How long has the supplier been established?
- What are the specific costs associated with its product, i.e. a one-off purchase price, an annual renewable licence, a charge per user, etc.?
- How much is charged for technical support?
- Does the supplier provide consultancy and, if so, at what rates?
- Is the system scalable? If you suddenly increase your product line by 200 per cent could the system grow automatically to cope with the expansion?
- Can the supplier recommend any third-party developers that make use of their RDBMS?
- Is there an active independent user group?
- Can the supplier provide references for businesses in your industry sector using their software?
- Does the supplier offer training in the RDBMS and, if so, at what typical cost?

Supply Chain Software

Ensuring that your own business performs effectively and efficiently is important. However, you probably have to rely on other businesses to supply you with products or services and to supply your products and services to customers. Therefore, you also have to ensure that they operate as effectively and efficiently as possible for you too. Getting this supply chain right can be one of the biggest challenges facing a business.

Supply chain software helps to automate your supply chain. It allows you to monitor and exchange information about orders and deliveries to and from partners, suppliers and customers. This enables you to conduct business with greater speed and accuracy.

This guide explains how supply chain software can benefit your business and how to choose the right system. It also looks at the changes you may have to make to your existing business processes and culture to accommodate the system as well as potential information security issues.

Benefits of Improving the Supply Chain

Supply chain software helps make your supply chain and customer order processes more transparent. As such, it gives you a better understanding of your processes, which brings many benefits.

For example, you can forecast demand and supply more accurately-this allows you to plan your business around customer demands, rather than around your production capabilities. This in turn helps to cut waste-you produce only what is needed, when it is needed and where it is needed.

Supply chain software streamlines your business processes by computerising them. This, together with integration via the internet, speeds up communication between partners and suppliers. Orders are sent more quickly and accurately, and partners can collaborate on a project online.

The main benefits from making these changes are improved performance in delivering on time and lower inventory levels. You can also benefit from better responsiveness to unforeseen events, eg machine failures, staff absences, delivery delays, the receipt of wrong or faulty goods, missing goods, urgent customer orders and human error.

Additional Benefits Include:

- improved planning and scheduling capabilities, due to better visibility
- reduced administration costs, because orders are sent electronically
- reduced costs for logistics, warehousing and manufacturing, due to better planning
- improved decision-making, due to real-time knowledge of sales rates, inventory and production rates
- improved customer service, due to more effective order tracking and automated massaging-eg letting customers know if deliveries will be late
- fewer data errors, due to automated processes.

Assess the Business Requirements

Not every business will gain sufficient benefits from supply chain software to justify the investment. Therefore, it's important to analyse your business requirements to see what the likely need is.

To do this, you need to identify the different processes involved in the supply chain, measure how well they perform, and compare this performance with best practice and marketplace needs. When understanding what your business priorities are, you should try to identify and distinguish between different process types. This will help you assess the likely benefits to be expected from the use of supply chain software. These processes are as follows:

Planning-a process that aligns resources to meet anticipated demand. Planning is a process that's carried out for the long term. It balances aggregated demand-the total demand across all customers for all products-with resources, to ensure that appropriate resources are in place to fulfil requirements when they arise.

Execution-processes that are initiated by actual customer demand or, in some cases, planned forecasts. These include scheduling manufacturing and fulfilment processes, and movement of products, materials and components.

Enable-processes that prepare and manage the information and relationships upon which planning and execution rely, such as agreeing common terminology and part numbers, and other parameters such as ways of expressing size and quantity. Begin by mapping out your supply chain by charting the flow of goods and information through your business. Identify:

- areas where you need to exchange information with partners
- bottlenecks in your supply chain.

Work out Costs Associated with Your Supply Chain, Such as:

- transport
- distribution
- warehousing
- inventory costs.

Use this information to identify where supply chain software will bring the greatest benefits, what business functions you want it to support, and whether this justifies the cost of implementing the software.

Changing Business Processes and Culture

Technology and software play an important part in improving supply chain processes. However, making effective improvements can also involve substantial changes to existing processes and culture inside and outside the business.

Consultation

As a first step, consult with both your suppliers and your customers. You should do this because:

- some businesses may not be used to sharing the quantity and quality of information that is often transferred in a computerised supply chain solution
- customers may highlight existing problems with-and where you can improve on-your current system

Information Sharing

Sharing of information can bring about substantial improvements without any investment in software. Instead, many of the solutions to supply chain issues are found in cultural change.

For example, agreements can be negotiated with both customers and suppliers. These make a general framework to cover multiple purchases, allowing for products to be ordered or cancelled as and when needed without the need for individual purchase contracts. You may then identify changes to quantities, intervals and delivery patterns that benefit all parties.

Information shared between supply chain partners can include:

- inventory levels
- demand forecasts
- customer orders
- delivery information.

Cultural Challenges

Within the organisation, changes to purchasing management can revolutionise supply chain performance. Using other techniques such as keeping stock to a minimum or availability of material at an optimum level, rather than providing incentives for purchasing staff to obtain goods at the absolute lowest cost, can reduce costs and improve performance.

Automation and Integration

For supply chain automation to work effectively, the system must be able to get information on what's happening within your company. Without this information, it can't keep existing or prospective customers accurately informed about their orders.

For companies involved in distribution, warehousing, logistics and transport, this means keeping the system informed about what goods are in transit and where, and what capacity is available now and in the future. This enables the system to respond to customer queries regarding delivery dates and times, to inform customers in the event of any delays or other mishaps, and to quote rapidly and accurately for new work. This type of information may also be on the computer system of another business if your business has outsourced some or all of these functions.

Integration

For companies involved in manufacturing, this entails tight integration with internal business systems and, in turn, with machines on the shop floor.

Tracking

Material will need to be tracked through the business in a way that provides information quickly, accurately and comprehensively. This can be done using a tracking technology such as barcodes or radio frequency identification (RFID). Find out about the basic components of an RFID system on the RFID Centre website-Opens in a new window.

Scheduling

Ideally, job scheduling-eg on the shop floor-should operate automatically, and in real time, in order to be flexible enough to respond to changes and unexpected events. For job planning and scheduling to work in a tightly run supply chain, it must realistically take into account limitations such as staff numbers, machines or material.

Security Issues

Supply chain automation increases both the amount of data that you share and the number of other companies that you share it with. If you don't take appropriate precautions, it could be easier for employees to give away sensitive information, for partners to steal information or commit fraud, and for external parties to gain access to confidential data.

Internal Risk

Most security risks come from within the organisation, not outside it. Therefore you need to control, limit, monitor and manage your employees' access to your internal systems.

This control can be physical, eg a member of staff being prohibited from accessing a computer system kept in a locked office, or logical control, eg where the system software is password-protected. The business' security policy should specify the various levels of control and how they are managed.

Partner Risk

Traditionally, people do business with companies that they know and trust. However, once supply chain automation is in place, it becomes easier to do business with new partners that you don't know, adding to existing security risks.

You therefore need to ensure that transactions with your partners-eg payments and transfers of business-critical documents such as orders and invoices-are secure and authenticated to protect against theft and misuse.

Authentication means confirming that the document is actually from the person who claims to have sent it and that its contents have not been altered. You may also want to ask what security procedures partner companies have to protect data provided by your business.

If you share commercially sensitive information about product development, you should use non-disclosure agreements to reduce the risk of partners passing on this information.

You should implement appropriate password protection to limit access to commercially sensitive information to those who need it.

External Risk

A breach of security could lead to customers leaving you or refusing to use supply chain software. Antivirus software, firewalls, intrusion detection devices and traffic pattern monitoring will help you create an online trading environment that is as secure as possible.

Authorised Economic Operator (AEO) Status

If you trade within the European Union as part of an international supply chain and are actively involved in customs operations, you can apply for AEO status.

The AEO certificate is an internationally recognised quality mark which tells people that:

- your customs controls and procedures are efficient and compliant

- you can be considered a secure and reliable trading partner in the supply chain.

AEOs may benefit from simplifications provided for under the customs rules, or from facilitations of customs controls relating to security and safety.

Here's how Supply Chain Software Improved my Business

The Hi-Technology Group Limited, based in Waterlooville in Hampshire, offers a total manufacturing solution from concept design, rapid tooling and advanced injection moulding. A division of the company, Hi-tech Mouldings Ltd, installed enterprise resource planning (ERP) software to overhaul its entire supply chain. The software has revolutionised the way the business operates, saving time and money and improving customer service. Project manager Chris Moore explains what was done.

What I did

Select a Solution Provider

"There are several routes to automating your supply chain and you have to research the options. Having mapped out our existing supply chain, consulted customers and identified areas for improvement, we attended an ERP vendor forum. It gave us the opportunity to explore different systems and ask questions.

"We decided to go for an 'off-the-shelf' package rather than a bespoke system, but not necessarily because of the cost. We wanted to use the software to rethink our entire supply chain strategy so the plan was to buy the best software to meet our specific requirements and adapt our operation to fit.

"We set up a project team and asked department heads for a wish list of what they would like to see the software achieve. The list was sent to the selected five ERP vendors and we short-listed three to give in-house demonstrations before making our final selection."

Plan the Implementation

"Our chosen solution providers, Lilly Software Associates, were excellent throughout. Working with them, we planned a timetable to implement the software system. It involved integrating everything from customer quotations and ordering, through raw material procurement and workshop scheduling, to despatch and invoicing. The installation, data transfer and testing took several months, but it was worth taking the time to get it right.

"Part of the implementation plan involved staff training and demonstrations to ensure everyone knew exactly what to expect when the new system went live. Thorough planning meant that we didn't lose a single day of production."

Use it to the Full

"One of our criteria in choosing supply chain software was that it had to have potential to develop with our business. We get regular updates from our supplier plus ongoing technical support. We also include an in-house review of the system in our monthly management meeting to monitor performance and plan improvements.

"From the first monthly meeting after going live, it was clear the project had been a success.

"Paperwork is streamlined, because it's all generated from the same system. Estimates are faster and more accurate. Raw materials arrive through the factory door just when we want them and order progress can be tracked at the touch of a button. Overall efficiency has improved because everyone in the business has instant access to all the information they need.

"The system is also a decision-making tool. For example, the data it generates enabled us to spot a potential bottleneck in our forward order schedule. As a result, we have invested in two new machines within the last six months."

What I'd do Differently

Don't Underestimate the Work

"To get the most out of supply chain software, you have to invest time as well as money. Even knowing that, we probably underestimated the amount of work involved."

Investigate Grants

"Supply chain software is a big investment. We funded it ourselves and expect to see a return on our investment within 18 months. But looking back, we may have been able to get financial support through our local Business Link to reduce some of the initial consultancy and setup costs."

Open Source Software

Open source software can be obtained by businesses for little or no cost. Developed and supported globally by IT professionals it provides an alternative to more traditional forms of proprietary software. Open source software is available for most business needs, including content management systems, databases, office tools, operating systems, internet related applications and IT security.

Unlike proprietary software, open source gives you access to the source code, providing you with the opportunity to develop the software for your own business requirements. Whilst most open source solutions lack the customer support and legal protection provided by proprietary software, open source can provide businesses with powerful, secure, well supported and cost effective solutions.

This guide will help you understand how you can use open source software in your business, and how to get training and support. It looks at some of the issues with open source software and shows you where to download some of the most popular applications. There is also additional information for IT professionals.

Open Source Software

Cost Benefits of Open Source Software

Many business owners choose to use open source software because it has little or no up-front cost. This is obviously a huge benefit, especially to new businesses, but you need to consider budgeting for support, training, and in the case of more complex applications, consultancy.

You should take time to assess the total cost of ownership for any software you intend to deploy. Will it require additional hardware, or will it need specialised technical staff? As with proprietary applications the vast proportion of the total cost of any open source software will be the cost of operations and of maintenance.

One key advantage of open source over the proprietary alternatives is that it simplifies your licence management issues. There's no need to ensure that all your servers and desktops have the right type or number of licences-you just need to download the software once and install it as many times and places as you want or need.

It's important to comply with the license restrictions, as these have the same legal basis as proprietary software licences. It's also important to read licences carefully, as there are many different open source licences, with as many different requirements.

Training and Support Options for Open Source Software

Support for open source applications can come from three different routes. In many cases a self-service approach using online community resources and search engines works well. More complex problems can be solved by talking directly with the developers, and possibly paying for consultancy or taking out a support contract. Alternatively you will find a number of service providers who have certified key open source applications, and who offer a range of different support services.

Support services are starting to become available for more widely used open source software. There is also often an online community of people who use the software and share tips and hints, and these community resources are an invaluable resource. If something does go wrong with a less popular application, finding an IT specialist with experience of using the software can be difficult and also costly. You'll also find well known IT providers like Microsoft, Oracle, IBM and HP offering open source support, as well as providing tools for integrating open source with their own proprietary solutions.

Many of the more popular open source business models revolve around charging for support and training. Some developers allow users to obtain the software for free, but then charge for support. You can purchase package solutions from some software companies that provide software, along with a year's support, while other open source software providers will not offer any support at all.

You will also need to consider what level of training is needed for employees on how to use the software, who will carry out this training and what they charge. It's often worth investing in a 'train the trainer' approach with open source tools, building your own internal training skills to keep total costs to a minimum. Some businesses develop their own in-house support and training for open source software because this can be less costly in the long term.

There are some not-for-profit organisations, such as Seeds for Change, which may be able to offer your business free training, support and advice on open source software.

Examples of Popular Open Source Products and Types

Whatever applications your business needs-whether it is a word processing solution, accounting software, customer relationship management software or website applications-you'll find it easy to find an open source version. Numerous sites like Source Forge act as central repositories for open source applications, and are good places to look for new software.

It is important to remember that the quality of what is available may vary. It's a good idea to look for software with a lot of users, as there'll be a large community who can provide help and support. Popular software also makes it likely that there will be commercial support and training services.

Some popular open source software options include:

Office Software

- Abiword-word processing tool
- Alfresco-enterprise content management system
- Joomla-enterprise content management system
- Open Office.org-business productivity suite
- Drupal-content management
- Chandler-contact management and collaboration
- SugarCRM-customer relationship management
- MySQL-database
- Ingres-database.

Operating Systems

- GNU/Linux (various versions or distributions include Debian, Fedora, Gentoo, Ubuntu and Red Hat)-operating system
- Open Solaris-operating system
- FreeBSD-operating system
- Android-mobile phone platform.

Internet-Related Applications

- Juice-podcasting
- Mozilla Firefox-web browser
- Mozilla Thunderbird-email client
- Pidgin-instant massaging

- Zimbra-email and collaboration server
- Apache-web server
- Zope-web application server
- PHP-web application platform
- Wordpress-blog hosting platform
- MediaWiki-information sharing platform.

IT Security

- Smoothwall-firewall and security tools
- Wireshark (aka Ethereal)-security application
- KeePass-password management
- Clam AV-antivirus software.

Images/Multi-Media

- GIMP-image processing/graphics editing
- VLC-multimedia file playback
- Ogg-open video and audio codecs.

Development Tools

- Ruby on Rails-rapid web application development
- Eclipse-integrated development environment.

Before downloading and installing open source software you should carry out the same due diligence as you would for proprietary applications. Check on the internet for reviews to get an idea of what other people think about the software and any issues they have had with it, and also read through any online support forums to understand any possible issues.

How to Gather Detailed Information on Specific Software

Before deciding to start using any open source software it is a good idea to do some research to see what other people think of it. There are several things you can do:

- Check whether the software has its own website where you can learn more about its uses.
- Learn about the team behind the application, and their plans for its future.
- Look for online reviews and join any community forums for users to see what other people think of the software.

- Contact other businesses through the community support group (if there is one) to ask about their experiences of using the software.
- Find out whether there is an IT support company with specialist knowledge of the software. See whether they will do some consultancy work with your business to assess whether the software will suit your needs.
- Find advice on the Free Software Foundation website-Opens in a new window.
- Understand the licence in use. Find information on the restrictions and benefits of most common open source licences on the Open Source Initiative's website-Opens in a new window.
- Contact your local university to see whether they can offer any advice-many universities and higher education establishments make use of open source software and some also have a commercial open source operation.

Choosing an IT Consultant

As open source software becomes more popular there are more IT consultants with expertise around some of the packages available. Some newer or less popular software may have less help and support available. Because of this some businesses decide to develop their own in-house expertise.

If you are going to appoint an IT consultant-for implementation help and advice, training or ongoing support-you should look for someone with experience of the specific software package if possible.

Getting a recommendation from someone else is a good way to find an IT consultant. You could contact other businesses through the software's community support group (if there is one) to ask whether any can recommend a consultant. You could also contact your local university to see whether they can offer any advice-many universities and higher education establishments make use of open source software.

Before appointing a consultant there are several questions you should ask. These include:

- Have they worked with businesses similar to yours in the past? You could also ask to see references or to be put in contact with one of its customers.

- How long have they been working with the particular piece of open source software? Who is the member of staff that will be your key contact and how experienced are they?
- What do they charge and when and how will the help be available? Is there a 24-hour helpline, for example? How quickly can they help if there is a problem?
- Do they offer training for your staff?
- Have other businesses had any major problems with implementing the software and will the software work with your existing systems?

Licensing and Legal Issues

Open source licences can be a source of some confusion. In practice open source licences give you access to the source code of an application, along with the ability to make changes. In general you will find that most licences allow you to use software for most common business uses. It's a good idea to read the terms of any software licence before you use the software to understand its terms and conditions. Most licences are written in plain English, and are very straightforward. It's important to note that you will get little or no warranty.

Open source licences take advantage of the ability of a licence to give rights above and beyond those enshrined in copyright law. This includes the ability to edit, modify and share the underlying source code-letting you tailor the software to your business needs.

Legal Issues

There are a number of legal issues to be aware of when using open source software. It's important to ensure that you remain compliant with the licence associated with the software you're using-especially if you're making your own changes to the software.

The Free Software Foundation, an organisation that protects the rights of free software users and developers, can investigate businesses that breach licence terms. This organisation monitors open source implementations to look for licence breaches, and try to ensure businesses comply with open source and free software licences.

There is always a risk that the open source software may not have been as rigorously tested as other software on the market. However, it can also be argued that because the code has usually been seen and modified by developers worldwide, it could in fact have fewer flaws than other software on the market. This can act as a balance to the extremely limited warranties offered with open source applications, which leave you with little recourse in the event of a significant failure or outage.

Information for IT Professionals

One of the key benefits of open source software is that a user has access to the source code. As a result open source software provides flexible business solutions, allowing you to customise and extend applications to meet your needs. Developers can respond to business requirements and innovate quickly, drawing on a mix of in-house resources, consultants, service providers and the open source community. However, when changing or adding to open source code it is important to look at the license to see what your legal obligations are.

Legal Requirements for Open Source Development

Open source licenses include the ability to edit, modify and share the underlying source code-letting you tailor the software to your business needs. But there are a variety of open source licenses, and they each differ in their legal requirements.

Three of the most common licenses are the GNU General Public License (GPL), the Lesser GPL License (LGPL) and the Berkeley Standard Distribution License (BSD).

The GPL requires any changes you make to the source code to be made available to other users of the software. The LGPL lets you mix elements of open source software with new proprietary applications, without making the whole application publicly available. The BSD lets you do whatever you want with the source code, without the requirement to share it with the rest of the world.

If you're planning on building open source tools into software and selling it, it's worth looking for software that comes with dual licences-an open source version and a paid-for version that lets you keep any changes you make. The commercial license releases businesses from the requirement to make changes to the software open source.

Intellectual Property

If a licence requires any modifications be made available to the wider community, make sure you don't include passwords and specific business intellectual property, which might increase risks to your business. While most data protection and other business regulations don't apply to source code, it's important that you do apply appropriate governance to any software release procedure.

Payroll Software

Using payroll software can speed up the process of calculating pay accurately, and making payments on time. It can reduce the burden of understanding complex payroll legislation and payroll systems operation. As a consequence, it can also reduce administrative costs.

Payroll is a business-critical operation for every organisation-people must be paid accurately and on time. It is therefore essential to train staff properly, and implement procedures and disaster recovery plans to ensure payroll system continuity.

It is important to select a reliable supplier. Unlike most other business functions, you are dependent on a payroll supplier not only for training, support and help if things go wrong, but also for regular updates when tax and other figures change, and when there are alterations to legislation.

The Advantages of Payroll Software

The most obvious benefit of payroll software is that payroll calculations-such as tax and National Insurance deductions-can be completed in a fraction of the time that they take to work out manually. Year-end reporting is also usually automated, and both payslips and annual reports are archived in case copies are needed later.

Time Recording

Payroll systems can also incorporate, or integrate with, timesheet systems that record employee attendance or time worked. In this way, information about hours worked, whether collected automatically as a user or operator logs into a system, or manually entered into an electronic form, can be automatically transferred into the payroll system.

Reporting

Using basic payroll data, together with data on attendance and hours worked, payroll systems can provide a wealth of reports. This allows in-depth analysis of staff costs for the business as a whole, across departments and even individual jobs and contracts.

Storing Personnel Records

Most organisations will also keep other data about employees, such as records of annual leave. This type of information is usually associated with the broader human resources function. You can get payroll systems that will record these additional types of information, avoiding the need for a separate software package.

Planning

The ability of payroll packages to provide forecasts means you can plan staff costs and budgets by entering hypothetical numbers to see the exact total cost of an employee.

Assess the Business Requirements for Payroll Software

Not every business needs payroll software. If there are no complications, and if the business is relatively small, manual payroll calculations can be quite straightforward.

Bought Software Versus HM Revenue & Customs (HMRC) CD-Rom

Whether or not you need to buy software depends largely on the size of your business. If you only have a few employees, the cost of the software may outweigh the time you save using it.

Payroll software usually requires an annual subscription, in addition to the initial purchase cost, in order to obtain regular updates to tax and National Insurance rates, and information on changing legislation that can affect payroll calculations.

HMRC now offers a basic calculator for tax and National Insurance contributions, and provides this free of charge to all employers, on CD-Rom. Although this cannot yet replace either a manual or computerised system completely, it can save time in producing payroll calculations and may be sufficient for some smaller businesses.

Who Will use the Software?

When choosing the best option for you, consider the expertise available within your business. For example, who handles your payroll when the company accountant is absent? You may find it easier to train someone else to operate the basic payroll run if they have the benefit of a suitable software package, rather than having to carry out the calculations manually.

What Will Happen if There's a Problem?

You should also consider business continuity. If you manage payroll using a computer, that computer will become business-critical. Therefore you will need to plan support, backups of data and disaster recovery plans. It is always possible to revert to a manual system if there is an emergency, but you should be aware that using payroll software makes you reliant on your computer system.

Payroll Software Capabilities

Payroll software can do many pay-related calculations. However, you will still need to input and maintain certain data for each of your employees.

What Payroll Software Can Do

Any payroll software will take over the routine calculation of ordinary payroll requirements such as tax and National Insurance contributions (NICs). It will also calculate the NICs that you have to pay as an employer. It will allow you to pay people at monthly or weekly intervals, as appropriate.

Payroll Software will also:

- calculate student loan and other deductions
- produce payslips for your employees
- produce payment reports to allow you to pay employees, showing the amount to be paid to each employee
- keep records of payments and deductions
- produce year-end reports and documentation for you and your employees
- produce the necessary figures or documentation when an employee leaves.

What Payroll Software Can't Do

While payroll software will do automatic calculations for you, there will still be administrative work for you to do.

In addition to inputting an employee's details when they start their employment, you will need to make changes when their rates of pay increase or decrease. You will also need to change tax codes when notifications are received. You may also need to enter details of hours worked and overtime.

There are also many possible deductions from pay such as employer loans and pensions. Even if the software can automatically calculate some or all of these, you will still need to key in the details for each employee to whom they apply. This information will have to be updated when appropriate.

Payroll Software Operation

Once computerised, the payroll function should be operated by someone with appropriate knowledge and training. The operator will need to understand the relevant accountancy practices and statutory requirements, especially if you plan to use manual operation in the event of a system failure.

Backup Plans

You need a backup plan for when the usual operator is ill, on holiday or otherwise unavailable. Alternatively, you may want to consider making arrangements for your business' accountants to provide emergency cover.

You should have backup copies of the payroll data, of which at least one should be stored off-site and with appropriate security, eg in a fireproof safe. You may find it most practical for both security and continuity purposes to run payroll software on a dedicated computer and printer to avoid any disruption to the payroll system by the failure of other software.

Privacy

You need to comply with the Data Protection Act 1998, even if your use of personal data does not require you to register with the Information Commissioner. You must keep only essential information-it should be kept securely for no longer than is necessary, in order to preserve confidentiality and prevent unauthorised access.

Access to payroll information should be controlled using appropriate passwords and, ideally, physical protection such as an office to which access is restricted.

Similarly, you will need to secure paper-based information, such as payslips, probably by employing physical security, eg keeping them locked away. Trial runs and tests, such as a payroll reports run to check that employee data has been entered correctly and that calculations are being performed correctly, should be destroyed.

Security

There are additional security measures you may need to take. If possible, at least two people should be involved in managing the payroll process, from inputting data to authorising the payroll run. Actual payments should only be made with whatever authorisation is usually appropriate in your business.

Comprehensive, accurate and timely reporting can help to reveal any discrepancies, such as mistakes in inputting hours, rates of pay and other data.

Payroll Software Functionality

Any payroll software will carry out basic calculations for pay, such as tax and National Insurance deductions. However, if you need to make other deductions you should check that any payroll software you use can handle these.

Pay Intervals

Weekly and monthly pay intervals are standard, but if you have different requirements you should check that these are supported. You may also want to check whether the software can handle pension scheme administration.

Multiple Usage

Smaller businesses may only require support for a single payroll operator at a time, but you should check that multiple user operation is available just in case you need it in future.

Reporting

Some basic end-of-year reports will be included as standard, but check that everything you need is supported. If necessary, look for a package that will calculate and prepare P11D forms and provide the relevant figures to give to employees to allow them to complete their tax returns.

Data Presentation

All payroll software will tell you the amounts that need to be paid to employees and HM Revenue & Customs (HMRC), but check that this information can be used in a way that meets your requirements. For example, you may want the software to print cheques for you, or just to give you figures to help write cheques yourself or use for electronic payment.

Personnel Records

Additional features may include the calculation and recording of holiday entitlements, self-service to allow employees to request or book annual leave online, and tracking sick leave.

In addition, some packages may be able to keep records such as job position history, previous employment history, education and academic qualifications, references, skills and competencies and training records.

Integration

Integration with the main accounting system to enable payroll costs to be automatically transferred is highly desirable. Expenses information is required to complete P11D forms, so it helps if the payroll system offers or integrates with expense reporting systems. If the system can record information regarding car administration, this can also help with the preparation of data used in completing P11Ds.

Reporting and Analysis Using Payroll Software

At a minimum, payroll software must produce payslips. However, it is also useful if you can run pay and personnel-related reports.

Payslips

Before you acquire any software, check whether it can print onto normal stationery or whether a special size or pre-printed stationery is required, and if so, how much it costs. It usually makes more sense to print any necessary forms directly onto blank paper or labels if the quantities are small. It can also be useful to be able to reprint payslips in the event of a problem.

Check whether the software needs special stationery for employee P60 forms at the tax year-end. Again, printing the form onto plain paper is often the better option. To ensure privacy, payslips should be printed on a printer that employees do not have access to. In some cases, you may prefer to use security stationery that cannot be read until opened by the recipient. If this is important, you should also check that the software is compatible with such stationery.

Reports

Payroll systems will provide information either on paper or electronically to update nominal ledgers, and a whole range of other reports are possible. Some will allow a high level of detail in the information passed to the ledgers, allowing accounting to distinguish between departments, managers and even individual jobs.

Software can also report on compliance with National Minimum Wage legislation and, if time and attendance information is recorded, the Working Time Regulations. If sickness and holidays are recorded in the payroll package, then these can readily be reported on too, together with other absences such as maternity, adoption and paternity leave.

Choosing a Payroll Software Supplier

Payroll software is extremely complex and it is essential that you choose a dependable supplier. Check that the supplier is successful, financially viable and can provide excellent references. These factors should take precedence over the temptation to choose existing suppliers.

HM Revenue & Customs (HMRC) Accredited Software

Ensure that software is accredited under the HMRC Payroll Standard Accreditation Scheme. This scheme covers accreditation in:

- calculation of tax and National Insurance contributions
- electronic exchange of HMRC returns and payments
- customer service
- handling of statutory records, credits and deductions.

The Scheme is updated regularly and all software packages are tested annually to ensure that they remain compliant with current legislation. Find out about the Payroll Standard Accreditation Scheme at the HMRC website-Opens in a new window.

An alternative is to use the HMRC Employer CD-Rom, which comes as part of the New Employer Starter Pack. You can order the pack by contacting the HMRC New Employer Helpline on Tel 0845 60 70 143. You can read about the Employer CD-Rom on the HMRC website-Opens in a new window.

Electronic Filing

Electronic filing of HMRC returns and payments can save time and trouble. Any supplier should provide electronic filing for some forms, and ideally all those that can be filed electronically.

If you employ fewer than 50 employees you can get a tax-free payment from HMRC if you file certain end-of-year forms online. Read our guide on how to file returns online.

Ask potential suppliers how quickly they've responded to producing software for new electronic submissions.

4

Computer Age in Business

The Information Age, also commonly known as the Computer Age or Information Era, is an idea that the current age will be characterized by the ability of individuals to transfer information freely, and to have instant access to knowledge that would have been difficult or impossible to find previously. The idea is linked to the concept of a Digital Age or Digital Revolution, and carries the ramifications of a shift from traditional industry that the Industrial Revolution brought through industrialization, to an economy based around the manipulation of information. The period is generally said to have begun in the latter half of the 20th century, though the particular date varies. Since the invention of social media in the early 21st century, some have claimed that the Information Age has evolved into the Attention Age.

The term has been widely used since the late 1980s and into the 21st century.

The Internet

The Internet was originally conceived as a distributed, fail-proof network that could connect computers together and be resistant to any one point of failure; the Internet cannot be totally destroyed in one event, and if large areas are disabled, the information is easily re-routed. It was created mainly by ARPA; its initial software applications were email and computer file transfer.

It was with the invention of the World Wide Web in 1989 that the Internet truly became a global network. Today the Internet has become the ultimate platform for accelerating the flow of information and is, today, the fastest-growing form of media.

What's more is that the very notion of our actions, our endeavors and especially our mistakes, being perfectly archived is somewhat terrifying to say the least, no matter what level of accepted virtue or morality we may possess. There is a stronger sense of urgency to obtain success and well being in these modern times. People are more intellectually engaged than ever before, because of The Internet.

Progression

In 1956 in the United States, researchers noticed that the number of people holding "white collar" jobs had just exceeded the number of people holding "blue collar" jobs. These researchers realized that this was an important change, as it was clear that the Industrial Age was coming to an end. As the Industrial Age ended, the newer times adopted the title of "the Information Age".

At that time, relatively few jobs had much to do with computers and computer-related technology. There was a steady trend away from people holding Industrial Age manufacturing jobs. An increasing number of people held jobs as clerks in stores, office workers, teachers, nurses, etc. The Western world was shifting into a service economy.

Eventually, Information and Communication Technology—computers, computerized machinery, fiber optics, communication satellites, Internet, and other ICT tools—became a significant part of the economy. Microcomputers were developed and many business and industries were greatly changed by ICT.

Nicholas Negroponte captured the essence of these changes in his 1995 book, Being Digital. *His book discusses similarities and differences between products made of atoms and products made of bits. In essence, one can very cheaply and quickly make a copy of a product made of bits, and ship it across the country or around the world both quickly and at very low cost.*

Thus, the term "Information Age" is often applied in relation to the use of cell phones, digital music, high definition television, digital cameras, the Internet, computer games, and other relatively new products and services that have come into widespread use.

Information Revolution

The term information revolution (sometimes called also the "information*al* revolution") describes current economic, social and technological trends beyond the Industrial Revolution.

Many competing terms have been proposed that focus on different aspects of this societal development.

The British polymath crystallographer J. D. Bernal (1939) introduced the term "scientific and technical revolution" in his book *The Social Function of Science* in order to describe the new role that science and technology are coming to play within society. He asserted that science is becoming a "productive force", using the Marxist Theory of Productive Forces.

After some controversy, the term was taken up by authors and institutions of the then-Soviet Bloc. Their aim was to show that socialism was a safe home for the scientific and technical ("technological" for some authors) revolution, referred to by the acronym STR. The book *Civilization at the Crossroads*, edited by the Czech philosopher Radovan Richta (1969), became a standard reference for this topic.

Daniel Bell (1980) challenged this theory and advocated *Post Industrial Society*, which would lead to a service economy rather than socialism. Many other authors presented their views, including Zbigniew Kazimierz Brzezinski (1976) with his "Technetronic Society".

The main feature of the information revolution is the economic, social and technological role of information. Information is the central theme of several new sciences, which emerged in the 1940s, including Shannon's (1949) *Information Theory* and Wiener's (1948) *Cybernetics*. Wiener (1948, p. 155) stated also: "information is information not matter or energy". This aphorism suggests that information should be considered along with matter and energy as the third constituent part of the Universe; information is carried by matter or energy.

We can distinguish between information, data and knowledge. Data comes through research and collection. Information is organized data. Knowledge is built upon information. Data and information are easily transferrable; knowledge built by a person is not certain that it can be transferred to another. Following this, the notion of a "knowledge society" cannot be defined cogently.

Information is then further considered as an economic activity, since firms and institutions are involved in its production, collection, exchange, distribution, circulation, processing, transmission, and control. Labour is also divided into physical labour (use of muscle power) and informational labour (use of intellectual power).

A new economic sector is thereby identified, the Information Sector, which amalgamates information-related labour activities. Porat (1976) measured the Information Sector in the US using the input-output analysis; OECD has included statistics on the Information Sector in the economic reports of its member countries.

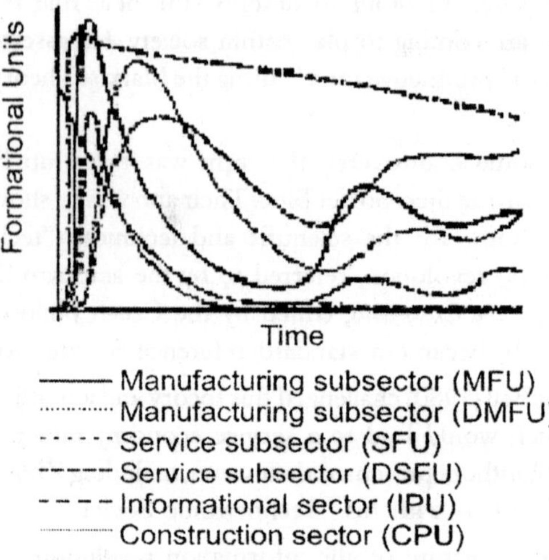

Modelling the Informational Revolution.

Source: Veneris (1984)

Veneris (1984, 1990) explored the theoretical, economic and regional aspects of the Informational Revolution and developed a systems dynamics simulation computer model.

These works can be seen as following the path originated with the work of Fritz Machlup who in his (1962) book "The Production and Distribution of Knowledge in the United States", claimed that the "knowledge industry represented 29% of the US gross national product", which he saw as evidence that the Information Age has begun. He defines knowledge as a commodity and attempts to measure the magnitude of the production and distribution of this commodity within a modern economy. Machlup divided information use into three classes: instrumental, intellectual, and pastime knowledge. He identified also five types of knowledge: practical knowledge; intellectual knowledge, that is, general culture and the satisfying of intellectual curiosity; pastime knowledge, that is, knowledge satisfying non-intellectual curiosity or the desire for light entertainment and emotional stimulation; spiritual or religious knowledge; unwanted knowledge, accidentally acquired and aimlessly retained The term Information Revolution may be preferred to terms such as "Information Economy/Society", in order to relate to the widely used terms Agricultural Revolution and Industrial Revolution. The activities which constitute the growing Information Sector did not come up with the Information Revolution. They existed, in one form or the other, in all human societies, and eventually developed into institutions, such as the Platonic Academy, Aristotle's Peripatetic school in the Lyceum, the Museum and the Library of Alexandria, or the schools of Babylonian astronomy. The Agricultural Revolution and the Industrial Revolution came up when new informational inputs were produced by individual innovators, or by scientific and technical institutions. During the Information Revolution all these activities are experiencing continuous growth, while other information-oriented activities are emerging.

Fiang Irving (1997) identified six 'Information Revolutions': writing, printing, mass media, entertainment, the 'toolshed' (which we call 'home' now), and the Information Highway. In this work the term 'information revolution' is used in a narrow sense, to describe trends in communication media. The following fundamental aspects of the theory of the Informational Revolution can be given (Veneris 1984, 1990); these define also the Informational Revolution:

1. The object of economic activities can be conceptualised according to the fundamental distinction between matter, energy, and information. These apply both to the object of each economic activity, as well as within each economic activity or enterprise. For instance, an industry may process matter (e.g. iron) using energy and information (production and process technologies, management, etc.).
2. Information is a factor of production (along with capital, labour, land (economics)), as well as a product sold in the market, that is, a commodity. As such, it acquires use value and exchange value, and therefore a price.
3. All products have use value, exchange value, and informational value. The latter can be measured by the information content of the product, in terms of innovation, design, etc.
4. Industries develop information-generating activities, the so-called Research and Development (R&D) functions.
5. Enterprises, and society at large, develop the information control and processing functions, in the form of management structures; these are also called "white-collar workers", "bureaucracy", "managerial functions", etc.

6. Labour can be classified according to the object of labour, into information labour and non-information labour.
7. Information activities constitute a large, new economic sector, the information sector along with the traditional primary sector, secondary sector, and tertiary sector, according to the three-sector hypothesis. These should be restated because they are based on the ambiguous definitions made by Colin Clark (1940), who included in the tertiary sector all activities that have not been included in the primary (agriculture, forestry, etc.) and secondary (manufacturing) sectors. The quaternary sector and the quinary sector of the economy attempt to classify these new activities, but their definitions are not based on a clear conceptual scheme, although the latter is considered by some as equivalent with the information sector.
8. From a strategic point of view, sectors can be defined as information sector, means of production, means of consumption, thus extending the classical Ricardo-Marx model of the Capitalist mode of production. Marx stressed in many occasions the role of the "intellectual element" in production, but failed to find a place for it into his model.
9. Innovations are the result of the production of new information, as new products, new methods of production, patents, etc. Their diffusion manifests saturation effects (related term: market saturation), following certain cyclical patterns and creating "economic waves", also referred to as "business cycles". There are various types of waves, such as Kondratiev (54 years), Kuznets (18 years), Juglar (9 years) and Kitchin (about 4 years) distinguished by their nature, duration, and, thus, economic impact.
10. Innovations cause structural-sectoral shifts in the economy, which can be smooth or can create crisis and renewal, a process which Joseph Schumpeter called vividly "creative destruction".

How to Take Your Business to Internet

Since the invention of the Internet, the world has never been the same. Many brick-and-mortar stores cannot keep up with the ever-booming Internet marketing business. This is mainly due to the extremely low cost of doing business online. For the people who think the Internet marketing is a risk, they have not understood how to do properly it. There are many types of free advertising that you can do for your business online.

Taking your business online can be a cost-effective and extremely profitable move. Nevertheless, before you throw up any type of random website in hopes of making it big, there are a few learning curves you have to get over. Knowing how to drive targeted traffic to your website is one of these learning curves. What this means is that you have to know the mindset of your customers. Having a good knowledge of your customers should be any businesses goal. When advertising online, it is all about mindset. What is the person thinking about when they type in certain keywords into the search engines?

For instance, if I were to type in the search engines this "how to rank my website in the search engines" I am then looking for information about ranking a website in the search engines. However, if I type something like this "hiring a search engine optimization expert" I am looking to buy for a search engine optimization expert. This is called the commercial intent of your visitors.

Each of the search queries I listed above have a specific way of driving traffic to your website. Take the information-based search, if you want to drive traffic from this type of query, then you simply write an article on whatever keyword that is typed. For queries that are based around buying something, you would then want to provide a review.

Driving traffic to your online website is the lifeblood of your Internet success. Without quality targeted traffic there is no point in having a website. After you have built up enough traffic to your site, you now need to start capturing that traffic for recurring business. You do this by capturing their name in e-mails and building a responsive list.

By providing a newsletter to your traffic, you can then have them frequently return to your website. Having a newsletter gives you a good advantage of building trust with your customers, these increases their ability to buy something from you.

Before you, consider starting an online Internet business, making a strategic plan of how to get targeted traffic, and then how to compound that traffics with a newsletter is your first task to overcome. Once you have mastered getting traffic to your site everything else is simple.

As our economy has become increasingly dependent on computers, more and more retailers have joined the electronic age. But some are still hanging back, continuing to do things the "old-fashioned way." While there may be a certain satisfaction in tracking inventory and balancing accounts by hand, pencil and paper techniques definitely belong in the dust bin. With the rest of the world "going electronic," sticking with outdated methods will outdate you as well.

One company that plugs retailers into the electronic age is ARS Solutions Ltd., headed by Jeff Helland. The company develops point-of-sale and inventory management software, and services about 700 retailers nationwide.

Three years ago ARS took a survey which indicated that about 60 percent of retailers had some kind of a computer in their business. This number is higher today, but just because a retailer owns a computer, that doesn't mean he uses it.

"Where the numbers really got small was in what they used computers for," Helland said. "One person might be doing inventory management, another may be doing a little bookkeeping, someone else may be using it for target ranges, and membership and range fees. But a fair percentage of them are just collecting dust."

So? What difference does it make if you're part of the 30-something percent of retailers who don't own computers, or who use them for paperweights?

"What it comes down to is that computers are involved in so many different things in business today," Helland said. "There are a lot of places a computer can either save you money or create new revenues. But if you never go through the learning process, you never know how to use those functions. It's not just what you miss, it's that you don't know what you're missing."

Once you've gotten your accounts payable up and running, you'll to see what a computer can do for you. Then you can begin to surf the Internet, track your inventory, and do many other useful tasks.

5

Cloud Computing and its Role in Business

Cloud Computing

Cloud computing is Internet-("cloud-") based development and use of computer technology ("computing"). In concept, it is a paradigm shift whereby details are abstracted from the users who no longer need knowledge of, expertise in, or control over the technology infrastructure "in the cloud" that supports them. It typically involves the provision of dynamically scalable and often virtualized resources as a service over the Internet. The term *cloud* is used as a metaphor for the Internet, based on how the Internet is depicted in computer network diagrams and is an abstraction of the underlying infrastructure it conceals. Typical cloud computing providers deliver common business applications online which are accessed from a web browser, while the software and data are stored on the servers.

These applications are broadly divided into the following categories: Software as a Service (SaaS), Utility Computing, Web Services, Platform as a Service (PaaS), Managed Service Providers (MSP), Service Commerce, and Internet Integration. The name cloud computing was inspired by the cloud symbol that is often used to represent the Internet in flow charts and diagrams."

Overview

Comparisons

Cloud computing can be confused with:

1. Grid computing — "a form of distributed computing, whereby

a 'super and virtual computer' is composed of a cluster of networked, loosely coupled computers acting in concert to perform very large tasks"

2. Utility computing — the "packaging of computing resources, such as computation and storage, as a metered service similar to a traditional public utility, such as electricity";
3. Autonomic computing — "computer systems capable of self-management".

Indeed, many cloud computing deployments depend on grids, have autonomic characteristics, and bill like utilities, but cloud computing tends to expand what is provided by grids and utilities. Some successful cloud architectures have little or no centralized infrastructure or billing systems whatsoever, including peer-to-peer networks such as BitTorrent and Skype, and volunteer computing such as SETI@home.

Characteristics

In general, cloud computing customers do not own the physical infrastructure, instead avoiding capital expenditure by renting usage from a third-party provider. They consume resources as a service and pay only for resources that they use. Many cloud-computing offerings employ the utility computing model, which is analogous to how traditional utility services (such as electricity) are consumed, whereas others bill on a subscription basis. Sharing "perishable and intangible" computing power among multiple tenants can improve utilization rates, as servers are not unnecessarily left idle (which can reduce costs significantly while increasing the speed of application development). A side-effect of this approach is that overall computer usage rises dramatically, as customers do not have to engineer for peak load limits. In addition, "increased high-speed bandwidth" makes it possible to receive the same response times from centralized infrastructure at other sites.

Economics

Diagram showing economics of cloud computing versus traditional IT, including capital expenditure (CapEx) and operational expenditure (OpEx)

Cloud computing users can avoid capital expenditure (CapEx) on hardware, software, and services when they pay a provider only for what they use. Consumption is usually billed on a utility (e.g., resources consumed, like electricity) or subscription (e.g., time-based, like a newspaper) basis with little or no upfront cost. A few cloud providers are now beginning to offer the service for a flat monthly fee as opposed to on a utility billing basis. Other benefits of this time sharing-style approach are low barriers to entry, shared infrastructure and costs, low management overhead, and immediate access to a broad range of applications. In general, users can terminate the contract at any time (thereby avoiding return on investment risk and uncertainty), and the services are often covered by service level agreements (SLAs) with financial penalties.

According to Nicholas Carr, the strategic importance of information technology is diminishing as it becomes standardized and less expensive. He argues that the cloud computing paradigm shift is similar to the displacement of electricity generators by electricity grids early in the 20th century.

Although companies might be able to save on upfront capital expenditures, they might not save much and might actually pay more for operating expenses. In situations where the capital expense would be relatively small, or where the organization has more flexibility in their capital budget than their operating budget, the cloud model might not make great fiscal sense. Other factors impacting the scale of any potential cost savings include the efficiency of a company's data centre as compared to the cloud vendor's, the company's existing operating costs, the level of adoption of cloud computing, and the type of functionality being hosted in the cloud.

Architecture

The majority of cloud computing infrastructure, as of 2009, consists of reliable services delivered through data centres and built on servers with different levels of virtualization technologies. The services are accessible anywhere that provides access to networking infrastructure. Clouds often appear as single points of access for all consumers' computing needs. Commercial offerings are generally expected to meet quality of service (QoS) requirements of customers and typically offer SLAs. Open standards are critical to the growth of cloud computing, and open source software has provided the foundation for many cloud computing implementations.

History

The Cloud *is a term that borrows from telephony. Up to the 1990s, data circuits (including those that carried Internet traffic) were hard-wired between destinations. Then, long-haul telephone companies began offering Virtual Private Network (VPN) service for data communications. Telephone companies were able to offer VPN-based services with the same guaranteed bandwidth as fixed circuits at a lower cost because they could switch traffic to balance utilization as they saw fit, thus utilizing their overall network bandwidth more effectively. As a result of this arrangement, it was impossible to determine in advance precisely which paths the traffic would be routed over. The term "telecom cloud" was used to describe this type of networking, and cloud computing is in concept somewhat similar.*

The underlying concept of cloud computing dates back to 1960, when John McCarthy opined that "computation may someday be organized as a public utility"; indeed it shares characteristics with service bureaus that date back to the 1960s. In 1997, the first academic definition was provided by Ramnath K. Chellappa who called it a computing paradigm where the boundaries of computing will be determined by economic rationale rather than technical limits. *The term* cloud *had already come into commercial use in the early 1990s to refer to large Asynchronous Transfer Mode (ATM) networks.*

Loudcloud, founded in 1999 by Marc Andreessen, was one of the first to attempt to commercialize cloud computing with an Infrastructure as a Service model. By the turn of the 21st century, the term "cloud computing" began to appear more widely, although most of the focus at that time was limited to SaaS, called "ASP's" or Application Service Providers, under the terminology of the day.

In the early 2000s, Microsoft extended the concept of SaaS through the development of web services. IBM detailed these concepts in 2001 in the Autonomic Computing Manifesto, which described advanced automation techniques such as self-monitoring, self-healing, self-configuring, and self-optimizing in the management of complex IT systems with heterogeneous storage, servers, applications, networks, security mechanisms, and other system elements that can be virtualized across an enterprise.

Amazon played a key role in the development of cloud computing by modernizing their data centres after the dot-com bubble, which, like most computer networks, were using as little as 10% of their capacity at any one time just to leave room for occasional spikes. Having found that the new cloud architecture resulted in significant internal efficiency improvements whereby small, fast-moving "two-pizza teams" could add new features faster and easier, Amazon started providing access to their systems through Amazon Web Services on a utility computing basis in 2005. This characterization of the genesis of Amazon Web Services has been characterized as an extreme over-simplification by a technical contributor to the Amazon Web Services project.

In 2007, Google, IBM, and a number of universities embarked on a large scale cloud computing research project. By mid-2008, Gartner saw an opportunity for cloud computing "to shape the relationship among consumers of IT services, those who use IT services and those who sell them", and observed that "[o]rganisations are switching from company-owned hardware and software assets to per-use service-based models" so that the "projected shift to cloud computing... will result in dramatic growth in IT products in some areas and in significant reductions in other areas."

Political Issues

The Cloud *spans many borders and "may be the ultimate form of globalization." As such, it becomes subject to complex geopolitical issues, and providers are pressed to satisfy myriad regulatory environments in order to deliver service to a global market. This dates back to the early days of the Internet, when libertarian thinkers felt that "cyberspace was a distinct place calling for laws and legal institutions of its own".*

Despite efforts (such as US-EU Safe Harbor) to harmonize the legal environment, as of 2009, providers such as Amazon cater to major markets (typically the United States and the European Union) by deploying local infrastructure and allowing customers to select "availability zones." Nonetheless, concerns persist about security and privacy from individual through governmental levels (e.g., the USA PATRIOT Act, the use of national security letters, and the Electronic Communications Privacy Act's Stored Communications Act*).*

Legal issues

In March 2007, Dell applied to trademark the term "cloud computing" (U.S. Trademark 77,139,082) in the United States. The "Notice of Allowance" the company received in July 2008 was cancelled in August, resulting in a formal rejection of the trademark application less than a week later.

In November 2007, the Free Software Foundation released the Affero General Public License, a version of GPLv3 intended to close a perceived legal loophole associated with free software designed to be run over a network. Founder and president, Richard Stallman has also warned that cloud computing "will force people to buy into locked, proprietary systems that will cost more and more over time".

Key Characteristics

- Agility improves with users able to rapidly and inexpensively re-provision technological infrastructure resources..
- Cost is claimed to be greatly reduced and capital expenditure is converted to operational expenditure. This ostensibly lowers barriers to entry, as infrastructure is typically provided by a third-party and does not need to be purchased for one-time or infrequent intensive computing tasks. Pricing on a utility computing basis is fine-grained with usage-based options and fewer IT skills are required for implementation (in-house).
- Device and location independence enable users to access systems using a web browser regardless of their location or what device they are using (e.g., PC, mobile). As infrastructure is off-site (typically provided by a third-party) and accessed via the Internet, users can connect from anywhere.
- Multi-tenancy enables sharing of resources and costs across a large pool of users thus allowing for:
- Centralization of infrastructure in locations with lower costs (such as real estate, electricity, etc.)
- Peak-load capacity increases (users need not engineer for highest possible load-levels)
- Utilization and efficiency improvements for systems that are often only 10–20% utilized.
- Reliability improves through the use of multiple redundant sites, which makes cloud computing suitable for business continuity and disaster recovery. Nonetheless, many major cloud computing services have suffered outages, and IT and business managers can at times do little when they are affected.
- Scalability via dynamic ("on-demand") provisioning of resources on a fine-grained, self-service basis near real-time, without users having to engineer for peak loads. Performance is monitored, and consistent and loosely-coupled architectures are constructed using web services as the system interface.
- Security typically improves due to centralization of data, increased security-focused resources, etc., but concerns can

persist about loss of control over certain sensitive data, and the lack of security for stored kernels. Security is often as good as or better than under traditional systems, in part because providers are able to devote resources to solving security issues that many customers cannot afford. Providers typically log accesses, but accessing the audit logs themselves can be difficult or impossible. Furthermore, the complexity of security is greatly increased when data is distributed over a wider area and/or number of devices.

- Sustainability comes about through improved resource utilization, more efficient systems, and carbon neutrality. Nonetheless, computers and associated infrastructure are major consumers of energy.

Categories

Software as a Service

This type of cloud computing delivers a single application through the browser to thousands of customers using a multitenant architecture. On the customer side, it means no upfront investment in servers or software licensing; on the provider side, with just one app to maintain, costs are low compared to conventional hosting. Examples include:

- Oracle CRM On Demand
- Salesforce.com
- Workday
- Google Apps
- Zoho Office
- Box.net
- TradeBeam.com.

Utility Computing

This type of cloud computing delivers storage and virtual servers that IT can access on demand. Early enterprise adopters mainly use utility computing for supplemental, non-mission-critical needs, but one day, they may replace parts of the datacentre. Other providers offer solutions that help IT create virtual datacentres from commodity servers. Examples include:

- Tera's AppLogic

- Cohesive Flexible Technologies' Elastic Server on Demand
- Liquid Computing's LiquidQ.

Web Services in the Cloud

Closely related to SaaS, This form of cloud computing offers APIs that enable developers to exploit functionality over the Internet, rather than delivering full-blown applications. They range from providers offering discrete business services to the full range of APIs. Examples include:

- Strike Iron
- Xignite
- Google Maps
- ADP payroll processing
- U.S. Postal Service
- Bloomberg
- Conventional credit card processing services.

Platform as a Service

Another SaaS variation, this form of cloud computing delivers development environments as a service. You build your own applications that run on the provider's infrastructure and are delivered to your users via the Internet from the provider's servers. Like Legos, these services are constrained by the vendor's design and capabilities, so you don't get complete freedom, but you do get predictability and pre-integration. Prime examples include:

- Salesforce.com's Force.com
- Google App Engine
- Yahoo Pipes
- Engineyard.com
- Dapper.net
- Heroku.com
- Informatica
- Cloud Services Depot.

MSP (Managed Service Providers)

One of the oldest forms of cloud computing, a managed service is basically an application exposed to IT rather than to end-users, such as a virus scanning service for email or an application monitoring service (which Mercury, among others, provides). Examples include:

- Managed security services delivered by SecureWorks, IBM, and Verizon
- Anti-spam services as Postini, recently acquired by Google
- Desktop management services, such as those offered by Centre Beam or Everdream.

Service Commerce Platforms

A hybrid of SaaS and MSP, this cloud computing service offers a service hub that users interact with. They're most common in trading environments, such as expense management systems that allow users to order travel or secretarial services from a common platform that then coordinates the service delivery and pricing within the specifications set by the user. Think of it as an automated service bureau. Well-known examples include:

- Rearden Commerce
- Ariba.

Internet Integration

The integration of cloud-based services is in its early days. Examples include:

- OpSource Services Bus
- Workday ESB (enterprise service bus).

Database as a Service

The centralization in the cloud of Database services. This typically range from simple key-value storage engine, often characterized by reduced functionality (e.g., limited data model, reduced ACID properties) but almost linear scalability. In this class are worth mentioning:

- Amazon Simple DB
- Yahoo Peanut
- Google BigTable.

Another important class includes full-featured SQL DBMS hosted in the cloud, some examples are:

- Amazon Relational Database Services
- Microsoft SQL Services
- LongJump

- Intuit.

More ambitious research efforts are aiming at developing dedicated novel architecture for DB in the cloud:

- MIT effort "relationalcloud.com"
- 28msec Inc: "Building a database on S3".

Architecture

Cloud Computing Sample Architecture

Cloud architecture, the systems architecture of the software systems involved in the delivery of *cloud computing*, comprises hardware and software designed by a *cloud architect* who typically works for a *cloud integrator*. It typically involves multiple *cloud components* communicating with each other over application programming interfaces, usually web services.

This closely resembles the Unix philosophy of having multiple programs each doing one thing well and working together over universal interfaces. Complexity is controlled and the resulting systems are more manageable than their monolithic counterparts.

Cloud architecture extends to the client, where web browsers and/ or software applications access *cloud applications*.

Cloud storage architecture is loosely coupled, where metadata operations are centralized enabling the data nodes to scale into the hundreds, each independently delivering data to applications or users.

Types

Cloud Computing Types Public Cloud

Public cloud or *external cloud* describes cloud computing in the traditional mainstream sense, whereby resources are dynamically provisioned on a fine-grained, self-service basis over the Internet, via web applications/web services, from an off-site third-party provider who shares resources and bills on a fine-grained utility computing basis.

Hybrid Cloud

A *hybrid cloud* environment consisting of multiple internal and/or external providers "will be typical for most enterprises". A hybrid cloud can describe configuration combining a local device, such as a Plug computer with cloud services. It can also describe configurations combining virtual and physical, colocated assets—for example, a mostly virtualized environment that requires physical servers, routers, or other hardware such as a network appliance acting as a firewall or spam filter.

Private Cloud

Private cloud and *internal cloud* are neologisms that some vendors have recently used to describe offerings that emulate cloud computing on private networks. These (typically virtualisation automation) products claim to "deliver some benefits of cloud computing without the pitfalls", capitalising on data security, corporate governance, and reliability concerns. They have been criticized on the basis that users "still have to buy, build, and manage them" and as such do not benefit from lower up-front capital costs and less hands-on management, essentially "[lacking] the economic model that makes cloud computing such an intriguing concept".

While an analyst predicted in 2008 that private cloud networks would be the future of corporate IT, there is some uncertainty whether they are a reality even within the same firm.

Analysts also claim that within five years a "huge percentage" of small and medium enterprises will get most of their computing resources from external cloud computing providers as they "will not have economies of scale to make it worth staying in the IT business" or be able to afford private clouds.. Analysts have reported on Platform's view that private clouds are a stepping stone to external clouds, particularly for the financial services, and that future datacentres will look like internal clouds.

The term has also been used in the logical rather than physical sense, for example in reference to platform as a service offerings, though such offerings including Microsoft's Azure Services Platform are not available for on-premises deployment.

Criticism

Critics of cloud computing cite its seemingly broad and vague definition. Oracle CEO Larry Ellison observes that cloud computing has been defined as "everything that we currently do". Forrester VP Frank Gillett expresses similar criticism. Many technologies that have been branded as "cloud computing" have existed for a long time before the "cloud" label came into existence. Examples include databases, load balanced on-demand web hosting services, network storage, real time online services, hosted services in general, etc.

Role in Business

Eight Ways That Cloud Computing Will Change Business

When a major change arrives on the IT scene it's not always clear what the implications will be, if any, and so for large organizations a risk-managed wait-and-see attitude tends to prevail. Occasionally however some shifts offer cost savings, improvements to operations, or ways to tackle business problems that offer significant strategic advantage. The larger the benefit in one or more of these areas, then the more strategic the advance is and the greater potential it will impact the bottom line. Cloud computing is quickly beginning to shape up as one of these major changes and the hundreds of thousands of business customers of cloud offerings from Amazon (Amazon Web Services), Salesforce (Force.com), and Google (many offerings, including Google App Engine), including a growing number of Fortune 500 companies, is showing both considerable interest and momentum in the space.

Cloud Computing: A Delicate Balance of Risk and Benefit

To be clear, there are currently unanswered questions and inherent challenges — even some major risks — in adopting cloud computing for more that so-called "edge" computing of minor applications and non-critical business systems. Notably, these include security of enterprise data that stored in the cloud, risk of lock-in to cloud platform vendors, loss of control over cloud resources run and managed by someone else, and reliability.

On the other side of the coin are some benefits that can potentially change the game for many firms that are willing to be very proactive in managing potential downside. These include access to completely different levels of scale and economics in terms of the ability to scale very rapidly and to operate IT systems more cheaply that previously possible. Easier change management of infrastructure including maintenance and upgrades (cloud vendors extensively virtualize and commoditize the underlying components to make them non-disruptive to replace and improve) as well as offering improved agility to deploy solutions and choice between vendors, particularly when cloud interoperability becomes more of a reality than it is today. Cloud computing also offers an onramp to new computing advances such as non-relational databases, new languages, and frameworks that are designed to encourage scalability and take advantage of new innovations such as modern Web identity, open supply chains, and other advances.

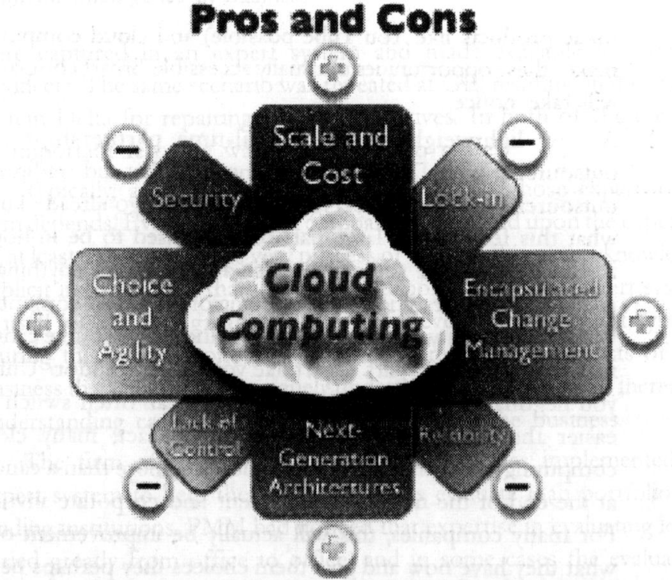

In fact, cloud computing holds the potential to dramatically change the businesses that adopt it, even if the technologies are only used internally. While these possibilities are only now starting to become clear, we can get a decent sense of these now:

Ways that cloud Computing will Change Business

1. The creation of a new generation of products and services. The economics of cloud computing lets innovative companies create products that either weren't possible before or are significantly less expensive than the competition (or just more profitable.) This part of cloud computing is an arms race and there are short windows of opportunity since competitors can often put the economic advantages of cloud computing into their product formulations fairly quickly once they see that it works for you. Where it gets interesting is that many business ideas that required prohibitive amounts of computing power, scale, or radically new business models (the aforementioned open supply chains and Global SOA) but couldn't be implemented due to existing technical limitations or cost-effectiveness, can now be realized. Every improvement in storage, processing power, or technology enables innovations that weren't possible before (high speed Internet, for instance,

made products like You Tube possible) and cloud computing makes these opportunities unusually accessible. Smart companies will take notice.

2. A new lightweight form of real-time partnerships and outsourcing with IT suppliers. Companies that did traditional outsourcing of their IT services a few years ago already know what this feels like; a large part of what used to be in-house is now being done somewhere else and changing anything is *hard*. But unlike traditional outsourcing of IT, cloud computing will provide agility and control that traditional outsource cannot match for the most part. Don't like your cloud vendor? Unless you negotiated a long-term contract, you can often switch far easier than changing IT outsourcers. In fact, many cloud computing relationships consist of nothing more than a cancel-at-the-end-of-the-month commitment and corporate invoice. For many companies, this will actually be improvement over what they have now and give them choices they perhaps never had when everything required internal execution or to go through the outsourcing supplier relationship.
3. A new awareness and leverage of the greater Internet and Web 2.0 in particular. Most companies are still notoriously critical of Web technologies as "not serious" computing. But the Web has grown up considerably in the Web 2.0 era and the challenges in scale, performance, and satisfying fickle audiences of millions has created technologies, solutions, and architectures that can address them in powerful yet economic ways that many enterprise systems are finding hard to match. When cloud computing is adopted by an organization, they will find themselves thrown into the pool with the rest of the online world in many ways, whether this is the employment of social tools, SaaS, non-relational databases or a host of other technologies in their new cloud. And in the end, this will serve them very well and allow many companies to acquire the skills and perspectives required to compete effectively in the 21st century.
4. A reconciliation of traditional SOA with the cloud and other emerging IT models. A great post this week from our very own Joe McKendrick illustrates how SOA is evolving because of the cloud. The advent of cloud technologies will have to be

dealt with and somehow encompassed by SOA initiatives that are already looking at their current toolset of heavyweight approaches and technologies with an eye towards seeking an onramp to change and improvement. Web-Oriented Architecture fits very well with cloud technologies which are heavily Web-based and it's a natural, lightweight way of building SOA at virtually every level of the organization. For many organizations, the cloud will likely be the straw that broke the back of traditional SOA and move it to a place where it will meet new business and technical requirements, faster rates of changes, and new business conditions.

5. The rise of new industry leaders and IT vendors. While we're seeing many of the top players in computing use their existing strengths to create successful cloud computing offerings, there were also be a new generation of companies that businesses generally aren't used to dealing with as suppliers. Amazon and Google are two firms that generally aren't regarded as deeply experienced in the enterprise, and there are many others. While it doesn't seem that we'll see many entirely new players compete with the big firms, it's certainly not out of the question (and given the opportunity, likely from an investment standpoint) that we'll see some very well-funded new cloud startups that lack the baggage of existing leaders (thereby moving very quickly) and bring a new sensibility (radical openness and transparency, new technologies, and Web-focus) that's often needed with cloud computing. We may see perhaps even before the downturn ends. Either way, the industry landscape will be remade by cloud computing as it is one of the very few new IT developments that will be very broadly adopted in the next several years.
6. More self-service IT from the business-side. Many cloud solutions, particularly as they relate to SaaS, will require increasingly less and less involvement from the IT department. Business users will be able to adopt many future cloud computing solutions entirely using self-service. This also heralds, as McKendrick indicates, that many of these scenarios will be much smaller and more numerous, tapping into the Long Tail of IT demand.
7. More tolerance for innovation and experimentation from

businesses. With fewer technical and economic barriers to creating new ways to improve the business (LOB, marketing, sales, customer service, IT, horizontal services), cloud computing will enable prototyping and market validation of new approaches much faster and less expensively that before. While legal, branding, and compliance will often struggle to keep up the pace with the rest of the organization, there will be gradual thawing of the glacial pace of change as business possibilities become, well, more possible in the cloud computing world. This won't fix the often broken innovation mechanisms in businesses, but then again, cloud computing is so accessible that many new internal entrepreneurs will use the tools to create new solutions anyway.

8. The slow-moving, dinosaur firms will have trouble keeping up more nimble adopters and fast-followers. Not adopting cloud computing doesn't spell the immediate demise of traditional companies that aren't good at making technology and cultural transitions (and make no mistake, cloud computing is a big cultural change), but it will pile onto other recent advancements and make it even harder to compete in the modern business environment. In the end, those too slow to adopt the benefits while managing the risk are likely going to face serious and growing economic and business disadvantage.

For many organizations in the short term the apparent potential of the individual changes above will often not be sufficient to them to make the transition to cloud computing, particularly as the cloud market is so new and major players such as IBM and HP have yet to arrive in full force. But gaining competency in cloud computing today by conducting pilots and building skills will server companies well and begin to position them for the future IT landscape. Longer term, cloud computing is increasingly appearing to be a transformative change in the business landscape.

How Risky is Cloud Computing?

Cloud computing is luring more businesses with its promise of minimal maintenance and low costs. But are companies putting their data at risk?

A new, free report released Friday by the European Network and Information Security Agency (ENISA) outlines the benefits and potential pitfalls of cloud computing. Based on an ongoing survey, the 123-page report, "Cloud Computing: Benefits, Risks and Recommendations for Information Security" (PDF), also offers recommendations to businesses on how to minimize the risks of entrusing their data to a cloud provider.

The benefits of cloud computing as described by ENISA are clear. Business content and services are always available. Companies can reduce costs by not overspending on the capacity of their own data centres. They can also scale up or down, depending on the services they use, and pay for those services only as needed. Internal IT is freed up by not having to implement or maintain certain hardware or software.

As more businesses hop onto the cloud, IDC expects worldwide spending on cloud services to hit $17.4 billion, revving up to $44.2 billion by 2013.

But Cloud Computing Poses Certain Key Risks

"The picture we got back from the survey was clear," Giles Hogben, editor of the ENISA report, said in a statement. "The business case for cloud computing is obvious—it's computing on tap, available instantly, commitment-free and on-demand. But the number one issue holding many people back is security—how can I know if it's safe to trust the cloud provider with my data and in some cases my entire business infrastructure?"

Though cloud-service providers promise 24-by-7 availability, their data centres can go down. Security is out of the hands of the customer, who must place trust in the service provider. Customers become dependent on a single provider and may face challenges if data and services need to be migrated to a different provider. By entrusting data to the cloud, companies could face risks and challenges from regulatory audits. Further, some cloud providers may not fully and properly delete data even if a customer requests it.

In its report, ENISA outlines measures companies can take when dealing with cloud-service providers.

Companies must perform risk assessments, comparing the potential risks of storing data in the cloud with keeping files in an internal data centre. Companies must also compare different cloud providers to narrow the list and then obtain service-level assurances from selected providers. Further, customers should clearly specify which services and tasks will be handled by internal IT and which by the cloud provider.

The report includes a checklist and detailed questions that customers can use when shopping for a cloud provider.

With the right provider, data can be safe and secure in the cloud. In fact, security with a cloud provider can be even more robust, flexible, and quicker to implement than when done internally. ENISA Executive Director Udo Helmbrecht noted in a statement: "The scale and flexibility of cloud computing gives the providers a security edge. For example, providers can instantly call on extra defensive resources like filtering and re-routing. They can also roll out new security patches more efficiently and keep more comprehensive evidence for diagnostics."

How Cloud Computing Will Change Business

Many businesses are struggling to understand what this shift means for them. They're feeling their way forward, trying to figure out how best to take advantage of it. "In this area, we're a bit behind, so this is a huge step for us," says Dr. Leo Hartz, chief medical officer for Blue Cross of Northeastern Pennsylvania, which has started using a cloud computing system to let its 300,000 members find medical histories and claims information with their mobile phones. "It's new, but I expect to see some big changes."

There are experiments popping up all over that offer lessons for other businesses. Serena Software has switched almost entirely to cloud services, even using Facebook as its main source of internal communications. Genentech (DNA) has made medical experts available to sales reps in the field with a couple of button clicks. Coca-Cola Enterprises (CCE) is equipping 40,000 mobile workers, including truck drivers, merchandisers, and sales staff, with portable devices so they're better connected to the home office while on the road. They can alert their bosses instantly about shifts in demand or problems they encounter. Such examples suggest the possibilities ahead for using these technologies to remake sales, distribution, and other parts of business.

It won't be easy for companies to make good on the opportunities. There is still a great deal of work to be done to get all these technologies functioning seamlessly and reliably. Tech companies have shifted a lot of the software applications that businesses typically handle for themselves over to the cloud, but many more have yet to be switched over.

Meanwhile, companies need increased reassurance that their data and communications will be secure and that the new services will be available whenever they need them. On May 14, an outage at Google left many customers unable to use its online applications. And while the tech industry has made it ever easier for information from different cloud services and devices to be fused together (personal profiles and calendars, for instance), a lot of the actual merging has yet to be done.

The shortcomings spell opportunity for plenty of companies in tech. Chipmakers such as Qualcomm (QCOM) and Intel (INTL) are creating products for portables that pack more capability on a single slice of silicon while reducing power consumption, making it easier to access information in the cloud from anywhere. Mobile-phone makers including Nokia (NOK) and Research in Motion (RIMM) are racing to come out with products aimed at business users that have all the ease-of-use of the iPhone (AAPL).

Hardware makers Hewlett-Packard (HPQ) and IBM (IBM), among others, are packing cloud technologies into their server computers. Software giants such as Microsoft and SAP (SAP) are developing cloud services. Salesforce.com (CRM) is providing mobile connections to its cloud software for corporate giants such as Avon and Genentech. And startups are coming out with technologies that reorganize our digital worlds. Silicon Valley's Xoopit, for instance, has built a specialized search engine capable of finding bits of information scattered among email systems, sales management programs, blogs, and online news sites. An executive could use the technology to pull together information about customer complaints from a variety of sources.

Virtual Personal Assistants

This is one of those turning points where small companies can explode onto the scene while industry giants miss out. One factor that puts some tech giants at a disadvantage is that the shift to a more personalized approach to computing is being led by companies born and raised in the consumer world. Apple and Google understand in their bones that simplicity and ease of use are essential to broad adoption of products and services. That lesson doesn't come so naturally to Microsoft and IBM.

But they are trying. For IBM, the change begins with encouraging its 400,000 employees to use tools it has created based on consumer social-networking sites. After IBM tests new consumer-like cloud computing capabilities internally, it launches them as services for customers. On Apr. 1, IBM unveiled LotusLive Engage, a cloud service for corporations that combines social networking and collaboration. IBM now is working to make it possible for Engage users to search the LinkedIn professional social networking site right from their Engage pages to find people outside their companies whose expertise they need.

One of the most promising aspects of cloud computing is that it enables the creation of so-called virtual personal assistants. These software confections know people's interests and needs and go off and do useful things for them on the Internet, like suggesting a restaurant for a client meeting or offering reminders of where you have taken the client before. With GPS in smartphones, computing systems know where we are. And with artificial intelligence software, computers can be taught what we expect of them and how to anticipate our needs.

Silicon Valley startup Siri last month introduced a service that puts sophisticated artificial intelligence in an easy-to-use form. The first applications are designed to help people arrange travel and entertainment, but the founders anticipate developing powerful tools specifically for business. Example: A salesperson asks her virtual assistant to help pull together the best pitch she can make to a particular customer. The assistant draws information from a variety of sources that the salesperson can use to create a proposal. "The goal is simple and practical: to help people perform tasks in their lives faster, easier, and in a more personalized way," says Adam Cheyer, Siri's vice-president for engineering.

Simple, yes. But it has taken nearly 20 years and a tremendous amount of innovation to get here. At last, though, the tech industry is beginning to make good on Gates' vision.

6

Artificial Intelligence in Business

Artificial Intelligence (AI)

Artificial intelligence (AI) encompasses a diverse number of computer applications, or components within applications, that use sets of rules and knowledge to make inferences. Unlike its roots as an esoteric discipline of trying to make computers emulate the human mind, modern AI—along with the technologies it has inspired—has many practical ramifications and delivers real benefits to users. In business applications, AI capabilities are often integrated with systems that serve the day-to-day needs of the enterprise, such as inventory tracking, manufacturing process controls, and customer service databases. Often, however, these newer, practical implementations of AI may not be labelled as such because of negative associations with the term.

What is Artificial Intelligence?

Defining AI succinctly is difficult because it takes so many forms. One area of agreement is that artificial intelligence is a field of scientific inquiry, rather than an end product. AI is difficult to define with any precision partially because several different groups of researchers with drastically different motivations are working in the field. Perhaps the best definition is that coined by M.L. Minsky, "Artificial intelligence is the science of making machines do things that would require intelligence if done by men."

History of Artificial Intelligence

Charles Babbage (1792-1871), an English mathematician, is generally acknowledged to be the father of modern computing. Around 1823 he invented a working model of the world's first practical mechanical calculator. Then, he began work on his "analytical engine," which had the basic elements of a modern-day computer. Unfortunately, he was unable to raise the funds needed to build his machine. Nevertheless, his ideas lived on.

Herman Hollerith (1860-1929), an American inventor, actually created the first working calculating machine, which was used to tabulate the results of the 1890 U.S. census. There ensued a series of rapid improvements to machines which allegedly "thought." The first true electronic computer, the Electronic Numerical Integrator and Computer (ENIAC), was developed in 1946. The so-called "giant brain" replaced mechanical switches with glass vacuum tubes. ENIAC used 17,468 vacuum tubes and occupied 1,800 square feet—the size of an average house. It weighed 30 tons. Scientists began at once to build smaller computers.

In 1959, scientists at Bell Laboratories invented the transistor, which marked the beginning of the second generation of computers. Transistors replaced vacuum tubes and sped up processing considerably. They also made possible a large increase in computer memory. Ten years later, International Business Machines Corp. (IBM) created third-generation computers when they replaced transistors with integrated circuits. A single integrated circuit could replace a large number of transistors in a silicon chip less than one-eighth of an inch square! More importantly, integrated circuits allowed manufacturers to dramatically reduce the size of computers. New software that made use of increased speed and memory complemented these third-generation computers—which themselves proved to be short lived.

Only two years after the appearance of integrated circuits, Intel Corp. introduced microprocessor chips. One chip contained a computer's central processing unit. Prior to that time, computers contained specialized chips for functions such as logic and programming. Intel's invention placed all of the computers' functions on one chip. Scientists continued to improve on computers.

Miniaturization of chips led to large-scale integrated circuitry (LSI) and very-large-scale integrated circuitry (VLSI). LSI and VLSI enabled software and printers to react faster with each other and with computers. They also contributed to the invention of microcomputers, which revolutionized the role of computers in business. More importantly, LSI and VLSI heightened scientists' interest in the development of AI.

Developments in Artificial Intelligence

AI is the construction and/or programming of computers to imitate human thought processes. Scientists are trying to design computers capable of processing natural languages and reasoning. They believe that once machines can process natural languages such as English or Spanish, humans will be able to give instructions and ask questions without learning special computer languages. When that day arrives, machines, like humans, will be able to learn from past experience and apply what they have learned to solve new problems. Scientists have a long way to go, but they have made what they believe is a giant step in that direction with the invention of "fuzzy logic."

Fuzzy Logic

Since their inception, computers have always acted on a "yes" or "no" basis. They simply have not been able to recognize "maybe." Even the most sophisticated computers, capable of performing millions of calculations per second, cannot distinguish between "slightly" or "very." This simple difference has confused AI scientists for years. However, an American researcher, Dr. Lofti A. Zadeh, of the University of California, presented a possible answer, which he termed "fuzzy logic."

The concept is based on feeding the computer "fuzzy sets," or groupings of concrete information and relative concepts. For example, in a fuzzy set for industrial furnaces, a temperature of 1,000 degrees might have a "membership" (relative value) of 0.95, while a temperature of 600 might have a membership of 0.50. A computer program might then utilize instructions such as, "the higher the temperature, the lower the pressure must be." This solution means that programmers can teach machines to compute with words, instead of numbers.

Historically, most complex mathematical models developed by programmers compute strictly with numbers. However, the fuzzy logic approach to AI did not catch on in the American scientific community. It did, however, among the Japanese.

Japan-based Hitachi, Ltd. developed an artificial intelligence system based on fuzzy logic that allowed an automated subway system in Sendai, Japan, to brake more swiftly and smoothly than it could under human guidance. The Japanese Ministry of International Trade and Industry budgeted $36 million in 1990 to subsidize the initial operation of a Laboratory for International Fuzzy Engineering. Development of fuzzy engineering also took hold in China, Russia, and much of Western

Europe. American scientists, however, pursued other aspects of Al. In the early 1990s, a University of North Carolina professor developed a microprocessor chip using an all-digital architecture, which would allow it to run in conventional computers. The chip can handle 580,000 "if-then" decisions per second, which is more than 100 times faster than the best Japanese fuzzy-logic chip can operate. Many U.S. companies have been experimenting with this and similar chips. The Oak Ridge National Laboratory is using the chip in robots to be employed in radioactive areas of nuclear power plants. The Oricon Corporation has used fuzzy logic in a signal analysis system for submarines. NASA has also experimented with using fuzzy logic to help dock spacecraft.

Expert Systems

Other Al applications are also in use; one is the so-called expert system. Expert systems are computer-based systems that apply the substantial knowledge of a specialist—be it in medicine, law, insurance, or almost any field—to help solve complex problems without requiring a human to work through each one. In developing such systems, designers usually work with experts to determine the information and decision rules (heuristics) that the experts use when confronted with particular types of problems. In essence, these programs are simply attempting to imitate human behaviour, rather than solving problems by themselves.

There are several advantages to expert systems. For example, they give novices "instant expertise" in a particular area. They capture knowledge and expertise that might be lost if a human expert retires or dies. Moreover, the knowledge of multiple experts can be integrated, at least theoretically, to make the system's expertise more comprehensive than that of any individual. Expert systems are not subject to human problems of illness or fatigue, and, if they are well designed, can be less prone to inconsistencies and mistakes. These benefits make them particularly attractive to businesses.

Companies also use expert systems for training and analysis. General Electric, for instance, developed a system called Delta that helps maintenance workers identify and correct malfunctions in locomotives. Digital Equipment Corporation uses XCON (derived from "expert configurer") to match customers' needs with the most appropriate combination of computer input, output, and memory devices. The system uses more than 3,000 decision rules and 5,000 product descriptions to analyze sales orders and design lay-outs, ensuring that the company's equipment will work when it arrives at customers' sites. XCON catches most configuration errors, and eliminates the need for completely assembling a computer system for testing and then breaking it down again for shipment to the customer. The system is expensive, however. DEC spends $2 million per year just to update XCON. In fact, cost is one of the most prohibitive factors involved in the development of Al systems. However, when such a system is implemented effectively, the money it saves in staff hours and costs from averted human errors can quickly recoup development costs. In large corporations the savings can accrue in the tens of millions of dollars per year.

A moderate-sized system, consisting of about 300 decision rules, generally costs between $250,000 and $500,000 to design. That is a great deal of money to spend on creating systems that do little more than play chess—which was what some designers did back in the 1960s.

Experimental Games

Scientists in the 1960s developed machines that could play chess in an attempt to create machines that could think by themselves. They made tremendous strides in developing sophisticated decision trees that could map out possible moves, but those programs included so many potential alternatives that even contemporary supercomputers cannot assess them within a reasonable amount of time. They reduced the number of alternatives, which allowed the machines to play at the chess master level. To simulate the thinking process, the computers processed large amounts of data on alternative moves. Some of these experiments continue through the present. A highly publicized success in this area came in 1997 when an IBM supercomputer named Deep Blue beat world chess champion Garry Kasparov in a match.

Neural Networks

Neural networks go one step further than expert systems in bringing stored knowledge to bear on practical problems. Instead of just leading the user to the appropriate piece of knowledge that has been captured in the system, neural networks process patterns of information to arrive at new abilities they weren't equipped with on day one. In a sense, they learn to do things for the user based on special preparation that involves feeding the system data which it then analyses for patterns. This approach has proven highly effective in a number of fields, including finance, information technology management, and health care.

For instance, a neural network might be employed to predict which loan applicants are too risky. Rather than programming the computer with exact, user-defined criteria for what constitutes a risky applicant, the neural network would be trained on a large volume of application data from past loans— especially on details about the problematic ones. The neural network would process the data thoroughly and arrive at its own evaluation criteria. Then as new applications come in, the computer would use this knowledge to predict the risks involved. As time passes, the neural network could receive periodic (or even continuous) retraining on new data so that it continues to hone its accuracy based on current trends. Real-life systems such as this have enjoyed a high success rate and have been able to reduce the number of bad loans at the lending institutions that use them.

Applications of AL in the Business World

Al is being used extensively in the business world, despite the fact that the discipline itself is still in the embryonic stages of development. Its applications cross a wide spectrum. For example, Al is being applied in management and administration, science, engineering, manufacturing, financial and legal areas, military and space endeavours, medicine, and diagnostics.

Some Al implementations include natural language processing, database retrieval, expert consulting systems, theorem proving, robotics, automatic programming, scheduling, and solving perceptual problems. Management is relying more and more on knowledge work systems, which are systems used to aid professionals such as architects, engineers, and medical technicians in the creation and dissemination of new knowledge and information. One such system is in use at Square D, an electrical component manufacturer. A computer does the design work for giant units of electrical equipment. The units generally share the same basic elements but vary in required size, specifications, and features. However, as is the case with most Al-type systems, human intervention is still required. An engineer is needed to check the computer-produced drawing before the equipment is put into production.

Senior managers in many companies use Al-based strategic planning systems to assist in functions like competitive analysis, technology deployment, and resource allocation. They also use programs to assist in equipment configuration design, product distribution, regulatory-compliance advisement, and personnel assessment. Al is contributing heavily to management's organization, planning, and controlling operations, and will continue to do so with more frequency as programs are refined.

AI is also influential in science and engineering. The applications developed were used to organize and manipulate the ever-increasing amounts of information available to scientists and engineers. AI has been used in complex processes such as mass spectrometry analysis, biological classifications, and the creation of semiconductor circuits and automobile components. Al has been used with increasing frequency in diffraction and image analysis; power plant and space station design; and robot sensing, control, and programming. It is the increased use of robotics in business that is alarming many critics of artificial intelligence.

Robots are being utilized more frequently in the business world. In 1990, over 200,000 robots were in use in U.S. factories. Experts predict that by the year 2025 robots could potentially replace humans in almost all manufacturing jobs. This includes not only the mundane tasks, but also those requiring specialized skills. They will be performing jobs such as shearing sheep, scraping barnacles from the bottoms of ships, and sandblasting walls. However, there are jobs that robots will never be able to perform, such as surgery. Of course, there will still be a need for individuals to design, build, and maintain robots. Yet, once scientists develop robots that can think, as well as act, there may be less of a need for human intervention. Thus, the social ramifications of Al is of major concern to people today.

The Future of Artificial Intelligence

In spite of its great advances and strong promise, Al, in name, has suffered from low esteem in both academic and corporate settings. To some, the name is inexorably—and unfavorably—associated with impractical chess-playing computers and recluse professors trying to build a "thinking machine." As a result, many developers of Al theories and applications consciously shun the moniker, preferring instead to use the newer jargon of fuzzy applications, flexible software, and data-mining tools. In avoiding the label Al, they have found more receptive audiences among corporate decision-makers and private investors for their Al-inspired technologies.

Thus, while the practices and ideas known as Al are hardly dead, the name itself is drifting toward obscurity. This is true not only because of the perceived stigma, but also as a consequence of the diversity and heterogeneity of ways in which Al concepts have been implemented. Furthermore, these concepts are verging on ubiquity in software applications programming. Such disparate objectives as building a customer order system, implementing a self-diagnostic manufacturing system, designing a sophisticated search engine, and adding voice-recognition capabilities to applications all employ AI theories and methods. Indeed, Ford Motor Company was slated to implement an engine-diagnostic neural network in its car computers beginning in the 2001 model year. With Al so entrenched in modern software development, it has lost many of its distinctions from software generally.

Can Your Business use Artificial Business

Artificial intelligence (AI) can be thought of as the art of making computers do things that would require intelligence or judgment if done by humans.

For example, computers approve American Express purchases, diagnose diesel locomotive faults for GE, configure VAXs for Digital, advise on tax matters for Arthur Andersen, schedule production for Westinghouse, and assign rooms for Holiday Inns. Every Fortune 500 company has AI applications online, in development, or as the subject of a feasibility study.

Pattern recognition, computer vision, and robotics all employ AI, as do computer programs for chess playing, automated reasoning, and problem solving. Natural language applications of AI range from low-level spelling and grammar checkers to speech recognition and machine translation. There's now an English to Spanish translating application on the market for microcomputers.

AI Applications in Business

The chief business use of AI is in expert systems, which assist human experts in solving difficult problems. All of the specific examples just mentioned are expert systems. Expert systems embody the knowledge and reasoning of human experts. They aid managers in understanding their businesses and in establishing control of business processes. In addition, they secure valuable intellectual resources for the company and enforce uniform application of policy.

When Campbell Soup's chief engineer was approaching retirement age, his knowledge and experience in keeping the huge cookers running were captured in an expert system and made available to younger engineers. The same scenario was repeated at GE, resulting in the expert system Delta for repairing diesel locomotives. In both of these cases, an important resource was not allowed to retire.

Typically, a firm has many employees upon whose expertise the firm depends. Even the smallest company will depend upon the expertise of at least one person. The very process of making this expert knowledge explicit in such a way that it can be incorporated into an expert system is itself one of the greatest benefits of developing an expert system. During this process, one can become aware of many aspects of the business that had been only vaguely understood previously. This increased understanding can lead to greater control over the business.

The firm of Peat, Marwick, Main (PMM) has implemented an expert system to help their various offices evaluate loan portfolios of lending institutions. PMM had noticed that expertise in evaluating loans varied greatly from office to office, and in some cases the evaluation was even being performed by partners because of the lack of expertise at lower levels. Their problem was to take the expertise of those few persons known as expert evaluators of loan portfolios and make it available, at least in some meaningful part, to employees throughout the company. PMM's success in doing so had the added benefit of establishing uniform standards for loan evaluations at their various offices so there were no longer any significant differences between the way a loan might be evaluated in Minneapolis and the way a similar loan would be evaluated in Memphis.

As a side benefit after a couple of years, employees have tended to consult the system much less frequently, presumably because they have absorbed much of the expertise embodied within the system. In other words, the expert system is proving to be a long-term training tool for employees.

Competitive Aspects of Expert Systems

The usual considerations of maximizing desirability and feasibility apply equally well to expert systems concerning traditional computer applications. A more distinctive issue is to decide which tasks are appropriate for expert systems and which ones are better handled by other methods. Researchers G. Gorry and M. Scott-Morton proposed a framework for decisions that can be useful in selecting those that can benefit most from expertise, whether human or artificial.

Unstructured (on the vertical axis) and how levels of managerial action can be analysed in terms of operational control, management control, and strategic planning (on the horizontal axis). Structured tasks (the first row), of course, usually require very little expertise and can be handled with traditional algorithmic solutions, whereas unstructured tasks (the third row) may very well resist the imposition of any structure, including that of an expert system. Semi-structured tasks seem to be the ones most typically chosen for expert system development.

Some of the classic successes in expert systems have been semi-structured tasks at the level of operational control, such as Digital's XCON system for configuring computer systems. Many expert systems, however, have been developed to aid in decisions at the managerial and strategic levels; and the competitive potential of applications at these levels is, of course, even greater than that of applications at the operational level. Yet there is no reason why even unstructured tasks cannot benefit from expert systems provided that there are human experts who can explain to others what they do.

Finally, potential expert system applications can be evaluated in terms of their position in the value chain (i.e., within a business, the arrangement of tasks that add value). As with other types of technology, the relevant question is whether expert systems are being retrofitted to low value-added applications or being used to exploit opportunities further up the value-added axis.

Expert System Life Cycle

A variety of issues emerge in the development stage of expert systems. Prototyping, however, is the most important expert system development tool and typically consumes a large share of resources. The two parts of an expert system—the knowledge base (the representation of expert knowledge) and the shell (the remainder of the system)—require separate development and maintenance skills.

It is relatively easy to build an impressive prototype of an expert system in a fairly short time. Completing the system, however, typically takes much longer.

Finally, expert system projects are often seen as risky, since the technology is relatively new and the applications tend to address unstructured problems. This risk needs to be considered in any commitment to development of an AI application. Such risk can be minimized by seeking the counsel of experienced AI consultants.

Getting Started With AI

The way to start an AI project is the same as with any other information system application. If a firm is large enough, it will have information system specialists. If not, the firm will probably depend upon an outside consultant for information systems needs. In either case, the initial steps are the same and are the traditional ones—conduct a needs analysis and a feasibility study together with a careful evaluation of costs and benefits. It is important to choose an application that is suited for an expert system—one that will provide cost savings large enough to justify the investment and its risk, or one that gives a firm a strategic advantage in the marketplace. The evaluation of costs and benefits is particularly important in the case of expert systems, since their relative riskiness and their typically lengthy development time require an unusually careful analysis of expected future returns. The analysis and design of expert systems can depend upon the skills of a knowledge engineer—someone with experience in helping persons with expertise in a firm to articulate that expertise in such a way that it can be incorporated into an expert system. A company's personnel can and should develop the skills of knowledge engineers over time by starting with small, manageable projects. It is more feasible in most cases, however, to call upon consultants who already have such experience.

Risks and Rewards

AI and expert systems provide a wide range of opportunities for automation beyond those of more restricted, traditional computer applications. Yet the risks and applications of new technologies to problems that are difficult to define may deter one from taking advantage of them. At the same time, a wait-and-see attitude may be even more risky, since AI and expert systems can give one's competition an advantage. As with any other project, careful analysis and planning usually translate into tangible benefits. Broadly speaking, information and expertise are assets of the corporation. Expert systems can be a tool to help solve stubborn problems, a tool for leveraging expertise. Those firms that implement expert systems in their operations, as well as at the managerial and strategic levels, may be able to move ahead of their competition.

Above all, the very experience with AI and expert systems can be leveraged. Those who can invest in such potentially valuable technology are positioned to reap the greatest benefits. Mr. Byrne is a doctoral candidate in accounting at Memphis State University. Dr. Franklin is a professor in the Mathematical Sciences department and a member of the Institute for Intelligent Systems at MSU.

Artificial Intelligence Techniques Enhance Business Forecasts

Computer-Based Analysis Increases Accuracy.

Today's business world is driven by customer demand. Unfortunately, the patterns of demand vary considerably from period to period. This is why it can be so challenging to develop accurate forecasts. Forecasting is the process of estimating future events, and it is fundamental to all aspects of management. The goals of forecasting are to reduce uncertainty and to provide benchmarks for monitoring actual performance. Emerging information technologies and artificial intelligence (AI) techniques are being used to improve the accuracy of forecasts and thus making a positive contribution to enhancing the bottom line. A new generation of artificial intelligence technologies have emerged that hold considerable promise in helping improve the forecasting process including such applications as product demand, employee turnover, cash flow, distribution requirements, manpower forecasting, and inventory. These AI based systems are designed to bridge the gap between the two traditional forecasting approaches: managerial and quantitative.

Organizations develop forecasts to support planning and decision-making processes. Specific operations forecasting applications include product demand, inventory levels, manpower levels, scrap rates, and raw materials requirements. Forecasts can also be used as motivational tools. Technology based forecasts tend to focus on new product/service development. For example, how long will it take before the DVD is the primary media platform in the home? Economic forecasts deal with business parameters such as interest and inflation rates.

Forecasting Approaches

Generally speaking, forecasts are based on quantitative analysis, qualitative analysis or a combination of both. Often quantitative forecasting is referred to as objective analysis while qualitative forecasting is called managerial or judgmental analysis. Typically, there is tension between these two approaches. Quantitative forecasts, which are often favoured by operations, tend to be developed using a bottom up approach while managerial-based forecasts, usually preferred by the marketing group, are approached from a top down perspective. For example, a primary marketing goal is to insure adequate supply while operation's focus is on minimizing inventory. The resolution of these two approaches is how forecasting errors occur and presents an opportunity for using artificial intelligence methods. Quantitative forecasting can be characterized by one of the two basic techniques:

- Time Series-The future will tend to look and behave like the past. For example, gasoline prices for the next six months will continue along the same lines as they have over the past six months.
- Relational-The future is dependent on the direction of a variety of factors. For example, new housing starts might be a function of interest rates and local weather conditions.

A time series is a set of data points recorded over successive time periods. Examples include monthly billables, weekly unit product demand and quarterly inventory levels and stock prices. A relational database consists of the recording of several variables for a number of observations. For example, a financial relational database could consist of revenues, earnings and assets for the *Fortune 500*.

The following graphic highlights the typical forecasting process. The resultant forecasts are evaluated by comparing predictions with actual results. This assessment is accomplished by examining the error terms. An error term is the difference between the prediction and the actual outcome. Based on an error assessment, the forecasting process is continually updated through the adjustment of model inputs.

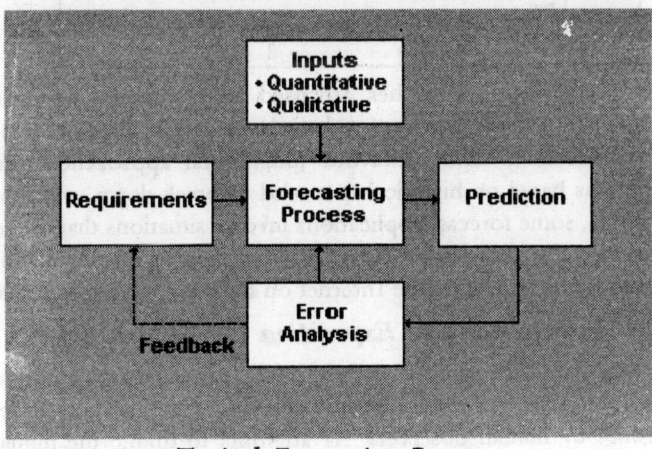

Typical Forecasting Process

Typically, no one forecasting approach is best in all situations. Instead, it is most appropriate to use a combination of different forecasting techniques in arriving at composite estimates. Furthermore, it is usually a good idea to provide interval or range estimates as well as a single point forecast.

Timeframe and Data

Two major issues in the forecasting process are the time horizon and extent of data availability. The following graphic illustrates the relationship between qualitative and quantitative forecasting as a function of time horizon and data content.

Judgmental vs. Objective Forecasting

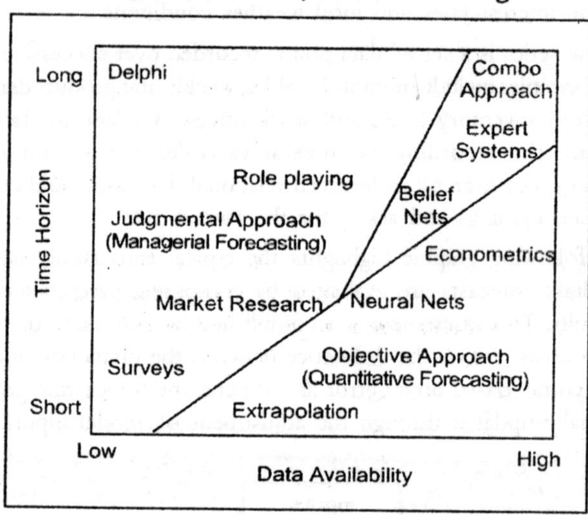

Often, objective approaches are used when there is sufficient supporting data and the horizon is relatively short. On the other hand, long-term forecasts tend to favour judgmental approaches since extrapolations based on historical data tend to break down over time. Furthermore, some forecast applications involve situations that do not have a history. For example, consider receiving the assignment, in 1985, of estimating the impact of the Internet on business by the year 2000.

Artificial Intelligence Use Expanding

What is AI? AI is generally defined as a computer-based analytical process that exhibits behaviour and actions that are considered "intelligent" by human observers. AI attempts to mimic the human thought process including reasoning and optimization. The overall market for AI related systems is growing rapidly. Presently, the United States accounts for over 60 percent of an estimated $900 million global AI market. One purpose of AI is to help organize and supply information for the management decision-making process in such a way as to improve overall efficiency and performance. Three of the more commonly used AI systems in forecasting are:

- Neural Nets emulate elements of the human cognitive process, especially the ability to recognize and learn patterns. The architecture consists of a large number of nodes that serve as calculators to process inputs and pass the results to other nodes in the network. These systems have the advantage of not requiring prior assumptions about possible relationships. One application of neural nets might be forecasting employee turnover by category based on such factors as tenure with the firm, managerial level, and gender.
- Expert Systems summarize the totality of available knowledge and rules. "Knowledge" is stored in a set of "if-then" rules. The knowledge base can be obtained by interviewing experts or integrating sets of data. For example, predicting upcoming weather conditions based on current temperatures, humidity levels, season of year, and geographical location.
- Belief Networks describe the database structure using a tree format. The nodes represent variables and the branches the conditional dependencies between variables. Belief nets generate conditional probabilities for a variety of future outcomes. For example, estimating the chances of various product sales levels based on such traditional factors such as marketing and R&D budgets as well as market signals like customer complaints.

These AI systems can be employed for both forecast classification (e.g., preferred customer vs. marginal customer) and prediction (e.g., annual sales). The following table provides a simple illustration of how AI could be used to refine a marketing strategy based on three customer behaviour factors: profit margin, retention probability and potential long-term value to the firm.

Each of these factors is characterized as either low or high. In practice, a more complex characterization scheme with more factors and more levels (e.g., low, medium, high) can be used. This table shows the appropriate qualitative strategy given each set of circumstances. Customers would be characterized in terms of their demographics and prior purchasing behaviour. Quantitative forecasts can also be developed along the same lines.

Profit Margin	*Retention Probability*	*Long Term Value*	*Strategy*
Low	Low	Low	Reduce marketing resources
Low	Low	High	Market distinct product portfolio
Low	High	Low	Examine up-sale opportunities
Low	High	High	Market missing products
High	Low	Low	Refocus marketing effort
High	Low	High	Re-attract these customers
High	Low	Low	Increase marketing resources
High	High	High	Pursue these customers

Used in this way, the system can automate the process of both qualifying and quantifying marketing prospects and forecasting demand. Other related AI capabilities include:

- Identify similar purchasing patterns within a given time frame.
- Segment databases into related factors.
- Detect relationships and sequential patterns.
- Develop categorization and estimation models.

Used in combination with traditional forecasting, AI can help ameliorate friction that may exist between objective and managerial oriented approaches. More specifically, it integrates the best features from both classical approaches in structuring a virtual forecasting system.

The human brain contains on the order of 10^{11} neurons. While this number is impressive the number of synapses, estimated at 10^{16}, is truly unbelievable. This is equivalent to the number of printed characters in all of the books contained in the United States Library of Congress 300 times over! By contrast a typical forecasting application might contain a few thousand neurons.

Results Talk

The following list presents some examples where organizations have improved bottom line profitability by improving the forecasting process.

1. Hyundai Motors reduced delivery time by 20% and increased inventory turns from 3 to 3.4.
2. Reynolds Aluminum reduced forecasting errors by 2% that resulted in a reduction of 1 million pounds in inventory.
3. Unilever reduced forecasting errors from 40% to 25% yielding resulting in multi-million dollar savings.
4. SCI Systems reduced on-hand inventory by 15% resulting in $180 million in annual savings.

Literacy grew out of the collision of the steam engine and the printing press. What will the Internet's linguistic impact be? We may be in for some real surprises. Will this process cause sophisticated artificial intelligence to finally burst onto the scene?

Improve your Forecasts

In a turbulent business environment, forecasting can lead to significant competitive advantage as well as to costly mistakes. Forecasting errors impact organizations in two ways. The first is when faulty estimates lead to poor strategic choices, and the second is when inaccurate forecasts impair performance within the existing strategic plan. An example of the former would be to increase the level of vertical integration based on a forecast of stable demand when demand actually turned out to be highly unstable. An example of the latter would be to significantly increase facility capacity based on a forecast of strong demand when, in fact, demand turned out to be soft. Either way there will be a negative impact on profitability. The following process outlines a plan for improving forecast accuracy using artificial intelligence support systems:

1. Evaluate and characterize the current forecasting system.
2. Measure the current level of error.
3. Compare error levels with industry norms.
4. Specify new requirements.
5. Characterize the economic impact of improved forecasts.
6. Identify alternative AI forecasting options.
7. Select best approach(s).
8. Develop implementation schedule.
9. Identify potential bottlenecks and problem areas.
10. Implement new system and monitor performance.

A primary objective for using AI is to better integrate the managerial and quantitative estimates and thereby reducing the forecasting errors. Organizations that currently utilize AI may increase the accuracy of forecasts by improving data collection methods and expanding efforts to gather market intelligence. Past customer behaviour is often a reliable data source of future behaviour. Finally, as in other areas of knowledge management, it is critical to maintain strong support for the forecasting process from the entire management team. Visit the following site for more on how AI is impacting business:

Scope of Artificial Intelligence in Business

Business applications utilize the specific technologies mentioned earlier to try and make better sense of potentially enormous variability (for example, unknown patterns/relationships in sales data, customer buying habits, and so on). However, within the corporate world, AI is widely used for complex problem-solving and decision-support techniques in real-time business applications. The business applicability of AI techniques is spread across functions ranging from finance management to forecasting and production.

In the fiercely competitive and dynamic market scenario, decision-making has become fairly complex and latency is inherent in many processes. In addition, the amount of data to be analysed has increased substantially. AI technologies help enterprises reduce latency in making business decisions, minimize fraud and enhance revenue opportunities.

Importance of AI

Enterprises that utilize AI-enhanced applications are expected to become more diverse, as the needs for the ability to analyze data across multiple variables, fraud detection and customer relationship management emerge as key business drivers to gain competitive advantage.

Artificial Intelligence is a branch of Science which deals with helping machines, finds solutions to complex problems in a more human-like fashion. This generally involves borrowing characteristics from human intelligence, and applying them as algorithms in a computer friendly way. A more or less flexible or efficient approach can be taken depending on the requirements established, which influences how artificial the intelligent behaviour appears.

AI is generally associated with Computer Science, but it has many important links with other fields such as Maths, Psychology, Cognition,

Biology and Philosophy, among many others. Our ability to combine knowledge from all these fields will ultimately benefit our progress in the quest of creating an intelligent artificial being.

Emergence of AI in Business

Artificial Intelligence (AI) has been used in business applications since the early eighties. As with all technologies, AI initially generated much interest, but failed to live up to the hype. However, with the advent of web-enabled infrastructure and rapid strides made by the AI development community, the application of AI techniques in real-time business applications has picked up substantially in the recent past.

Computers are fundamentally well suited to performing mechanical computations, using fixed programmed rules. This allows artificial machines to perform simple monotonous tasks efficiently and reliably, which humans are ill-suited to. For more complex problems, things get more difficult... Unlike humans, computers have trouble understanding specific situations, and adapting to new situations. Artificial Intelligence aims to improve machine behaviour in tackling such complex tasks.

Together with this, much of AI research is allowing us to understand our intelligent behaviour. Humans have an interesting approach to problem-solving, based on abstract thought, high-level deliberative reasoning and pattern recognition. Artificial Intelligence can help us understand this process by recreating it, then potentially enabling us to enhance it beyond our current capabilities.

Applications of AI

The potential applications of Artificial Intelligence are abundant. They stretch from the military for autonomous control and target identification, to the entertainment industry for computer games and robotic pets, to the big establishments dealing with huge amounts of information such as hospitals, banks and insurances, we can also use AI to predict customer behaviour and detect trends.

AI is a broad discipline that promises to simulate numerous innate human skills such as automatic programming, case-based reasoning, decision-making, expert systems, natural language processing, pattern recognition and speech recognition etc. AI technologies bring more complex data-analysis features to existing applications.

Business applications utilize the specific technologies mentioned earlier to try and make better sense of potentially enormous variability (for example, unknown patterns/relationships in sales data, customer buying habits, and so on). However, within the corporate world, AI is widely used for complex problem-solving and decision-support techniques in real-time business applications. The business applicability of AI techniques is spread across functions ranging from finance management to forecasting and product

Artificial Neural Networks

An artificial neural network (ANN), often just called a "neural network" (NN), is a mathematical model or computational model based on biological neural networks. It consists of an interconnected group of artificial neurons and processes information using a connectionist approach to computation. In most cases an ANN is an adaptive system that changes its structure based on external or internal information that flows through the network during the learning phase. In more practical terms neural networks are non-linear statistical data modelling tools. They can be used to model complex relationships between inputs and outputs or to find patterns in data.

Real Life applications of ANN

The tasks to which artificial neural networks are applied tend to fall within the following broad categories:

- Function approximation, or regression analysis, including time series prediction and modelling.
- Classification, including pattern and sequence recognition, novelty detection and sequential decision making.
- Data processing, including filtering, clustering, blind source separation and compression.

Application areas include system identification and control (vehicle control, process control), game-playing and decision making (backgammon, chess, racing), pattern recognition (radar systems, face identification, object recognition and more), sequence recognition (gesture, speech, handwritten text recognition), medical diagnosis, financial applications (automated trading systems), data mining (or knowledge discovery in databases, "KDD"), visualization and email spam filtering.

The proven success of Artificial Neural Networks (ANN) and expert systems has helped AI gain widespread adoption in enterprise business applications. In some instances, such as fraud detection, the use of AI has already become the most preferred method. In addition, neural networks have become a well-established technique for pattern recognition, particularly of images, data streams and complex data sources and, in turn, have emerged as a modelling backbone for a majority of data-mining tools available in the market. Some of the key business applications of AI/ANN include fraud detection, cross-selling, customer relationship management analytics, demand prediction, failure prediction, and non-linear control.

A majority of the enterprises adopt horizontal or vertical solutions that embed neural networks such as insurance risk assessment or fraud-detection tools, or data-mining tools that include neural networks (for instance, from SAS, IBM and SPSS) as one of the modelling options.

Artificial Intelligence in Manufacturing

As the manufacturing industry becomes increasingly competitive, sophisticated technology has emerged to improve productivity. Artificial Intelligence in manufacturing can be applied to a variety of systems. It can recognize patterns, plus perform time consuming and mentally challenging tasks. Artificial Intelligence can optimize your production schedule and production runs. In order for organizations to meet ever increasing customer demands, and to be able to survive in an environment where change is inevitable, it is crucial that they offer more reliable delivery dates and control their costs by analysing them on a continual basis. For businesses, being capable of delivering high quality goods at low costs and short delivery times is akin to operating in a whirlpool environment like the Devil's Triangle, and this is no easy task for any organization. Managing so that production takes place at the right time, on the right equipment, and using the right tools will minimize any deviations in delivery dates promised to the customer. Utilizing equipment, personnel and tools to their maximal efficiency will no doubt improve any organization's competitive strength. In return, proper utilization of these capabilities will result in lower costs for the organization

Optimal scheduling of jobs on equipment, without the use of computer software, is a truly difficult undertaking. Performing planning using the "Deterministic Simulation Method" will provide you with schedules that will indicate job loads per equipment. Even in the case limited to a single piece of equipment, as the number of jobs to schedule on that equipment increases, finding the right solution in the

"Possible Solutions Set" becomes next to impossible. And in the real world, the difficulties arising from the large size of the solutions set due to the recipes formed by jobs, equipment and products, and shaped by the technological restrictions, as well as the complexity in finding a close to ideal solution, are readily apparent.

Research and studies are being conducted worldwide on the subject of scheduling. Software vendors working in this area follow developments closely, and they are coming out with new products to better meet demands. "Genetic Algorithms", "Artificial Intelligence", and "Neural Networks" are some of the technologies being used for scheduling

Advantages

- View your best product runs and the corresponding settings.
- Increase efficiency and quality by using optimal settings from past production.
- Artificial Intelligence can optimize your schedule beyond normal human capabilities.
- Increase productivity by eliminating downtime due to unpredictable changes in the schedule.

Artificial Intelligence in Financial Services

AI has found a home in financial services and is recognized as a valuable addition to numerous business applications. Sophisticated technologies encompassing neural networks and business rules along with AI-based techniques are yielding positive results in transaction-oriented scenarios for financial services. AI has been widely adopted in such areas of risk management, compliance, and securities trading and monitoring, with an extension into customer relationship management (CRM). Tangible benefits of AI adoption include reduced risk of fraud, increased revenues from existing customers due to newer opportunities, avoidance of fines stemming from non-compliance and averted securities trade exceptions that could result in delayed settlement, if not detected.

Warren Buffet is known as the ultimate investor in this age. So good is he, in fact, that artificial intelligence software developed in Carnegie Mellon that predicts stock movements was named after him by. But can machines really take the place of human traders, much less surpass them? When Deep Blue defeated Chess Grandmaster Kasparov in 1997, AI was propelled into the limelight. Indeed, if a machine can whiz through the intricacies of the ultimate game of strategy, why not beat man in other fields as well – thereby facilitating work, decreasing costs and errors and increasing productivity and quality. This study focuses on applying AI in Finance, particularly in stock trading. In the field of Finance, artificial intelligence has long been used. Some applications of Artificial Intelligence are

- Credit authorization screening
- Mortgage risk assessment
- Project management and bidding strategy
- Financial and economic forecasting
- Risk rating of exchange-traded, fixed income investments
- Detection of regularities in security price movements
- Prediction of default and bankruptcy
- Security/and or Asset Portfolio Management.

Artificial intelligence types used in finance include neural networks, fuzzy logic, genetic algorithms, expert systems and intelligent agents. They are often used in combination with each other. When AI first appeared a decade ago, it generated mass media hype but delivered inconsistent results. A number of those who praised its ability were paralyzed in the end. One such case is Fidelity Investments. In this paper, we set the stage by describing how traditional stock trading differs from AI-powered stock trading. We define the various AI systems available and also explore the various solutions available in the market, their IT foundations and how salient they are. Then, we move into how AI systems for stock trading will affect traders, companies and individuals. Benefits, risks and competitive strategy will be defined and real-world examples cited, as grounding for our recommendations in the end. Recommendations include getting management buy-in, implementing the system and managing the whole structure to succeed.

Artificial Intelligence in Marketing

Advances in artificial intelligence (AI) eventually could turbo-boost customer analytics to give companies speedier insights into individual buying patterns and a host of other consumer habits.

Artificial intelligence functions are made possible by computerized neural networks that simulate the same types of connections that are made in the human brain to generate thought. Currently, the technology is used mostly to analyze data for genetics, pharmaceutical and other scientific research. It's seeing little use in CRM right now, though it has tremendous potential in the future

AI-enhanced analytics programs also provide survival modelling capabilities — suggesting changes to products based on use. For example, customer patterns are analysed to learn ways to extend the life of light bulbs or to help decide the correct dosage for medications.

High-tech data mining can give companies a precise view of how particular segments of the customer base react to a product or service and propose changes consistent with those findings. In addition to further exploring customers" buying patterns, analytics could help companies react much more quickly to the marketplace.

According to Meta Group vice president Liz Shahnam, intelligent agents could let companies make real-time changes to marketing campaigns. "New technologies would have the model refreshed on the fly based on each new incoming piece of customer information — reaction to the campaign — for a more targeted offer,"

Artificial Intelligence in HR

It is widely believed that the role of managers is becoming a key determinant for enterprises' competitiveness in today's knowledge economy era. Owing to fast development of information technologies (ITs), corporations are employed to enhance the capability of human resource management, which is called human resource information system (HRIS). Recently, due to promising results of artificial neural networks (ANNs) and fuzzy theory in engineering, they have also become candidates for HRIS. The artificial intelligence (AT) field can play a role in this, especially; in assuring that the fuzzy neural network has the characteristics and functions of training, learning, and simulation to make an optimal and accurate judgment according to the human thinking model. The main purposes of the study are to discuss the appointment of managers in enterprises through fuzzy neural network, to construct a new model for evaluation of managerial talent, and accordingly to develop a decision support system in human resource selection. Therefore, the research methods of reviewing literature, in-depth interview, questionnaire survey, and fuzzy neural network are used in the study. The fuzzy neural network is used to train the concrete database, based on 191 questionnaires from experts, for getting the best network model in different training conditions. In order to let decision-makers adjust weighted values and obtain decisive results of each phase's scores, we adopted the simple additive weighting (SAW) and fuzzy analytic hierarchy process (FAHP) methods in the study. Finally, the human resource selection system of Java user interface has been constructed by FNN in the study.

Conclusion

It is difficult for business to see general relevance from AI. This is probably one of the reasons for the compartmentalization of AI into things like Knowledge Based Systems, Neural Networks, and Genetic Algorithms etc. Some of these separate sub topics have been shown to be very useful in solving certain difficult business and industrial problems and consequently funding bodies influence research directions by encouraging work on these more application based areas. This can have a positive effect for business benefit and has lead to some very useful systems that have found their way into the heart of business activity. Business should not lose sight of where AI could go because there are many potential benefits to current and new businesses of future research. The idea of robotic domestic workers is still far fetched but companies are making progress even here. There is already a Robot Vacuum Cleaner marketed by Electrolux and doubtless improved systems with better functionality will follow.

I would like to close by quoting from Tom Peters, a leading management guru: "When you think you've reached the top, tear down everything and do it all over again. If you don't, your competitor will." To this, I would like to add my own: "If your competitor won't, new investors will enter the market segment who will do the same job better."

Potential Benefits of Artificial Intelligence Applications

Improve Training

Train employees, customers, and partners faster and more reliably using simulated scenarios and automated coaching, performance evaluation, and feedback. Increase the effectiveness of simulation-based training for safety, hazardous conditions, emergency response, and other critical situations (e.g., pilots, nuclear power plant operators, military personnel, and equipment operators.

Improve Products and Services

Enhance the competitiveness of your company's product or service by automating some of its functions or by making it easier to use.

Leverage Corporate Knowledge

Make corporate expertise more widely available throughout your company to improve the quality of decisions. Save, retrieve, and build on corporate expertise that is often lost when employees leave or transfer within the company.

Improve Collaboration

Help geographically-distributed employees, customers, and partners work together more effectively by providing intelligent, computer-assist supporting collaboration.

Automate Unpleasant Tasks

Automate boring, dangerous or unpleasant tasks, reducing the need for employees to work in these conditions.

Complement Your Employee's Reasoning Skills

Complement the reasoning abilities of humans (pattern recognition and association) with those of computers (data retrieval, logical analysis).

Business Intelligence through Hybrid Intelligent System Approach: Application to Retail Banking

Continuing business in today's competitive world is full of uncertainty and risk. Capturing new customers and retaining the existing ones is a challenge. To bring efficiency and cost advantage, organizations have to learn to manage not only the organizational resources intelligently but also precious expertise within the organization and learn from the experience. To bring efficiency and cost advantages, analytical tools help managers to model the problems, create various scenarios, perform sensitivity and what-if analysis, forecasting, etc. as a component of decision making process to manage and use resources well and optimally. Analytical methods are scientific techniques and tools to analyse the problems and find the solutions to the managerial decision problems. While analytical tools assist and support managers in making decisions, they don't assist in accumulating, reusing and managing precious expertise available in the organizations. Intelligent systems are best suited to do this. They facilitate to acquire, extract, preserve, use and apply the knowledge in the organization and thereby making it intelligent. These systems bring expertise and use the past experience of organization to deal with new problems. Facilitate to preserve the corporate knowledge (which a valuable asset of any organization) even after the decision maker leaves the organization.

The retail portfolio of banks has been growing at fast pace and volume is increasing. Consumers demand quick and effective service. The manager has to manage between prompt service v/s better assessment of customer and minimization of risk. Getting best business out of the customer, the managers have to understand and analyse the customer-well, profile them and look for right cross-selling and up-selling opportunities. Along with increase in retail customers, there is increase in number of transactions. To keep track of transactions manually for possible fraudulent or suspicious transaction is very difficult job and may not be technically possible to do. The RBI has already come with comprehensive KYC (Know Your Customer) and AML (Anti-Money Laundering) guidelines to take care of such issues. The banks are offering new and customized products. The products are becoming complex and it takes time for customer to understand the products, their features etc. In such an environment intelligent systems play a very crucial role in automating some of these tasks and supplement managers in their decision-making and to be compliant. [1,5,11]. In the following sections we have proposed and discussed a hybrid intelligent approach to address the applications in retail banking. The section 2 describes the basic intelligent framework used in the system, section 3 discusses the application of this approach to retail banking. 2 Hybrid Intelligent System Approach and Framework 2.1 Hybrid Intelligent Systems The widely used intelligent systems in management are expert systems, neural networks, case-based reasoning, fuzzy systems and genetic algorithms [9]. Brief definition of intelligent systems we discussed in the paper is given bellow.

Expert System

It is a system that stores explicit knowledge (about a particular application area) and uses it. It acts as an expert consultant to solve the problems by using and applying the knowledge intelligently. Knowledge consists of the facts: data about the problem to be solved and a set of rules to solve the problem. In Q & A (Question and Answer) mode, expert system works like a doctor asking series of relevant questions (to know symptoms) and gives expert opinion (diagnosis) based on answers (symptoms). *Case Based Reasoning* A CBR system contains *case-base*, a repository of solved problems (cases). It digs out the implicit expertise in the past cases and uses it to address a new problem (problem case). It finds out the most closely matching case/

s with the problem case and recommends the decisions by re-using, and adapting the decisions in those cases. The CBR system contains domain and conceptual knowledge to match, reuse and adapt cases. *Artificial Neural Networks* Simulate the working of biological nervous systems; upon training them to solve the problem by providing the past data, they learn complex relationships, patterns, etc. in the data. They hold this learnt relationship, patterns etc. (as an implicit knowledge) and use it to solve new problems.

Intelligent systems differ in ways they get, store and apply the knowledge, deal with uncertainty and incomplete information and knowledge, adapt to new knowledge, maintain the knowledge and so on [2,4]. Comparison between expert system, neural network and case-based reasoning technology. Expert systems are good when expertise is available and easy to extract from the human experts and various knowledge sources. Neural networks can learn and model complex relationships. Case-based reasoning helps to dig out the hidden expertise/knowledge in already solved problems (with partial domain knowledge) and use that to solve new problems of similar kind. Fuzzy systems deal with ambiguity and uncertainty in human decision making while genetic algorithms are based on evolution principal and suitable for applications involving searching best solutions and optimizing. Each of these systems has some inherent weaknesses and strengths. This makes them less suitable for solving problems using a single technique. For example problem with expert systems is extracting knowledge from experts, which is time consuming and costly, expert systems can not learn on their own and adapt, but these systems are good in giving qualitative explanations and justifications for decisions they make. While, neural networks are best in learning and adapting but they are poor in explaining their results.

Integrating these techniques enhance their overall strengths and lessen weaknesses thereby helping to solve overall problem in effective way [2,4]. Various strategies, architectures, models and classification schemes have been suggested by many authors to integrate various intelligent systems for practical applications [2,3,4,6,7]. Some of them based on functionality and characteristics of intelligent systems while others based on techniques and mechanisms used to integrate the systems. However, the final goal is to model the problem by taking advantages of strengths to achieve effectiveness and efficiency. Combining analytical methods and intelligent systems gives advantages of having and applying knowledge about the problem and solving problem using various mathematical modelling techniques.

The major advantages of combining these two types of systems are: a) understanding of operation and results of the decision support system in consistent and objective manner; b) the quantitative results are transformed to qualitative explanations, which are easier to understand, and are often of greater significance to the decision makers, c) using domain knowledge about the problem, knowledge about usability and suitability of analytical techniques, etc. before starting decision-making process, d) the objectiveness and completeness of the results are ensured: the combination of both increases the objectives of the final results, e) solving the problem not only considering quantitative facts but also analysing the problem qualitatively, and, f) managing and controlling overall decision making process intelligently.

A Hybrid Intelligent System Framework the architecture of framework that integrates various intelligent systems. This framework is used to develop, deploy and run web-applications and decision support systems backed by integrated architectures of expert system, neural network, case-based reasoning, genetic algorithms and analytical methods. The framework is completely web-based and supports thin client and server-based computing. All the intelligent systems use XML (eXtensible Markup Language).

The framework has XML-database access layer to extract, map and transform the data from data sources. The framework uses a unique and novel way of integrating various intelligent systems and data sources in web environment [8]. Representing the problem as well as result (output) as a case in a common XML format makes it flexible to store, interchange, and use the session data across various intelligent systems. Framework allows to host multiple expert system, CBR and neural network systems.

Hybrid Intelligent Systems and Retail Banking

1 Retail Banking The retail banking functions other than transaction support have been broadly classified into following broad areas:

   a. Customer Analysis: Understanding and analysing customer well, their preferences. Profiling and segmentation. Looking for right marketing, cross-selling opportunities and up-selling opportunities to right people and so on.

b. Decision Support: Evaluating customer, credit rating and scoring etc.

c. Help-Desk and Self-Service: Providing help to customer on products and services. Facilitating them to explore information such as statements, past transactions and so on.

d. Transaction Monitoring: Continuously monitoring the transactions to detect suspicious and abnormal transactions.

e. Information Retrieval: Managers and decision makers can access required information quickly and easily.

2 Hybrid Approach to Retail Banking, how retail functionality discussed in above paragraph is implemented using hybrid intelligent framework. The domain generic vocabulary required for modelling various applications is divided into three broad groups: customer, product and transaction. Customer group has set of parameters, which represents almost all information about customer like *Name*, *Sex*, *Age*, etc.

The information about the customer, product and transaction is extracted from the databases is mapped and transformed into instances at run-time. This makes the approach independent of database and database schema. The intelligent system layer has rule-based expert system engine, neural network modules, case-based reasoning engine and libraries of analytical methods. This layer has repository of various neural network models, case schemas and global expert system rules. These models and rules are logically separated into groups depending upon the applications. These intelligent systems and models use the data extracted, mapped and transformed to common vocabulary.

Customer Analysis

Intelligent systems play very important role in analysing a new customer and existing customers. The combination of expert system and case-based reasoning is used. Expert systems has been used to put set of standard and common-sense rules to understand and analyse the customer. These rules are defined in consultation with domain experts or derived from automated learning tools. For example, set of rules to determine to whom to target when a new product is introduced, rules to customize customer preferences and on. Each customer's information is treated as case and all customer database as a case-base. Modelling a customer using case-based reasoning gives edge over other automated learning techniques because they are supplement by domain knowledge. In CBR the domain knowledge plays very important role in searching and intelligent matching. This helps to profile the customers based on conceptual similarity rather than just numbers and figures. For example, a neural network may not understand the difference between two designations or qualifications. However, in CBR, the knowledge component takes care of this. It takes the new customer into the profile of nearest conceptually matching ones (cluster). One can study the characteristics of the cluster and understand many things like what is the age profile, what kind of products these people buy, what kind of communication channel they respond etc.

Automated Help Desk Help-desk operations can be automated through web-based systems backed by expert system and case-based reasoning techniques. There is lot of information made available on websites on products and services. But most of time, the visitor wants specific information and customized answers rather than ending up with reading, understanding and evaluating through lots of web pages. This really requires knowledge of searching the right information. Similarly help-desk executives need to be trained for new products and services. Automated help-desk provide expert interface like human experts that guides the customer intelligently on the path leading towards the right product. This enables customers to find the right and the best product suitable for them or they are looking for, subject to their profiles, needs, objective and constraints. These interfaces are intelligent capable of engaging the customers like intelligent sales person through series of questions and answers. The questions and answer options may be put in a simple layman's language (including multilingual) to be understood by average customer instead using technical jargons. The system can control the flow of questions intelligently (avoid asking irrelevant questions), by judging what user wants, based on user answers. Automated web-based help-desks not only help customers to find right product in an easy way but also help organizations to capture such conversations with visitors to keep track of what kind of customers visit, show interest in what kind of products. Such information organizations can use for cross-selling opportunities, keeping track of user profiles, their expectations, popular products, target promotional materials etc.

Transaction Monitoring

Whenever a transaction is about to authorize, the statistics like *average transaction amount*, *max amount transacted* so far, *minimum duration between two transactions*, *standard deviation of transaction amount and time* etc. is generated. The expert system compares current transaction with statistics generated to detect deviations. Expert system has rules to check consistency and inspect the transaction. For example, a simple rule to generate alert 'Odd transaction time' whenever a credit card transaction happens between midnight to morning at grocery merchant location. There can be personalized customized rules depending upon customer's requests. A CBR system can be modelled which conceptually matches current transaction with past ones in terms of *location*, *time*, *amount*, *date*, *type*, etc. and find the deviation. CBR system can also be managed to match the customer transaction pattern with the fraudulent ones.

Information Retrieval & Reporting Most of the time, required information is not found quickly and easily and it takes lot of time in searching. Expert system and case-based reasoning systems can help to find out required matching information quickly and easily. Report interfaces backed by expert system facilitate to retrieve or drill-down the information from databases about the customer, product and transactions in very interactive Q & A way. The approach of simple Q & A is heuristic and can be mapped to SQL (Structured Query Language) engine, can lead to right information the decision-maker is looking for easily and quickly avoiding remembering technical syntax of ad-hoc SQL queries. For example, a manager may be looking for most profitable customers in a particular locality or the list of customers to whom a particular product can be marketed etc. Expert systems and CBR can be customized to take care of common needs of users.

Intelligent systems play very crucial role in automating expertise and reusing organizational experience. Hybrid approach is more suitable to retail banking because it involves analysis of lot of data with different perspectives. Retail banking involves various tasks and needs better analysis and understanding of customers, products and transactions. Using only one intelligent technique for analysis may not be suitable or would play limited role. The intelligent retail-banking framework described above integrates various intelligent systems along with analytical methods. Banking organizations would definitely going to benefit from hybrid approach for better and quick customer service, better management of in-house expertise, reuse of experience of dealing with customers, monitor transactions closely and better help-desks for products. Apart from these, intelligent systems bring consistency, objectivity in decision-making along quick response and flexibility.

Mobile Computing: Characteristics, Business Benefits, and the Mobile Framework

Mobile computing is a versatile and potentially strategic technology that improves information quality and accessibility, increases operational efficiency, and enhances management effectiveness. A successive examination of the characteristics and benefits of mobile computing is used to achieve this goal.

As a starting point, a definition of mobile computing is provided. Next, the technologies that make mobile computing possible (hardware, software, and communications) are examined. The discussion of mobile computing technologies leads into an overview of the types of applications that are commonly found on mobile computers. With this background established, the following two sections demonstrate the ability of mobile computing to improve both information quality and information accessibility. Using this knowledge in conjunction with mobile computing case examples, the ability of mobile computing to improve operational efficiency is subsequently supported. Then, the ability of mobile computing to increase management effectiveness is similarly supported.

The previously discussed improvements in information quality, information accessibility, operational efficiency, and management effectiveness are then used to demonstrate that mobile computing is a versatile technology. Additionally, three separate existing frameworks for understanding the strategic nature of information technology are used to illustrate the strategic qualities of mobile computing.

As with any technology, mobile computing must be used appropriately in order to attain the benefits that have been discussed. To this end, a set of heuristics called the MOBILE framework is developed by the author to assist information technology professionals in achieving the stated benefits of mobile computing. The MOBILE framework assists information technology professionals by defining the types of problems, opportunities, and directives that are best addressed through mobile computing technology.

Before concluding, the paper discusses the continuous evolution and change that is occurring within the field of mobile computing. Two examples of new technologies that will impact mobile computing in the future are examined. The paper concludes with a review of the material covered and a reassertion of the stated benefits of mobile computing.

Mobile Computing Defined

The term "Mobile computing" is used to describe the use of computing devices—which usually interact in some fashion with a central information system—while away from the normal, fixed workplace. Mobile computing technology enables the mobile worker to: (a) create; (b) access; (c) process; (d) store; and (e) communicate information without being constrained to a single location. By extending the reach of an organization's fixed information system, mobile computing enables interaction with organizational personnel that were previously disconnected. Throughout this paper, the concept of mobile computing will be further refined through: (a) an examination of the technologies that make mobile computing possible; (b) an analysis of the many benefits of mobile computing; and (c) the presentation of the MOBILE framework, that provides guidance on when mobile computing is best applied to a problem, opportunity, or directive. Mobile computing is an extremely versatile, capable, and exciting technology that offers many otherwise unattainable benefits to organizations that choose to integrate it into their fixed information system.

Mobile Computing Technology

Mobile computing is accomplished using a combination of: (a) computer hardware; (b) system and applications software; and (c) some form of communications medium. Powerful mobile solutions have recently become possible because of the availability of: (a) extremely powerful and small computing devices; (b) specialized software; and (c) improved telecommunications. ("SOLID White", 1998) This section provides a brief overview of the general types of hardware, software, and communications mediums that are commonly integrated to create mobile computing solutions.

Hardware

The characteristics of mobile computing hardware are defined by the: (a) size and form factor; (b) weight; (c) microprocessor; (d) primary storage; (e) secondary storage; (f) screen size and type; (g) means of input; (h) means of output; (i) battery life; (j) communications capabilities; (k) expandability; and (l) durability of the device. Using these hardware characteristics, mobile computing hardware can be grouped into the following general categories: (a) Palmtop; (b) Clamshell; (c) Handheld Penkey; (d) Penslate; and (e) Laptop. The following table—based on an amalgamation of data—depicts the prevalent characteristics of mobile computing hardware in each category. (Buyer's Guide, 1998) (Intermec Technologies, 1999) (Product Comparison Guide, 1999) (Intermec Technologies, 1999a)

Users need and want access to their data wherever they go, and they will use a wide assortment of mobile computing devices to get it. Except for possibly high-end laptops, none of the categories of mobile computing hardware are replacements for a loaded desktop PC. Instead, each category of device fills a niche that helps to satisfy the demands created by mobile users' many computing needs. Although a lot of mobile hardware has many eye-catching characteristics, the decision about which hardware to employ should be based entirely on clear business needs. (Radcliff, 1998) Defining these needs, and having a solid strategic plan for how the new hardware will be used, is the best way to avoid disappointment and missed opportunities. (Paisner, 1998) While many specific makes and models of hardware exist, the general categories of mobile computing hardware depicted in the previous table adequately characterize the majority of mobile computing devices available today. References to mobile computing hardware during the subsequent analysis of the benefits of mobile computing will make reference to these categories.

Software

Mobile computers make use of a wide variety of system and application software. The most common system software and operating environments used on mobile computers include: (a) MSDOS; (b) Windows 3.1/3.11/95/98/NT; (c) Windows for Pen Computing; (d) Windows CE; (e) PenDOS; (f) PenRight!; (g) Palm OS; (h) Psion EPOC32; and (i) Unix. (Buyer's Guide, 1998) (Boling, 1998, xiii-xv) These operating environments range in capabilities from a minimalist graphically-enhanced-pen-enabled DOS environment (PenDOS and PenRight! for DOS) to the powerful capabilities of Windows NT.

Each operating system/environment has some form of integrated development environment (IDE) for application development. Most of the operating environments provide more than one development environment option for custom application development. For example, Windows ons between mobile devices. This allows the developer to concentrate on the application and not the specifics of the hardware being utilized. (Besaha, 1998)

All mobile computing application software does not have to be custom-designed. Prewritten application software can be purchased for many application areas, such as sales force automation. Additionally, many companies that develop mobile computing software offer systems integration services, and will work with the client to modify their existing application to fulfil the client's specific needs.

Communications

The ability of a mobile computer to communicate in some fashion with a fixed information system is a defining characteristic of mobile computing. The type and availability of communication medium significantly impacts the type of mobile computing application that can be created.

Modes of Communication

The way a mobile computing device communicates with a fixed information system can be categorized as: (a) connected; (b) weakly connected; (c) batch; and (d) disconnected. (Muller, 1998, 112-113) The connected category implies a continuously available high-speed connection. The ability to communicate continuously, but at slow speeds (i.e. < 28 Kbps), allows mobile computers to be weakly connected to the fixed information system. A batch connection means that the mobile computer is not continuously available for communication with the fixed information system. In the batch mode, communication is established randomly or periodically to exchange and update information between the mobile computer and fixed information systems. Mobile computers may operate in batch mode over communication mediums that are capable of continuous operation, reducing the wireless airtime and associated fees. Disconnected mobile computers allow users to improve efficiency by making calculations, storing contact information, keeping a schedule, and other non-communications oriented tasks. This mode of operation is of little interest because the mobile device is incapable of electronically interacting and exchanging information with the fixed organizational information system. Exchange of information with a disconnected mobile computing device can only be accomplished by manually entering information into the device or copying from the device's screen and manually entering the information into the fixed information system. This mode of information exchange is no more efficient than using paper and is effectively nonexistent, since virtually all modern mobile computing hardware is capable of some form of native electronic data communications.

Available Technologies

There are many communications technologies available today that enable mobile computers to communicate. The most common of these technologies are: (a) Wireless Local Area Networks (WLANs); (b) Satellite; (c) Cellular Digital Packet Data (CDPD); (d) Personal Communications Systems (PCS); (e) Global System for Mobile communications (GSM); (f) RAM and ARDIS data networks; (g) Specialized Mobile Radio (SMR) service; (h) one and two-way paging; (i) plain old telephone system (POTS); (j) Internet; (k) infra-red; (l) docking (serial, parallel, LAN); and (m) disk swapping. These diverse communications technologies make available a continuum of connectivity that provides communications capabilities ranging from manual-assisted batch transfers to high-speed continuous communication.

Making the Choice

The specific mobile application, hardware, software, and operating location/environment determine which communications mediums are appropriate to use for a mobile computing solution. (Muller, 1998, 303-392) Achieving the desired communication capability requires matching the communications medium with the appropriate mobile computing hardware. Most mobile computing hardware is designed to take advantage of multiple communications mediums. Specialized hardware and software is also available which enables many mobile computing devices to utilize communications mediums for which they were not originally designed. Again, the desired operating location and environmental conditions within which the mobile device will operate must significantly impact the choice of communications medium. The proper selection and utilization of the communications medium ensures that the mobile computing device is capable of reliable communications to support the mobile computing application and fulfil the business need.

Mobile Computing Applications

The real power of mobile computing becomes apparent when

mobile hardware, software, and communications are optimally configured and used to accomplish a specified mobile task. Although many varied applications exist, mobile computing applications can generally be divided into two categories—horizontal and vertical.

Horizontal

Horizontal applications have broad-based appeal and include software that performs functions such as: (a) email; (b) Web browsing; (c) word processing; (d) scheduling; (e) contact management; (f) to-do lists; (g) massaging; (h) presentation. These types of applications usually come standard on Palmtops, Clamshells, and laptops with systems software such as Windows 95.

Vertical

Vertical applications are industry-specific and only have appeal within the specific industry for which the application was written. Vertical applications are commonly used in industries such as: (a) retailing; (b) utilities; (c) warehousing; (d) shipping; (e) medical; and (f) law enforcement and public safety. (Dhawan, 1997, 15-57) These vertical applications are often transaction oriented and normally interface with a corporate database.

Application Categories

The specific requirements of a mobile computing application generally determine the type of hardware and operating environment required to support the application. The common types of applications for each category of mobile computer. (Pen Computer Solutions, 1999) (Dhawan, 1997, 78)

This list is by no means exhaustive. Other application areas include: (a) mining; (b) forestry; (c) agriculture; and (d) surveying. (Lauzon Computer, 1997) The application areas depicted in the table demonstrate the general capabilities offered through mobile computing. Many of these application areas will be examined in further detail during the subsequent sections of this paper that discuss the benefits of mobile computing.

Content Dimension

Mobile computing enables information to be captured at its source, that is, its point of creation. The obvious advantage of this type of data capture is that it eliminates the need to reenter the data at a later time by transcribing it into a computer from the original paper copy. Besides eliminating redundancy, source data capture with mobile computing offers additional advantages. Complex and complete information can be quickly and easily captured through special mobile input devices such as barcode readers. The amount of information captured by special input devices and the speed with which it is captured could not be duplicated by human-based input means. The software application on the mobile computing device can be programmed to use error-checking routines that ensure the captured data is complete and free from errors. Furthermore, the software can use context sensitive questions and intelligent forms to ensure that the proper scope of information is retrieved and that no extra, unnecessary or irrelevant information is accepted. The mobile computing device may also perform preprocessing on the data that is being collected before it is ultimately transferred to a fixed information system. Since the information being transferred from the mobile device to the fixed information system is high quality, the information that is transferred back from the fixed information system to the mobile computing device will generally also be of higher quality. Mobile computing application software can be used to intelligently request information from the central fixed information system, so the mobile device only receives the desired information from the central system. These characteristics of mobile computing enable it to improve the content dimension (accuracy, relevance, completeness, conciseness, and scope) of information quality.

Form Dimension

Mobile computing applications use hardware and software that are specifically configured so that information can be viewed in a format that is: (a) easy for the mobile user to use; and (b) unambiguous. Since the information that is transmitted or stored in the mobile device is in digital format, it can normally be: (a) viewed in either a detailed or summary form; (b) sorted as required; (c) manipulated into tables or charts as required; and (d) viewed on the screen or printed out. Mobile computing applications can use a wide variety of devices which enhance the ability of the mobile worker to capture and distribute data. Mobile computers can take advantage of: (a) barcodes; (b) magnetic stripe readers; (c) portable printers; (d) signature capture; (e) smart cards; (f) radio frequency identification; (g) voice recognition; (h) still image capture; (i) video image capture; and (j) the Global Positioning System

(GPS). (Intermec Technologies, 1998) Additionally, the internal storage and processing capability of mobile computers allow immediate access to large quantities of localized digital information. For example, a utility employee may carry a mobile device that contains a CDROM with maps of the entire city within which she works. From this discussion, it can be seen that mobile computing improves the form dimension of information quality by improving the characteristics of clarity, detail, order, presentation, and media.

Overall Quality

Mobile computing improves the time, content, and form dimensions of information quality. Since each dimension is improved, the resulting overall quality of information generated by an organizational information system that utilizes mobile computing is also improved.

Improved Information Accessibility

Mobile computing enables improvements in information accessibility. The degree of improvement is directly dependent upon the mobile hardware and communications equipment in use. For example, a Penslate computer that is operating in the connected mode via a wireless local area network will have much greater information accessibility than a clamshell mobile computer that is operating in batch mode and only connects randomly throughout the day. The degree of information accessibility required—which defines the hardware and communications requirements—is determined by the business needs that are driving the mobile computing application. Mobile computing technology (hardware, software, and communications) provides a wide range of options that can be mixed and matched to fit the needs of each individual mobile computing application.

The improvements in information accessibility enabled by mobile computing result in improved information flow both to and from the central fixed information system. The mobile computer enables quick and efficient information retrieval from the central information system. The ability to access central information and make fixed or ad hoc queries of corporate databases enables employees to get the information they need to complete the job. The mobile computer also enables transmission of current operational data, in native digital format, from the mobile user to the central fixed information system.

Once transmitted to the fixed information system, the data from the mobile user can be processed and made available for all other users of the central information system. Thus, the information available to a mobile user from the central information system reflects current information from other mobile users as well. Mobile computing eliminates the delay that occurs when an employee must physically return to the office at the end of the day and submit paper forms so that data entry personnel can enter the information into the central information system.

Even employees that are not continuously connected to the fixed organizational information system via a wireless link will experience significantly improved information accessibility through mobile computing. One phone call at the end of the day from the mobile user via a standard modem is all that is required to transmit the entire day's transactions to the central computer, saving travel and data entry time. Additionally, any scheduling or assignment changes for the mobile employee for the following day can be transmitted to the employee during the same phone call.

Mobile computing also significantly speeds information accessibility when other media, such as: (a) facsimile; (b) audio files; or (c) still images are concerned. Digital images or audio files can be accessed by the mobile user or transmitted from the mobile user to the central fixed organizational information system. If matched properly to the work environment and task to be accomplished, the mobile computer will always be in the possession of the mobile worker during the course of the day. Especially in the connected or weakly connected modes of operation, this means that the mobile employee may be contacted throughout the workday via the mobile computing device. Additionally, it means that the employee has access to other mobile employees via email or other massaging schemes. As with many mobile computing applications, the type of mobile application and the hardware, software, and communications used to support it will normally determine the degree and type of information accessibility.

The direct measurable results of improved information accessibility—both to and from the mobile worker—are many. They include: (a) improved customer service; (b) reduced cycle times; (c) greater accuracy; (d) fewer complaints; and (e) a reduction in required intermediate support staff. Improved information accessibility can also support many other improvements such as: (a) elimination of extra travel; (b) reduction of selling times; and (c) saving lives.

Increased Operational Efficiency

Mobile computing enables improvements in the operational efficiency of organizations that integrate the technology into their fixed information systems. It enables the computing power and information contained within the fixed information system to be structured around the optimum work flow of a mobile worker, instead of altering the mobile worker's work flow to meet the optimum configuration for computing. The mobile computer stays with the mobile employee, instead of the employee being required to travel to the computer. Mobile computing can improve efficiency in many ways, including: (a) saving time; (b) reducing waste; (c) cutting cycle times; (d) reducing rework; (e) enabling business process reengineering; (f) improving accuracy; (g) decreasing time spent on customer complaints; and (h) reducing unnecessary travel. (Dhawan, 14) Representative examples from actual real-world mobile computing implementations will be presented to demonstrate the ways in which mobile computing can improve the operational efficiency of an organization.

Field Sales

The operational efficiency of sales personnel is significantly enhanced through mobile computing. An excellent example of these improvements can be seen by examining how mobile computing improves the efficiency of remote insurance and financial planning sales. The mobile computer frees the sales agent to meet with the client at the client's home, office, or other location. Customer data is collected, estimates and comparisons are immediately calculated, the customer decides on the program of choice, the central computer is immediately updated, and the customer is enrolled in the insurance or financial planning program. (Dhawan, 34) Without mobile computing, this sales process would take days instead of minutes. In addition to accessing and updating customer account information, mobile sales personnel can accomplish tasks such as printing invoices or other information to leave with the customer. (Automated Wireless, 1999)

Transportation and Shipping

The transportation and shipping industries benefit greatly from mobile computing. Using mobile computers in conjunction with GPS/GIS and an accompanying vehicle information system (VIS), the operations of an entire transportation fleet can be managed from a central location. The central office knows the location, status, and condition of all vehicles, and operators have two-way communication with the operations centre. Using this information, vehicles can be optimally dispatched to maximize efficiency as measured by: (a) time; (b) fuel consumption; and (c) delivery priority. (Dhawan, 52) The mobile computers enable significant performance improvements, achieved simultaneously with operational cost reductions.

Averitt Express, a North Carolina trucking company that specializes in less-than-truckload deliveries, significantly improved its operational efficiency with a mobile computing solution that utilizes Penkey computers and continuous wireless connectivity. Before the mobile computing solution was introduced, the company managed its trucking assets using a manual tracking system and two-way voice radio. The system was not providing the desired efficiency or quality of customer service that Averitt needed for competitiveness. Using the new system, dispatchers enter customer pickup information directly into the central computer, which automatically selects and notifies the appropriate truck via the driver's Penkey computer. Drivers record information about deliveries, such as the time of delivery and the person who signed for it, on the mobile computer. This information is automatically transmitted to the central computer and customer service representatives can use it to provide better delivery information to customers. Since the introductions of the mobile computing solution, operations are more efficient and customers are happier. (Intermec Technologies, 1998a)

General Dispatching

Mobile computers used in conjunction with Global Positioning System (GPS) and Geographical Information System (GIS) data allow significant improvements in the operational efficiency of various dispatch operations. (Dhawan, 27) For example, the central computer at a taxi company can track the location and status of all its taxicabs and electronically dispatch the most appropriate car to a customer's location. Additionally, the central computer can calculate an accurate approximation of when the taxi will arrive, enabling improved customer service.

Hotel Operations

Connecting the cleaning and hospitality staff of a hotel with mobile computing can significantly improve the efficiency of hotel operations. As guests check out and rooms are vacated, the central computer wirelessly signals cleaning staff that the rooms are ready for cleaning. Problems that are identified during cleaning, such as broken appliances or faulty plumbing, are immediately communicated to the mobile maintenance team for action. As soon as cleaning is complete and repairs are accomplished, the cleaning staff member wirelessly updates the central computer and the room is immediately available for check-in by a new guest. The same system can be used to efficiently direct mobile hospitality personnel in response to guest requests for information and service. (Dhawan, 57)

News Reporting

Mobile computers dramatically improve the efficiency of news media operations. Reporters equipped with mobile computers and accompanying electronic devices can cover a news or sporting event, take digital video or still photographs, digitally record audio interviews, compose the text of the news story, and transmit the completed product back to the central agency for editing and immediate publication. (Dhawan, 56) In the media industry, the timing and quality of news coverage is critical. Mobile computing increases the quality of the information from the media crews and significantly decreases the time required to process and transmit the story for publication.

Health Care

Mobile medical care, whether in-home, on the road, or within a hospital, is more efficient with mobile computing. The mobile healthcare worker can access patient records for reference purposes, and is able to update records with current diagnosis and treatment information. Emergency medical technicians (EMTs) responding at the scene of an accident can use mobile computers to capture patient information, treatments accomplished, vital signs, and other critical data. This information is wirelessly transmitted to the receiving hospital, which then prepares to receive and treat the patient, or recommend another hospital facility with more appropriate treatment facilities—depending upon the nature and severity of the injuries. The more efficient hand-off between ambulance EMTs and hospital staff made possible by mobile computing can save lives that otherwise might have been lost. (Dhawan, 44-46)

Car Rental Agencies

Car rental agencies have taken advantage of the improved operational efficiency made possible by mobile computing. Using handheld computers, rental company employees can now process a rental car return without the customer ever being required to enter the office. The process works as follows: (a) The customer arrives with a car for drop-off; (b) an employee greets the customer, receives the keys to the vehicle, and performs an interior and exterior vehicle inspection; and (c) upon inspection completion, the employee uses the mobile computer to settle the account and record the car as returned. Additionally, the vehicle cleaning and maintenance staff is automatically notified when the vehicle is returned, so it can quickly be returned to a rentable status.

Fieldwork

Almost any form of fieldwork can be made significantly more efficient through the application of mobile computing. Parking control officers and utility inspectors are two examples of field workers who can receive operational benefits from mobile computing. Parking control officers use handheld computers to check the registration and violation history of parking offenders. Parking violations are issued immediately and towing/backup can be requested when required. Utility inspectors have historically used paper forms to capture information such as consumer power consumption and utility equipment status (transformers, transmission towers, etc.). Using mobile computers, inspectors can be given instructions on inspections to be accomplished and information can be captured and validated at the source. (Dhawan, 50-51)

Mobile Automation

General business travellers also reap the benefits of mobile computing. Email, spreadsheets, presentations, and word processing are the four primary tasks accomplished by these business travellers. Laptops, Palmtops, and portable Clamshell computers with usable-size keyboards enable businesspeople to stay in touch and accomplish the tasks they need for job effectiveness. (Gillin, 1998) Using powerful mobile computers in conjunction with high-speed connectivity, mobile workers can perform work normally accomplished at the office while on the road or in the field. (Dhawan, 77)

Results

These examples have demonstrated the types of operational efficiency improvements that can be gained through the use of mobile computing technology. The improvements in efficiency made possible by mobile computing are impressive. Mobile computing technology can be applied to a diverse range of problems and achieve similar improvements in operational efficiency.

Increased Management Effectiveness

Mobile computing technology can improve management effectiveness by improving information quality, information flow, and ability to control a mobile workforce. It makes the most current and accurate information available to both the mobile worker and the users of the fixed information system with which the mobile worker communicates. These benefits can be seen in all areas of the information system, from the fixed reports generated by a management information system all the way to ad hoc systems such as decision support and executive information systems.

Many of the management benefits of mobile computing have already been seen in the examples previously presented in the operational efficiency section of this paper. Companies like Averitt Express not only improved their efficiency through mobile computing, but they also improved their ability to manage operations. Often, it is the improved ability to manage operations that is partly responsible for the performance improvements seen in companies that introduce mobile computing technology. Several examples will be presented in this section, in order to further demonstrate the ability of mobile computing to improve management effectiveness.

Campus Access

Elected government officials, such as state senators, have dramatically improved their management effectiveness through the use of mobile computing. A wireless LAN is used to connect the senators to a campus-wide network. Through this network, senators access private and global information; allowing access to: (a) private files; (b) email; (c) current legislation; (d) scheduling information; and (e) many other services. Additionally, the mobile computer makes the senator continuously accessible to his or her office staff. (Dhawan, 49) This type of system can be implemented using laptops, pen-slates, or even hand-held computers, depending on the individual processing needs and information requirements of each senator. By staying in touch and having continuous access to current information and works-in-progress, senators are better able to manage their time and the many political requirements of the job.

Sears

Sears, Roebuck & Co. uses mobile computers to improve their ability to manage over 14,000 service technicians that are dispersed throughout the United States. Using specially designed, durable laptop computers and wireless connectivity, Sears directs the activities of its technician staff. Each morning, technicians download their schedule for the day, including customer information and service history. Throughout the day, the technicians record their progress on the mobile computer. During service calls, the technician uses the computer to accomplish tasks such as verifying the price and availability of repair parts. Once a service call is complete, the central dispatch facility is automatically notified via wireless communication. Technicians that finish service calls early, or that have cancelled appointments, can be dynamically redirected to another service call in the immediate area. The mobile computing solution has dramatically improved the ability of Sears to manage its mobile technician staff. (Flanagan, 1998)

Other

Stock traders use handheld mobile computers to gain immediate access to financial data and manage transactions. (Dhawan, 36) Airlines use handhelds with built-in barcode scanners to scan baggage as it is moved through the handling system, improving the ability to real-time track and manage baggage movement. (Dhawan, 41) Mobile computers and wireless networks have also proven to be a significant management tool to assist with coordination during disaster recovery operations.

Results

Just as mobile computing enables improved operational efficiency, it also enables improved management effectiveness. Mobile computers make more timely and accurate information available to managers. Mobile computers improve the manager's ability to track work in progress. They also improve the ability of managers to communicate with mobile personnel. Additionally, mobile computers provide better information to mobile employees, so they can make more informed decisions locally and minimize the need for management decisions from the central office.

Mobile Computing is Versatile

As can be seen from the previous examples, mobile computing is an extremely versatile technology. It can be instrumental in: (a) process reengineering; (b) reducing operational and administrative staff; (c) improving communications; (d) improving customer service; (e) reducing manufacturing costs; (f) shortening business cycles; and (g) many other benefits. The variety of hardware, software, and communications systems available and the many ways they can be integrated to solve problems add to the versatility of mobile computing. Mobile computers can be used in harsh outdoor environments as well as indoor office environments. They can be operated by workers while standing, walking, or driving. They can be operated by workers with no existing keyboard skills as well as those that work with gloves on or who normally only have one hand free. Anyone who understands how to use a pen and paper can easily be trained to use most mobile computers. (Lauzon Computer, 1997)

Examples of Versatility

The true versatility of mobile computing can be seen by recalling examples of how it is currently being utilized to enhance business and other operations. It delivers critical medical information from mobile emergency medical technicians to emergency rooms, so the doctors can be ready to treat the patient immediately upon arrival. It enables a salesperson to demonstrate product options, calculate delivery fees, check availability, verify customer credit, and accept payment all during one short visit. It makes it possible for a regional manager to quickly reference his region's current and past performance with a Penslate computer and WLAN connection; answering important questions without ever leaving the meeting table.

Versatility Summary

Yes, mobile computing is versatile. It extends the reach of an organizational information system and enables interaction with employees who otherwise would not have access. The versatility of mobile computing will continue to expand over the next few years as a predicted proliferation of new mobile computing devices and the expanded usage of existing devices comes to fruition. (Needle, 1998)

Strategic Nature of Mobile Computing

"The strategic role of information systems involves using information technology to develop products, services, and capabilities that give a company strategic advantages over the competitive forces it faces in the global marketplace." (O'Brien, 1996, p. 402) Mobile computing is a key enabling technology for the creation of strategic information systems.

Five Competitive Forces

Mobile computing's strategic nature can be seen by examining how mobile computing influences the five competitive forces that impact businesses. As discussed by O'Brien, (1996, pp. 402-408) the five competitive forces described by Michael Porter are: (a) rivalry among competitors; (b) threat of new entrants; (c) threat of substitute products; (d) bargaining power of suppliers; and (e) bargaining power of customers. An organization can counter these competitive forces by pursuing one or more of the following strategies: (a) cost leadership; (b) differentiation; (c) innovation; (d) growth; and (e) alliance. In each case, mobile computing information technology can be an important part of implementing the competitive strategy. Mobile computing can significantly reduce the operational costs associated with business processes. These savings can be passed on to the customer and enable a cost leadership strategy. Mobile computers can enable a more satisfying experience for the customer or an entirely new and innovative way of doing business, enabling a differentiation and/or innovation strategy. Mobile computers simplify: (a) the capture of data; (b) communication; and (c) the management of complex operations, thus enabling growth. Mobile computing technology enables real time tracking and management of business operations, which are both important for attaining the performance and reliability required for inter-organizational alliances such as just-in-time inventory agreements. Additionally, a strategic information system that is aligned with company goals and takes advantage of the benefits of mobile computing technology represents a significant barrier to entry for any other businesses that are considering entry into the market.

Categories of Strategic Systems

The strategic nature of mobile computing can be further seen by examining how it supports the primary categories of strategic information systems. Although a multitude of specific examples of strategic information systems exist, all these systems can generally be classified as belonging to one or more of four main types of strategic information systems. (Ward & Griffiths, 1996) The defining characteristics of these four categories of strategic information systems are: (a) those that change the nature of a relationship with consumers, customers, and/

or suppliers by sharing information via technology-based systems; (b) those that improve the organization's value-adding processes by more effectively integrating the use of information; (c) those that use information to develop, market, produce, and deliver enhanced or new services or products; and (d) those that support executive management decision-making in the areas of development and implementation of strategy, by providing them with information. Each of these categories is directly supported and enhanced by mobile computing. As seen in previous case examples, mobile computing can be directly responsible for changing the nature of relationships, improving key processes through information, enabling new products or services, and supporting executive decision making. These examples further support the assertion that mobile computing can play a major role in strategic information systems and thus is a strategic technology.

Strategic Value of Information Technology

The key categories of information technology application that define the sources of information technology strategic value have also been defined by Applegate, McFarlan, and McKenney (1996). They have defined these categories as: (a) process performance improvements; (b) individual/work group decision quality and workgroup improvements; and (c) competitive advantage. It has been shown that mobile computing improves business process performance. Mobile computing enables better individual decision quality by the mobile worker because the mobile worker with a mobile computer has access to more information and computing resources than one without. Potential for improved group decision making is also possible because more current and higher quality information is made available through the use of mobile computers.

Strategic Nature Summary

Regardless of the measure, it should be clear that mobile computing has many strategic characteristics. Capitalizing on these characteristics by incorporating mobile computing technology into the fixed organizational information system will only strengthen the strategic nature of the overall information system.

Achieving the Benefits of Mobile Computing (MOBILE Framework)

Accurately recognizing situations where mobile computing is an appropriate technology to address an organization's problems, opportunities, and directives is important if the promised benefits of mobile computing are to be achieved. In the spirit of—and partially based on—James Wetherbe's PIECES framework, as presented by Whitten & Bentley in their 1998 book *Systems Analysis and Design Methods*, I have developed a framework that specifically applies to mobile computing—the MOBILE framework. The MOBILE framework is used to determine when it is most appropriate to use mobile computing technology to address a problem, opportunity, or directive. The name MOBILE is derived from the first letter in each of the six categories that make up the framework.

The Six Categories Are

M the need for *mobility*

O the need to improve *operations*

B the need to break business *barriers*

I the need to improve *information* quality

L the need to decrease transaction *lag*

E the need to improve *efficiency*

Mobility

1. Freedom of movement is required to accomplish the task.
2. Information must be gathered, accessed, or processed during movement or while at a remote location.
3. Contact must be made while personnel are mobile or at remote locations.
4. The location or status of personnel must be known throughout the workday.

Operations

1. Current operations are not keeping pace with competitors due to a technological disadvantage.
2. Management is not able to properly oversee operations due to a lack of information.
3. Workers lack information required to operate at their full potential.
4. There is a significant economic, public safety, or crime prevention value that can be gained by improving the system. (Dhawan, 13)

Barriers

1. Geography. Business operations or expansion is hindered by the geographical dispersion of business activities. Key business processes or activities are not being accomplished where they are best performed or most needed.
2. Cost. Current processes carry significant costs in labour, inventory, operating locations, or travel expenses. (O'Brien, 415)
3. Structure. Current communications capabilities and the existing business structure lack the agility, ability, and information required to support innovative operations and strategic alliances. (O'Brien, 415).

Information

1. Information sent to or received from mobile personnel is not timely, current, or frequent enough.
2. Information sent to or received from mobile personnel is not accurate, complete, concise, or relevant enough.
3. Information sent to or received from mobile personnel is not clear, detailed, or presented appropriately.

Lag

1. The mobile worker cannot quickly complete a transaction while at the remote location because access to information or authorization from a central location is required.
2. Return trips to a remote location or multiple contacts are required to complete a transaction.
3. The continuation of any process is delayed until the mobile worker physically returns to the central business location with the collected information.

Efficiency

1. Data is input from paper, input more than once, or not captured at its source.
2. Method of data capture is slow, awkward, or labour intensive.
3. Questions must be re-asked or locations must be revisited because data was not completely or correctly gathered on initial visit due to a mistake or oversight.

4. Work cannot be completed at remote site due to lack of information from the central business location.
5. Travel time is wasted due to inefficient scheduling, dispatching, or the need to return to the home office for further instructions or information.
6. Materials or supplies are wasted by people or machines.

Businesses can decide if mobile computing is an appropriate technology to utilize by analysing their current operations and performance with respect to the MOBILE framework. If the problem, opportunity, or directive is one that is covered in the MOBILE framework, then mobile computing technology should be seriously investigated as part of the overall solution.

Technology will Change

When considering information technology, the only certainty is change. This change has implications for Systems Analysts and other information technology professionals who work closely with technology. The fact is that today's hot technology can be tomorrow's dinosaur. The functionality, technical implementations, and application heuristics of today may not be as applicable in the near future.

New Technologies

Exciting new technologies are being developed that will drastically alter and improve mobile computing capabilities. Two of these technologies are low earth orbit (LEO) satellites and wearable computers. Current LEO satellite developments promise ubiquitous and high-speed network access using extremely small and low power devices. Soon, it will be possible and economical to provide all mobile workers with a connected mode for all mobile computing operations. Advances in microcomputer, display, and natural interface technologies are making the first wave of commercially useful wearable computers possible. These devices are still in the experimental stages, and are not commonplace, but are finding applications in areas like aircraft inspection; where a hands-free operating environment and access to large amounts of information is required. In the future, wearable computers are predicted to replace the myriad of personal electronic devices (computers, cell phone, pagers, tape recorders, and cameras) with an integrated and unobtrusive wearable replacement that merges the user's work space with his or her information space. (Mann, 1998) (Jastrzembski, 1997)

The ways in which these types of technologies can be applied to solve problems is only limited by the creativity and skill of the developers.

Adapting to Change

The field of mobile computing is still evolving. Even more advanced and yet unimagined mobile technologies will certainly be discovered. Many of the advances will be evolutionary, but some will be revolutionary. The key to integrating these new technologies into the organizational information system will be forward thinking, adaptability, life-long learning, technical competence, an explorative spirit, and the use of tools such as the MOBILE framework. The result will be hardware, software, and communications systems that are even more mobile and more capable of accomplishing organizational objectives.

Mobile computing is an important, evolving technology. It enables mobile personnel to effectively communicate and interact with the fixed organizational information system while remaining unconstrained by physical location. Mobile computing may be implemented using many combinations of hardware, software, and communications technologies. The technologies must be carefully selected and the applications designed to achieve the business needs required from the overall organizational information system. The MOBILE framework can assist information technology professionals in determining the applicability of mobile technology to an organizational problem, opportunity, or directive. Mobile computing is a versatile and potentially strategic technology that improves information quality and accessibility, increases operational efficiency, and enhances management effectiveness.

Web Mining

Web mining-is the application of data mining techniques to discover patterns from the Web. According to analysis targets, web mining can be divided into three different types, which are Web usage mining, Web content mining and Web structure mining.

Web Usage Mining

Web usage mining is the process of finding out what users are looking for on internet. Some users might be looking at only textual data whereas some other might want to get multimedia data. Web usage mining also helps finding the search pattern for a particular group of people belonging to a particular region.

Web Content Mining

Web content mining is the process to discover useful information from text, image, audio or video data in the web. Web content mining sometimes is called web text mining, because the text content is the most widely researched area. The technologies that are normally used in web content mining are NLP (Natural language processing) and IR (Information retrieval). Although data mining is a relatively new term, the technology is not. Companies have used powerful computers to sift through volumes of supermarket scanner data and analyze market research reports for years. However, continuous innovations in computer processing power, disk storage, and statistical software are dramatically increasing the accuracy of analysis while driving down the cost. Example

Web Structure Mining

Web structure mining is the process of using graph theory to analyse the node and connection structure of a web site. According to the type of web structural data, web structure mining can be divided into two kinds.

The first kind of web structure mining is extracting patterns from hyperlinks in the web. A hyperlink is a structural component that connects the web page to a different location. The other kind of the web structure mining is mining the document structure. It is using the tree-like structure to analyse and describe the HTML (Hyper Text Markup Language) or XML (eXtensible Markup Language) tags within the web page.

Web Mining Pros and Cons

Pros

Web mining essentially has many advantages which makes this technology attractive to corporations including the government agencies. This technology has enabled ecommerce to do personalized marketing, which eventually results in higher trade volumes. The government agencies are using this technology to classify threats and fight against terrorism. The predicting capability of the mining application can benefits the society by identifying criminal activities. The companies can establish better customer relationship by giving them exactly what they need. Companies can understand the needs of the customer better and they can react to customer needs faster. The companies can find, attract and retain customers; they can save on production costs by utilizing the acquired insight of customer requirements. They can increase profitability by target pricing based on the profiles created. They can even find the customer who might default to a competitor the company will try to retain the customer by providing promotional offers to the specific customer, thus reducing the risk of losing a customer.

Cons

Web mining the technology itself doesn't create issues, but this technology when used on data of personal nature might cause concerns. The most criticized ethical issue involving web mining is the invasion of privacy. Privacy is considered lost when information concerning an individual is obtained, used, or disseminated, especially if this occurs without their knowledge or consent. The obtained data will be analysed, and clustered to form profiles; the data will be made anonymous before clustering so that no individual can be linked directly to a profile. But usually the group profiles are used as if they are personal profiles. Thus these applications de-individualize the users by judging them by their mouse clicks. De-individualization, can be defined as a tendency of judging and treating people on the basis of group characteristics instead of on their own individual characteristics and merits.

Another important concern is that the companies collecting the data for a specific purpose might use the data for a totally different purpose, and this essentially violates the user's interests. The growing trend of selling personal data as a commodity encourages website owners to trade personal data obtained from their site. This trend has increased the amount of data being captured and traded increasing the likeliness of one's privacy being invaded. The companies which buy the data are obliged make it anonymous and these companies are considered authors of any specific release of mining patterns. They are legally responsible for the contents of the release; any inaccuracies in the release will result in serious lawsuits, but there is no law preventing them from trading the data.

Some mining algorithms might use controversial attributes like sex, race, religion, or sexual orientation to categorize individuals. These practices might be against the anti-discrimination legislation. The applications make it hard to identify the use of such controversial attributes, and there is no strong rule against the usage of such algorithms with such attributes. This process could result in denial of service or a privilege to an individual based on his race, religion or sexual orientation, right now this situation can be avoided by the high ethical standards maintained by the data mining company. The collected data is being made anonymous so that, the obtained data and the obtained patterns cannot be traced back to an individual. It might look as if this poses no threat to one's privacy, actually many extra information can be inferred by the application by combining two separate unscrupulous data from the user

Web Mining-An Important Tool for Molding Business

Web mining is becoming the tool for success for those who adopt electronic means of operation for conducting their business. Web mining is the application of data mining techniques to discover patterns from the Web through content mining, structure mining, and usage mining. Web mining can contribute to a large extent in gaining a competitive advantage in your business. Your business goals should be well understood. We can explore areas where web mining can help you achieve these goals.

Customer Behaviour Analysis

Customer relationship management is one of the major applications of Web mining. A website should be designed to entice the customers. Web Mining analyses visitor's behaviour and makes predictions on their future interaction. This can be exploited to improve website performance and to recommend products or links based on user's behaviour. Visitors entering the site exhibits different behaviour. They might just surf through or the process might end up in a purchase. For understanding customer behaviour and thus improve the performance of your web site, certain standards should be used. Web metrics provide a method to evaluate the performance. There are certain standard notations used which is provide.

Number of repeat visitors and committed visitors should be increased. Customer service sites should be able to provide the required information in a short span of time. Customer data including personal information entered during log time is stored in customer database. The content delivery to the customer can be customized. Each user might be interested in specific products and features. New products can be recommended to the user by analysing their behaviour pattern. Market basket analysis can be carried out using the web data and there by improve the chances of cross selling, discount rates etc.

Information about the visitor's behaviour can be collected from Web logs which includes various log files like We can also analyze the pattern in which the user travelled from one web page to another of your website before making a purchase. Behaviour can be analysed to form user clusters who require same class of details. Information mined can be used to opt for the finest manner of interaction with customers. The decision made by a customer depends on his experience on the site. Provision can be provided to enter feedback. Data can be gathered and mined from web to achieve the final goal of turning visitors to buyers.

Web Mining in E-learning

E-learning is nothing but where learning happens with the aid of digital tools and content, with necessary interactions possible. E-learning is independent of location, time or space. A user who is exploring the web for self learning may not be a domain expert. Web sites and topics popular among other users exploring the same area can be found using web mining and recommended to the non-experts. Students or learners using E-learning sites will be differing from each other on various aspects like the rate at which they capture the lessons, domain expertise, personal interests etc. On the other hand, there will be many learners who show the same characteristics also. Interest of learners and relevance of topics to them can be mined from the user's profile created and the same can be made in designing and linking sites.

Giving the right combination of keywords is imperative for searching and finding what we require exactly. Query keywords can be grouped into clusters and information from the query result can be recommended to users. E-learning experience can be enhanced by providing the relevant information to the relevant learner with the assistance of Web mining.

Web Mining in Banking Industry

Internet banking was offered as a "value addition" for most customers. But now almost all the banks have ventured into this area. Enormous amount of data gets stored through banking transactions. Success factor is the amount of valuable knowledge that is extracted from this data store. Customer profile can be generated. This helps the bank executives in identifying the appropriate customer for certain category of products and the risk in allotting loan facilities. Credit card usage patterns can be identified and special offers can be provided.

Defaulters of payment can be identified easily. Banks like ICICI bank and HSBC bank identify the customers for certain offers like home equity loan using web mining. Bank can target at the customers who are likely to invest in mutual funds. Thus targeting the right customer and ensuring excellent service to these customers can be made a reality with the aid of web mining.

Limitations

Raw Web data will not be in a presentable form for analysis. Web data will have to be prepared for analysis. The software vendors providing Web Analysis claim of having sophisticated methods for data preparation. When you consider the data available for mining in log files on server side and client side, server records the date/time, bytes transferred, time taken for transaction etc. Client side counts every single visit and page view to a website. The server log may not contain correct usage pattern because of caching. Request for details from web sites which are already traversed may be served by web cache. This can be avoided by cache busting where browsers should be requesting for fresh copies at every user request.

Another problem is where responders are not genuine. For application like credit offers, frequent responses are not a positive sign. Introduction of incentives and other offers for attracting a customer will result in increase of cost of acquiring a new customer.

Web mining is an excellent tool for acquiring an enviable position in business and for sustaining and improving it. But the rate of success depends on the alignment of the outcome of web mining with the strategic goals of your business. Web mining has made its presence felt in the area of e-tailing, e-learning, e-hr and e-finance to list a few. Organizations moving along with these advantages provided by technology had always sailed to success.

More and more commerce-related transactions are becoming digital. This is happening not just in the supplier side of the value chain, but increasingly in the consumer side. The current market for the analysis of digital consumer data is in this burgeoning area of Internet e-commerce. Business Internet surveyors, such as Gartner and Jupiter, predict that over 5 billion dollars of business will be transacted on the Internet by next year.

Every customer action on a web site generates data-not just high level interactions such as buying something but also actions as simple as using a search engine or navigating through a site. All these interactions between digital service providers and the consumer can be recorded and stored in digital databases. These large data sets contain useful information helpful to business marketing strategies, both for retrospective analysis as well as data driven forecasting. Companies today are in the unprecedented position of being able to collect vast amounts of customer information relatively easily. As a result, by using Web Mining, companies can both analyse and predict the behaviour of their customers. Forrester Research Inc. say that 16% of large companies already expected more effective use of customer information to help them cut costs in 1999. They also predict that an additional 34% are banking on savings by 2001.

Web Analysis

All visitors to a web site leave digital trails which servers automatically store in log files. Web analysis tools analyse and process these web server log files to produce meaningful information. Essentially a complete profile of site traffic is created, for example how many visitors to the site, what sites they have come from and which of the site's pages are most popular. Web analysis tools provide companies with previously unknown statistics and useful insights into the behaviour of their online customers. While the usage and popularity of such tools may continue to increase, many e-tailers are now demanding more useful information on their customers from the vast amounts of data generated by their web sites. Jesus Mena, in his book "Data Mining Your Web Site", says that "current traffic analysis tools...are geared at providing high-level predefined reports about domain names, IP addresses, browsers, cookies and other machine-to-machine activity. These server activity reports simply do not provide the type of bottom-line analysis that e-tailers, service providers, marketeers, and advertisers in the business world have come to demand. These software packages (i.e. web analysis tools) originated from the need to report on the activity of the server and not on the behaviour of its visitors."

The result of the changing paradigm of commerce, from traditional brick and mortar shop fronts to electronic transactions over the Internet, has been the dramatic shift in the relationship between e-tailers and their customers. There is no longer any personal contact between retailers and customers. Customers are now highly mobile and are demonstrating loyalty only to value, often irrespective of brand or geography. A major challenge therefore is for e-tailers to identify and understand their new customer base. E-tailers need to learn as much as possible regarding the behaviour, the individual tastes and the preferences of the visitors to their sites in order to remain competitive in this new era of commerce. Web mining makes this possible.

So What is Web Mining?

Data mining is the technology used to discover non-obvious, potentially useful and previously unknown information from data sources. The potential of web mining is in the application of existing and new data mining algorithms to Internet data, which include Internet server logs, as well as external data on customer, sales, and products. Web mining may be sub-divided into web-content mining, webstructure mining and web-usage mining. Web-content mining is the extraction of information from Internet pages, common in the next generation of XML/RKF based search engines/web spiders. Web-structure mining is the application of data mining to reconstruct the structure of a web site or sites. Web usage mining is the mining of log files and associated data from a particular web site to discover knowledge on browser and buyer behaviour on that site. In short, Web Mining can be seen to apply existing analysis techniques together with cutting edge technology to the plethora of data that the internet is generating.

The Benefits of Web Mining

Web Mining enables e-tailers to leverage their online customer data by understanding and predicting the behaviour of their customers. For the first time e-tailers now have access to detailed marketing intelligence on the visitors to their web sites. The business benefits that web mining afford to digital service providers include-personalisation, collaborative filtering, enhanced customer support, product and service strategy definition, particle marketing and fraud detection. In short, the ability to understand their customers' needs and to deliver the best and most appropriate service to those individual customers at any given moment.:

Closing the Loop

Web mining plays a considerable role in the area of one-to-one marketing through content personalisation, ad targeting and profile building.

Web mining reveals layers of information about the markets and the data collected from web sites present enormous potential for direct marketing. Personalised messages can be delivered to individual people – the famous "segment of one". The opportunity to identify and target browsers and buyers of products and services with attractive offers and sales promotions has never been greater. Marketeers can fine tune their strategies by building customer or prospect profiles and using these to identify the segments upon which marketing activities are focused. For the first time, e-tailers have the capability to consider a cost-effective means of providing individually customised marketing communications.

Web mining fully supports 'web personalisation'. A web site can be tailored for each particular user's preference and profile information. This allows e-tailers to develop loyal and long lasting relationships with each individual visitor.

Conclusion

Many companies wanting an online presence believe that all they have to do is build a web site and sit back and reap the benefits. In most cases this has been a fruitless exercise and companies will be unable to improve the situation without first gaining a basic understanding of the visitors to their web site. Web mining puts e-tailers in the unprecedented position of being able to understand and predict the behaviour of their customers. Companies can now optimise their e-business sites for maximum commercial impact and personalise the online content of their web site.

It is those companies who adopt a web mining strategy NOW to learn about their customers who will gain the competitive edge in the new 'digital economy'.

Online Auction (New Business)

Online Auction Business Model

The online auction business model is one in which participants bid for products and services over the Internet. The functionality of buying and selling in an auction format is made possible through auction software which regulates the various processes involved.

Several types of online auctions are possible. In an English auction the initial price starts low and is bid up by successive bidders. In a Dutch auction, multiple identical items are offered in one auction, with all winning bidders paying the same price — the highest price at which all items will be sold (treasury bills, for example, are auctioned this way). Almost all online auctions use the English auction method.

Strengths of the Business Model

The Strategic Advantages of This Business Model Include

1. No time constraints. Bids can be placed at any time (24/7). Items are listed for a number of days (usually between 1 and 10, at the discretion of the seller), giving purchasers time to search, decide, and bid. This convenience increases the number of bidders.
2. No geographical constraints. Sellers and bidders can participate from anywhere that has internet access. This makes them more accessible and reduces the cost of "attending" an auction. This increases the number of listed items (i.e..: number of sellers) and the number of bids for each item (e.g.: number of bidders). The items do not need to be shipped to a central location, reducing costs, and reducing the seller's minimum acceptable price.
3. Intensity of social interactions. The social interactions involved in the bidding process are very similar to gambling. The bidders wait in anticipation hoping they will "win." Much like gambling addiction, some bidders may bid primarily to "play the game" rather than to obtain products or services. This creates a highly loyal customer segment. This can also skew the prices of items/services/goods in the auction.
4. Large number of bidders. Because of the potential for a relatively low price, the broad scope of products and services available, the ease of access, and the social benefits of the auction process, there are a large numbers of bidders.
5. Large number of sellers. Because of the large number of bidders, the potential for a relatively high price, reduced selling costs, and ease of access, there are a large number of sellers.
6. Network economies. The large number of bidders will encourage more sellers, which, in turn, will encourage more bidders, which will encourage more sellers, etc., in a virtuous circle. The more the circle operates, the larger the system becomes, and the more valuable the business model becomes for all participants.
7. Captures consumers' surplus. Auctions are a form of first degree price discrimination. As such, they attempt to convert

part of the consumers' surplus (defined as the area above the market price line but below the firm's demand curve) into producers' surplus.

Criticism

Auction sites, like garage sales, flea markets, classified advertisements and other independent sales venues, sometimes draw criminals wishing to sell stolen products, but for law enforcement organizations, finding stolen goods offered online is sometimes easier than more traditional detection methods.

Some criticism is levelled at online auction websites for uneven representation of items offered for sale. Descriptions may omit important information, and photos may not be adequate. Potential bidders can typically protect themselves by reading the text, studying photographs and asking questions of the seller before bidding. Another way you can get comfortable is by looking at the rating of the seller and the feedback they have received for past sales. The rating indicates the number of people they have done transactions with successfully. This can be an indicator of how trustworthy they are. Studies show that a large proportion of unsatisfactory online purchase experiences are the result of careless consumerism.

In the U.S., large retailers have lobbied Congress to require online auction sites to share private sales information about sellers, citing potential illegalities. Within the online auction community this is commonly viewed as an attempt at unfair market protection and trade restraint. Reduced overhead sometimes enables independent online sellers to offer goods at lower prices than large retailers.

Online auction selling has attracted millions of laid-off workers, as well as the disabled, parents of young children, retirees, pensioners and others that are unable to find employment in the mainstream workforce. Online auction venue corporations are accused of engaging in discriminatory trade practices that unfairly impact such customers. Presently, the trading practices of online auction venue corporations is not regulated by state or federal agencies.

Online Auction Tools

Online Auction tools is application software, that can either be deployed on a Web server or a Desktop. This software is used by customers of online auctions such as Ebay or Oztion.

Online Auction companies have opened up their applications to third party application developers to extend the capabilities and increase revenue. API interfaces were developed using XML which enable third party developers to build applications that use the back-end of the online auction. This software enable tools such as:

Auction Snipers: Auction Sniping Tools that allow consumers to place last minute bids

Auction Listing Tools: Services that aid in listing items on auction sites like Ebay, such as Vendio and Auctiva.

Auction Marketing: Services that display ads on behalf of auction sellers

Auction Portal Software: Auction Portal Software provides the auctioneers to develop their own auction system with the tools & service provided in the system. The system now adopts the Web 2.0 compatibility and able to match with the new data structures and technologies. This will help the entrepreneurs to step in the business of E-com.

Auction Listing Enhancements: Auction Seller Tools, to make the listing more attractive or easier for buyers to get access to information quicker

Offline Tools: Auction tools to access sites such as Ebay offline.

Use Online Auctions to Promote Your Business

When they first appeared on the scene, online auctions were used mainly by people looking to get rid of old heirlooms or collectors in niche markets (stuffed collectibles, etc.). Now, it seems like everyone is participating in online auctions. People are also beginning to realize that auctions can be a great way to promote a business and test products.

I have to admit it — I'm an eBay junkie. I'm probably on their site at least 4 or 5 times a week, looking for items to add to my various collections, and the more I visit, the more I'm seeing businesses using online auctions in creative ways. For instance, there are many people who have started to make their living solely through online auctions. However, if you don't want to become one of these "full-timers", you can still use online auctions to help you with your business. Here are a couple of thoughts on ways to do that:

- Use auctions to gauge new products. If you are considering adding a new product to your business, auctions are a great way to see what kind of demand there might be for it. Do an experiment — put one of the products up for auction and see how many people bid on it (you might even be able to track how many people look at the auction without making a bid). If you have good response from the auction, it can be a good indication that you should add the product to your inventory.
- Use auctions to determine prices. One question that I get a lot from clients is, "How much should I charge for so-and-so?". If you have this kind of question, auctions can be a great way to gauge prices. Put your item on auction and see how much people are willing to bid on it. Don't just look at the high bid — remember that there are some "insane bidders" out there — rather, look at the maximum bids from all bidders to get an idea of what customers are willing to pay for your product.

Link your auction to your business. Now, before I go any further, I have to warn you to read your auction service's policies CAREFULLY— many services will not allow you to put a direct link to your web site in your auction description.

Even if you can't put a link directly in your auction, you might still be able to promote your business. For instance, many services will have an "about me" page where you can put a link to your business. Also, there is nothing keeping you from linking the sites in the other direction— putting a link to your auctions on your web site, for instance.

One of the things that has always impressed me about the so-called "net gurus" is their ability to be creative in their advertising and promotion efforts. Online auctions seem to be a great candidate for that type of creativity.

SEO (Search Engine Optimization) Toolkit provides everything you need to promote and optimize your web pages for the search engines. Features include: Ranking, Keyword Density Analysis, Keyword Research, URL Submission, Optimization wizards, just to name a few. Award winning web site promotion software SubmitWolf can dramatically increase your web site traffic. Submit your web site details to thousands of Search Engines, directories and link pages.

Discover the best keywords to target on your website-

KeywordDiscovery compiles keyword search statistics from over 180 search engines world wide, to create the most powerful Keyword Research tool.

Steps to a Successful Online Auction Business

If you talk to just one eBay business owner in your lifetime, you'll be instantly infused with his infectious joy at finding he could start a successful business using the ubiquitous auction service. Now multiply that excitement by about 5,400, and you may come close to understanding the pervasive—almost evangelical—energy that ran rampant through this June's eBay Live!, the first-ever eBay convention that took place in California. Prospective eBay sellers and current Shooting Stars (a distinction awarded at certain levels of feedback) mingled with eBay staff members and suppliers like FedEx and AuctionWatch.com; maniacally collected the trading cards eBay produced for the event (for later auctions, of course); attended classes like Basic Selling and Customer Support; and perused the areas set up for specific eBay categories like Motors and Media.

Why did 5,400 people travel—many crossing distances of thousands of miles—just to mingle? Why are successful business owners so gushingly positive about their eBay experiences? The main reason: It's almost too easy. Anyone can sell something on eBay. You don't need a storefront; HTML skills, though handy, aren't required; and you don't need a merchant account to accept payments. You really don't need anything but a computer, an Internet connection, a printer and a digital camera. And with more than 420 million items up for auction and gross merchandise sales averaging $38 million a *day* in 2001, you know there's an audience out there for products.

But there is a difference between a part-time amateur seller and a successful business owner. If you aspire to become a Power Seller and really make this a successful, full-time business, you've got to get serious and treat it like a business. You need to understand the profit margins on your products. You have to appreciate the importance of customer support. You'll need to look at every aspect of your process as you grow to discover where you can streamline to save money and time and improve the way you serve your bidders.

So start out right. Do your research to decide if an auction site is the right place for your new business. In this article, we're primarily focusing on eBay—not because it's our favourite, but because it is the industry leader, and many auction maxims, like the importance of customer service, are universal. There are other options to choose from—Yahoo! Auctions, Amazon.com Auctions and uBid are just a few—so before you begin, do some research to truly find your perfect home. And now, read on for the 6 steps to starting an online auction business.

Familiarize your self with the Auction Environment

Before you sell anything, buy yourself a little present. "That way, you get to know how the system works," explains Marsha Collier, author of *Starting an eBay Business for Dummies* and a frequent instructor at eBay University. Bidding on an item not only puts you in the shoes of your future customers, but it will start boosting your feedback rating on the site. You don't have to spend a lot of money. There are some very low-cost items to be found on eBay—postcards, CDs by bands no one has ever heard of; even beads. Spend time surfing eBay, looking at the auctions of items you might sell. Which ones are getting the bids? What key words do they use? Do they have gallery photos that show up when bidders browse categories or search listings? Collier also suggests you search completed items (you'll find this option in advanced search) to see what items actually sold and for what price. This will help you determine if the products you're interested in have a market and a big enough profit margin on eBay.

Spend time in the Help section, too. This is where you'll start to understand the different types of auctions, the many features you can use when listing items, the rules and regulations of the site, the levels of feedback and what you can do when something goes wrong.

Finally, do some research on your own. Selling on eBay may be a cinch to set up, but good business sense is what guides you in the long term. Take advantage of business books, sites like ours, eBay guides like Collier's, and eBay's own resources, such as the aforementioned Help section and eBay University. eBay is genius at customer service and wanting to help their sellers succeed. Yes, it's self-serving—if they help you succeed in business, they'll get more money in their own coffers. But hey, you need all the help you can get, so why not go to the source?

Find a Focus

This is very likely your most important step of the process—where you decide what type of business to start. eBay is really just a sales outlet, like the mall or a catalog. Your real business is what you decide to sell on eBay.

Most folks find their inspiration in something they have experience with. PowerSeller Joshua Mandell spent his free time and extra money collecting baseball cards, and found once he started selling cards on eBay, he could better support his hobby/habit. "After six months of casual selling on eBay, I realized the potential for profitability, " says Mandell, who handles the ordering, sales and marketing, while his partner, Sabian Craig, does the shipping, customer service and inventory. Today, he averages 1,500 to 2,000 auctions each month and has sold to bidders in more than 35 countries.

Kathleen and Raymond Manning also had stock just waiting for eBay. Raymond had been looking to unload the inventory from video rental stores he'd owned during the 1980s and '90s, but thought brokers' offers for the videos were too low. Kathleen, a former banking VP, was laid off during a bank merger, began looking up some of the video titles on eBay and discovered the perfect market. "I have since sold thousands of tapes," says Kathleen, who works out of their Phoenix home. "During the past two years, my inventory has continued to grow as my husband—a true 'scrounger' as he likes to call himself—brings me more and more items to sell. There is truly an abundance of 'gold in the hills,' and our only constraint is time." To escape that constraint, Kathleen has recently enlisted her teenage daughter for help.

Once you begin browsing your closet and hobbies for things to sell, return to that completed item search. "Do research on the particular item you plan on selling, even if you only have one," suggests Collier. Collier provides this example: She recently inherited a Dwight D. Eisenhower commemorative plate. Thinking this was eBay gold, she looked it up. "It was worth six bucks," laughs Collier. "Not wanting to sell it for $6, I put it aside as something I'll sell in the future."

So if you think you think you've struck auction gold—for example, found a store clearing a particular item at dirt-cheap prices—do your research before you buy the lot of them. You may find out you can only get 25 cents more, which won't be worth your time, money or effort.

Setup your Office

It doesn't take much equipment to get started on the site, but what you do have, you need to organize well. First, you need a decent computer with a fast Internet connection—DSL or a cable modem will make a big difference when you're uploading photos to your auctions. Then you'll need a digital camera and possibly a scanner. Photos sell auctions—that's all there is to it. Going digital is the easiest, and, in the long run, cheapest option. Collier suggests, of course, going to eBay to find a discounted camera. Scanners can work if you're selling two-dimensional products, such as Mandell's baseball cards. And a good printer and office software suite is vital in any business.

Next item of business: Your storage area. When you're selling just a few items, it's easy enough to stack them on an empty closet shelf. But once you get into high volume, you've got to get organized or you'll go nuts and lose time and money to your inefficiency.

In Collier's eBay classes, she suggests enlisting an army of those clear plastic boxes you can get in several sizes at any discount store. They keep items clean, fresh-smelling (you'll notice many auctioneers tout their "smoke-free" households) and easily accessible. Place photos on the outside of the boxes for easy recognition when a customer e-mails a question about one of 75 items you have up for auction.

Now we come to what will surely be your favourite task: Shipping. It may be boring, but it's an extremely important aspect of your business. Streamline your shipping so items get sent out in a timely fashion—all the better for your feedback rating. And you want to watch your costs so that: a) you don't eat any costs; b) you don't inflate S&H so much it sends bidders running. The USPS is a candy store for eBay users, as so much packaging is available for free and even delivered to your house. Visit here to stock up. A postal scale may prove to be a worthwhile investment so you can avoid lines and buy postage online.

Last but not least: Your photo area. Devote a small table to this task. Collier suggests if you sell clothing or jewellery, used mannequins will prove their worth. Dress up your items; don't just toss them on the carpet or prop them against a wall that should've been re-wallpapered in 1973. An empty box and a piece of material do wonders as a pedestal. And if you really want to get fancy, consider some lighting as well.

List your Auctions

Now it's time for the nitty-gritty. You've done your research to determine if there's a market for your product and what you should expect to get for your tchotchke. Let's start a bidding war.

First things first: Your titles and descriptions. Your titles and gallery photos are what entice a bidder to view your auction. A lot goes into this—you can use all caps sparingly to make certain words jump out, carefully choose key words to attract searchers, or even pay extra for eBay goodies like highlighting ($5 a listing), bold type ($2), gallery photos (a mere quarter to have your photo show up on listings pages—this is Colliers' favourite bargain) and more. Again, go back to those "completed items" searches to see what's worked for those who've gone before you. And remember that every extra you get cuts into your bottom line, so be sure they're worth it.

As for descriptions, do your research on each and every item and lay out your terms as simply and thoroughly as possible so you're a pleasure to do business with. "You have to write your descriptions thoroughly. Describe the good parts—and the bad parts—of whatever the item is. Because what sells your items on eBay are your titles and your descriptions," says Collier. "That's the most important thing—it sets you apart from other people." This is also where you're going to set prices. Again, eBay offers several options for your auction, including:

- Fixed-Price Format. Bidders can buy the item at the price you set immediately, no auction at all.
- Reserve Price Auctions. You set the lowest amount—the reserve price—you're willing to accept for your item. Your opening bid may be below this, and bidders will be told if they don't reach your reserve price, which isn't disclosed unless you do so in your description.
- Dutch Auctions. If you have several of one item, you can sell them as a Dutch, or multiple, auction at either a fixed price or as an auction. If you do it as an auction, bidders can choose the amount and price they want. They can only be outbid if the total price (number of items bid on multiplied by bid price) is higher. All winning bidders pay the lowest successful bid.
- Buy It Now. This gives bidders the option to buy your item at a set price without having to wait for the auction to end. But when the first person bids, the option disappears. So for instance, you're selling a glass bowl with an opening bid of $1, but your Buy It Now price is $5. Someone can pay $5 and end the auction, or they can bid $1.50, and the Buy It Now option disappears.

Of course, each option has some restrictions and fees. You can also choose to have auctions of different duration—3-, 5-, 7-and 10-days. eBay, if nothing else, likes to provide lots and lots of options for sellers. Explore these in the Help section. As you sell more and more items, you'll discover which formula works best for you.

Customer Service

eBay is all about the "f" word: feedback. "The feedback rating is the core of the community, " says Collier. "Buying something from someone with a high positive feedback rating is always desirable from a buyer's point of view." It's also what separates the little guy from big companies. "People say that all the big retailers are starting to sell on eBay, so what chance [does the little guy have]? But there's no way a big company can give the customer service you can. [If a customer asks them a question about an item,] they have to go look for it in a big warehouse or read about it from a description. You can go over to the shelf, look at it and give the details. As an individual, you have a leg up on the big companies, especially if you specialize in a particular item you're very, comfortable with."

What exactly entails customer service on eBay? A few things, starting with your auction itself. Listing your S&H and payment policies upfront makes it easier to do business with you. Accepting several forms of payment can also ease customer's concerns. When someone e-mails you about an item, answer quickly, thoroughly and courteously. And of course, when someone wins a bid and completes payment, send the item out as soon as humanly possible, if not sooner.

Joshua Mandell mails his products all over the world, sends out monthly mailings to his loyal customers about his products up for sale, offers money-back guarantees, and basically bends over backward to make sure he pleases his customers. "If a person has a good experience, they'll tell a couple of people or maybe nobody. If that same person has a bad experience, they will tell everybody," says Mandell. "You must serve the customers with 2000 percent of everything you have at your disposal, or they will not come back. If you do, they will come back again and again!" Kathleen Manning also values her customers, and reflects it in her customer service. 'There is a true sense of community with eBay—an atmosphere of honesty and doing the right thing," says Manning. "I treat each of my buyers with courtesy, quality and customer service. You can't go wrong with this philosophy."

Bibliography

Aspray, William: *John von Neumann and the Origins of Modern Computing*, Cambridge, MA, The MIT Press, 1990.

Augarten, Stan: *Bit By Bit, An Illustrated History of Computers*, New York, Ticknor & Fields, 1984.

Bass, Thomas A: *The Eudaemonic Pie*, New York, Random House, 1985.

Baran, Paul A.: *The Political Economy of Growth*, New York, Modern Reader Paperbacks, 1975.

Baumann, P. R.: *Computer Assisted Instruction Programs in Geography: Five Climate Programs*, Oneonta, New York, 1970.

Bazilevskii, Y. Y.: *The Theory of Mathematical Machines*, Pergamon Press, Macmillan Co., New York, 1963.

Berezin, I. S.; N. P. Zhidkov: *Computing Methods, Pergamon Press*, Oxford and Addison-Wesley, Reading, Mass., 1965.

Borst, Arno: *The Ordering of Time: From the Ancient Computus to the Modern Computer*, Trans. Andrew Winnard, Chicago, IL, University of Chicago Press, 1993.

Brand, Stewart: *The Media Lab: Inventing the Future at MIT*, New York: Penguin, 1987.

Burke, Colin: *Information and Secrecy, Vannevar Bush, Ultra, and the Other Memex,* Metuchen, NJ, Scarecrow Press, 1994.

Burke, Frank M., *Valuation and Valuation Planning for Closely Held Businesses*, Englewood Cliffs, NJ, Prentice Hall, 1981.

Campbell-Kelly, Martin and William Aspray: *Computer, A History of the Information Machine*, New York, Basic Books, 1996.

Caviglioni O. : *Mapwise: Accelerated Learning Through Visible Thinking*, Network Educational Press, 2000.

Chandler, Alfred D.: *The Visible Hand: The Managerial Revolution in American Business*, Cambridge, MA: The Belknap Press of Harvard University Press, 1977.

Charles R. Morris: *Computer Wars, The Fall of IBM and the Future of Global Technology*, New York, Times Books, 1993.

Copeland, Tom, Tim Koller, and Jack Murrin, *Valuation: Measuring and Managing the Value of Companies*, New York, Wiley, 1994.

Cortada, James W.: *The Computer in the United States: From Laboratory to Market, 1930-1960*, Armonk, NY: M. E. Sharpe, 1993.

Crichton, Michael: *Electronic Life, How to Think About Computers*, New York, Alfred A. Knopf, 1983.

Dasgupta, Subrata: *Creativity in Invention and Design, Computational and Cognitive Explorations of Technological Originality*, New York, Cambridge University Press, 1994.

Dertouzos, Michael L. and Joel Moses: *The Computer Age, A Twenty-Year View*.Cambridge, MA, The MIT Press, 1979.

Desmond, Glenn, and John A, Marcell, *Handbook of Small Business Valuation Formulas and Rules of Thumb*, Valuation Press, 1993.

Edward A.: *Computers and Thought*, New York: McGraw-Hill, 1963.

Edwards, Paul N: *The Closed World: Computers and the Politics of Discourse in Cold War America*, Cambridge, MA, The MIT Press, 1996.

Fishman, Katherine Davis: *The Computer Establishment*, New York: McGraw-Hill, 1981.

G. C. Tootill: *Electronic Computers*, Baltimore: Penguin Books, 1967.

Gavino Morin: *Cyberspace and the Law: Your Rights and Duties in the On-Line World*, Cambridge, MA: The MIT Press, 1994.

Goldstine, Herman H.: *The Computer, From Pascal to von Neumann*. Princeton, NJ, Princeton University Press, 1972.

Gul, F. and Pesendorfer, W.: *The Foundations of Positive and Normative Economics*, New York, Oxford University Press 2008.

Hanson, Dirk: *The New Alchemists*, Boston: Little, Brown, 1982.

Harrigan, K. R.: *Strategies for Declining Businesses*. Lexington, MA: Heath, 1980

Hawkes, Nigel: *The Computer Revolution*, New York: E.P. Dutton, 1972.

Heims, Steve J.: *The Cybernetics Group*, Cambridge, MA, The MIT Press, 1991.

Heller, Robert: *The Fate of IBM*, London, Little Brown, 1994.

Herman H.: *The Computer: From Pascal to von Neumann*, Princeton, Princeton University Press, 1972.

Hollingdale, S. H., and G. C. Tootill: *Electronic Computers,* Baltimore: Penguin Books, 1967.

Holzmann, Gerald J. and Bjorn Pehrson: *The Early History of Data Networks,* Los Alamitos, CA, IEEE Computer Society Press, 1994.

Hsu, Jeffrey: *A Comprehensive Guide to Computer Bible Study. Up-to-Date Information on the Best Software and Techniques*, Dallas: Word, 1993.

James Keller: *Public Access to the Internet*, Cambridge, MA: The MIT Press, 1995.

James R.: *The Control Revolution: Technological and Economic Origins of the Information Society*, Cambridge, MA: Harvard University Press, 1986.

Kasper, Larry J.: *Business Valuations, Advanced Topics*, Westport, CT, Quorum Books, 1997.

Katherine Davis: *The Computer Establishment*, New York: McGraw-Hill, 1981.

Kawasaki, Guy: *The Computer Curmudgeon,* Indianapolis, Hayden Books, 1992.

Kidder, Tracy: *Soul of a New Machine*, New York, Avon, 1981.

Lee, J.A.N.: *Computer Pioneers,* Los Alamitos, CA, IEEE Computer Society Press, 1994.

Levy, Steven: *Hackers, Heroes of the Computer Revolution*, New York, Dell, 1984.

Lewis, Charles: *Premises and Prospects, TCP/IP and the Internet*, B.A. Thesis, New College of the University of South Florida, 1996.

Lukoff, Herman: *From Dits to Bits: A Personal History of the Electronic Computer*, Portland, OR, Robotics Press, 1979.

Malone, Michael S.: *The Microprocessor, A Biography,* Santa Clara, CA, TELOS, 1995.

Marris, R. L., and Wood, A.: *The Corporate Economy*, London: Macmillan, 1971.

Martin and William Aspray: *Computer: A History of the Information Machine*, New York: Basic Books, 1996.

Metropolis, N., J. Howlett, and Gian Carlo Rota: *A History of Computing in the Twentieth Century, A Collection of Essays*, New York, Academic Press, 1980.

Paul N.: *The Closed World: Computers and the Politics of Discourse in Cold War America*, Cambridge, The MIT Press, 1996.

Peirson, G., Bird, R., Brown, R., & Howard, P.: *Business Finance*, Roseville, 1990

Pogue, David and Joseph Schorr: *Macworld Mac & Power Mac SECRETS*, New York, IDG Books, 1994.

Pournelle, Jerry: *The User's Guide to Small Computers,* New York, Baen, 1984.

Ranade, Jay and Alan Nash: *The Best of Bye, Two Decades on the Leading Edge,* New York, McGraw-Hill, 1994.

Robert L.: *Software Creativity*, Prentice Hall PTR, 1995.

Rodgers, William: *Think, A Biography of the Watsons and IBM*, New York, Stein and Day, 1969.

Rose, Frank: *West of Eden, The End of Innocence at Apple Computer*, New York, Penguin, 1989.

Smith, Gordon V., and Russell Parr, *Valuation of Intellectual Property and Intangible Assets,* New York: Wiley, 1994.

Stern, Nancy: *From ENIAC to UNIVAC, An Appraisal of the Eckert-Mauchly Computers,* Bedford, MA, Digital Press, 1981.

Steve J.: *The Cybernetics Group*, Cambridge, MA: The MIT Press, 1991.

Stross, Randall: *The Microsoft Way, The Real Story of How the Company Outsmarts Its Competition*, New York: Addison-Wesley, 1996.

Weibull, J. W.: *Advances in Understanding Strategic Behaviour*, New York, Palgrave, 2004.

West, Thomas L.: and Jeffrey D. Jones: *Handbook of Business Valuation*, New York: Wiley, 1992.

Zachary, G. Pascal: *Showstopper! The Breakneck Race to Creat Windows NT and the Next Generation at Microsoft,* New York, The Free Press, 1994.

Index

A

B

C

D

E

F

G

H

I

L

M

O

P

R

S

T

W

□□□